PSYCHOLOGY AS THE DISCIPLINE OF INTERIORITY

Psychology as the Discipline of Interiority is the first collection of essays dedicated to the study and application of Psychology as the Discipline of Interiority – a new 'wave' within Analytical Psychology which pushes off from the work of C. G. Jung and James Hillman. The book reflects upon the notion of psychology developed by German psychoanalyst Wolfgang Giegerich, whose Hegelian turn sheds light on the notion of soul, or psyche, and its inner logic and 'thought', forming a radical new basis from which to ground a modern psychology with soul.

The book's theme – "the psychological difference" – is applied to topics including analytical theory, clinical practice, and contemporary issues, ranging from C. G. Jung's *Mysterium*, to case studies, to the nuclear bomb and the Shoah. *Psychology as the Discipline of Interiority* expounds upon the complexity, depth and innovativeness of Giegerich's thought, reflecting the various ways in which international scholars have creatively explored a speculative psychology founded upon the notion of soul. The contributors here include clinical psychologists, Jungian analysts, and international scholars.

With a new chapter by Wolfgang Giegerich and a foreword by David Miller, *Psychology as the Discipline of Interiority* will be essential reading for depth and clinical psychologists, Jungian psychoanalysts in practice and in training, and academics and students of post-Jungian studies. It is also relevant reading for all those interested in the history of philosophical thought and what it means to *think* in the highly sophisticated and technological world of the twenty-first century.

Jennifer M. Sandoval, PhD, is a licensed clinical psychologist in private practice in Los Angeles, USA.

John C. Knapp, PhD, is a licensed clinical psychologist in private practice in Chicago, USA.

PSYCHOLOGY AS THE DISCIPLINE OF INTERIORITY

"The Psychological Difference" in the Work of Wolfgang Giegerich

Edited by
Jennifer M. Sandoval and John C. Knapp

Routledge
Taylor & Francis Group

LONDON AND NEW YORK

First published 2017
by Routledge
2 Park Square, Milton Park, Abingdon, Oxon OX14 4RN

and by Routledge
711 Third Avenue, New York, NY 10017

Routledge is an imprint of the Taylor & Francis Group, an informa business

British Library Cataloguing in Publication Data
A catalogue record for this book is available from the British Library

Library of Congress Cataloging in Publication Data
Names: Sandoval, Jennifer M., editor. | Knapp, John C. (John Cortney), 1982- editor.
Title: Psychology as the discipline of interiority : "the psychological difference" in the work of Wolfgang Giegerich / edited by Jennifer M. Sandoval and John C. Knapp.
Description: Abingdon, Oxon ; New York, NY : Routledge, 2017. | Includes index.
Identifiers: LCCN 2016032189 | ISBN 9781138120785 (hbk. : alk. paper) | ISBN 9781138120884 (pbk. : alk. paper) | ISBN 9781315651378 (ebk.)
Subjects: | MESH: Giegerich, Wolfgang, 1942- | Jung, C. G. (Carl Gustav), 1875–1961. | Jungian Theory | Philosophy | Consciousness | Mind-Body Relations, Metaphysical
Classification: LCC BF109.J8 | NLM WM 460.5.J9 | DDC 155.2/644–dc23
LC record available at https://lccn.loc.gov/2016032189

ISBN: 978-1-138-12078-5 (hbk)
ISBN: 978-1-138-12088-4 (pbk)
ISBN: 978-1-315-65137-8 (ebk)

Typeset in Bembo
by Taylor & Francis Books

CONTENTS

ACKNOWLEDGEMENTS

Content in chapter 10 from ABC *Viewpoint,* 20 November 1983, is reproduced by permission of the Australian Broadcasting Corporation – Library Sales, © ABC 2016.

Material in chapter four is reprinted with the permission of Scribner, a division of Simon & Schuster, Inc. from *The Collected Works of W. B. Yeats, Volume I: The Poems,* revised by W. B. Yeats, edited by Richard J. Finneran. Copyright © 1940 by Georgie Yeats, renewed 1968 by Bertha Georgie Yeats, Michael Butler Yeats, and Anne Yeats. All rights reserved.

SOURCES AND ABBREVIATIONS

For frequently cited sources, the following abbreviations have been used:

CW: Jung, C. G. *Collected Works*. 20 vols. Ed. Herbert Read, Michael Fordham, Gerhard Adler, and William McGuire. Trans. R. F. C. Hull. Princeton: Princeton University Press, 1957–1979. Cited by volume and, unless otherwise noted, by paragraph number.

MDR: Jung, C. G. *Memories, Dreams, Reflections*. Rev. ed. Ed. Aniela Jaffé. Trans. Richard and Clara Winston. New York: Vintage Books, 1989. Cited by page number.

CONTRIBUTORS

Daniel M. Anderson, J.D., PhD is a registered psychologist in Los Angeles working in private practice and as a post-doctoral Fellow at the Reiss–Davis Child Study Center. Daniel received his doctorate from Pacifica Graduate Institute where he wrote his dissertation on "Giegerich's Psychology of Soul: Psychotherapeutic Implications." Daniel is a former member of the Executive Committee of the International Association for Jungian Studies (IAJS) and served as moderator for the IAJS online discussion group for over five years. He is currently a member of the Executive Committee of the International Society for Psychology as the Discipline of Interiority.

Marco Heleno Barreto, PhD, is a Jungian psychotherapist, working in private practice, and is also a teacher of philosophy at FAJE (Faculdade Jesuíta de Filosofia e Teologia) in Belo Horizonte, Brazil. He is the author of *Símbolo e Sabedoria Prática. C. G.Jung e o Mal-estar da Modernidade* (2008), *Imaginação Simbólica. Reflexões Introdutórias* (2008), *Pensar Jung* (2012) and *Homo Imaginans. A Imaginação Criadora na Estética de Gaston Bachelard* (forthcoming), all published by Edições Loyola, São Paulo. He has also contributed papers to many philosophical as well as psychological journals, including *Spring Journal, International Journal for Jungian Studies, Journal of Analytical Psychology* and *Jung Journal*.

Patricia Berry was for many years James Hillman's student, companion, and wife. She has been active in the Jungian world for nearly half a century, serving on faculties and boards of training institutions, and as President of the Inter-Regional Society of Jungian Analysts, as well as of the New England Society of Jungian Analysts. She teaches and lectures internationally and is the author of many publications including *Echo's Subtle Body: Contributions to an Archetypal Psychology*. Currently, she lives and practices in Woodacre, California.

Jordan Dessertine holds a Master of Arts from the School of Environmental Studies at the University of Victoria (Victoria, British Columbia) and a Bachelor of Arts from the Liberal Arts College at Concordia University (Montreal, Quebec). His scholarly interests range from the history of philosophy and consciousness to ecology, integral theory, dialogue studies and psychology as the discipline of interiority. Jordan first encountered Giegerich's works during his first year of graduate studies in 2013, which then led him to shape his thesis project around Giegerich's approach to psychology, with particular attention to its relationship to the contemplative apophatic tradition of *The Cloud of Unknowing*. The essay included in this collection is a condensed version of elements from that thesis project.

Wolfgang Giegerich is a Jungian analyst now living in Berlin. He is the author of numerous books and articles.

John Hoedl is a graduate of the C. G. Jung Institute in Zurich and is in private practice in Edmonton, Canada. Prior to beginning his training, he worked many years in Child Welfare Services in group homes, residential treatment centers, and with families of children in care. He is current president of the Western Canadian Association of Jungian Analysts. He is also a founding member and President of the International Society of Psychology as the Discipline of Interiority. John has lectured in a number of Canadian cities on themes related to Jungian psychology.

Philip Kime has an academic background in Philosophy and is an Analyst in private practice in Zurich.

John C. Knapp, PhD, is a licensed clinical psychologist who holds a doctorate in clinical psychology with an emphasis in depth psychology from Pacifica Graduate Institute. His research interests include Psychology as the Discipline of Interiority as relevant to contemporary phenomena such as the Shoah, nuclear bomb, or mass incarceration in America. He is in private practice in Chicago and Wilmette, IL.

David L. Miller, PhD, is Watson Ledden Professor Emeritus at Syracuse University and he was for many years a faculty member at Pacifica Graduate Institute in both the clinical psychology and mythological studies programs. He is an honorary member of the Inter-Regional Society of Jungian Analysts, the International Association of Analytical Psychology, and the International Society for Psychology as the Discipline of Interiority. Dr. Miller was a member of the Eranos Circle in Switzerland from 1975 until 1988 and he lectured at the Eranos Conferences on nine occasions during that period. He is the author of six books and more than one hundred articles since 1963. For more information see his website at: https://dlmiller.mysite.syr.edu/.

Greg Mogenson is a Jungian analyst practicing in London, Ontario, Canada. He is the editor of The Studies in Archetypal Psychology Series of Spring Journal Books and the Vice-President and founding member of the International Society for

Psychology as the Discipline of Interiority. The author of many articles in the field of analytical psychology, his books include *A Most Accursed Religion: When a Trauma Becomes God*, *The Dove in the Consulting Room: Hysteria and the Anima in Bollas and Jung*, *Greeting the Angels: An Imaginal View of the Mourning Process*, *Northern Gnosis: Thor, Baldr, and the Volsungs in the Thought of Freud and Jung*, and (with W. Giegerich and D. Miller) *Dialectics and Analytical Psychology: The El Capitan Seminar*. For more information visit his website at: www.gregmogenson.com.

Pamela Power, PhD, is a clinical psychologist and Jungian psychoanalyst with a private practice in Santa Monica, California. She is a member of the C. G. Jung Institute of Los Angeles where she teaches and supervises. She served as Clinic Director and Training Director at the LA Institute. She is also a member of the Inter-regional Society of Jungian Analysts as well as a member of the International Association for Analytical Psychology. She has lectured nationally and internationally on a range of topics. She has published numerous articles in *Psychological Perspectives*, the *Journal of Jungian Theory and Practice* and *Spring Journal*. Her chapter in *Shared Realities: Participation Mystique and Beyond*, edited by Mark Winborn, is entitled, "Negative Coniunctio: Envy and Sadomasochism in Analysis." Prior to becoming a psychologist, she trained as a classical musician and studied music theory and history.

Jennifer M. Sandoval, PhD, is a licenced clinical psychologist practicing in Orange County, CA. She received her doctorate from Pacifica Graduate Institute, her BA in theoretical mathematics from the University of California, Santa Cruz, and interned at the C. G. Jung Institute of Los Angeles. Her primary interests include the study of Analytical Psychology, Psychology as the Discipline of Interiority, and dialectical materialist perspectives within psychology and culture. Jennifer is the author of the forthcoming book, *A Psychological Inquiry into the Meaning and Concept of Forgiveness*, published by Routledge.

Yasuhiro Tanaka, PhD, is an Associate Professor at the Graduate School of Education, Kyoto University, for Clinical Psychology. He is Honorary-Secretary of the Association of Jungian Analysts, Japan, the Japan Association of Jungian Psychology, and the Japan Association of Sandplay Therapy. He was educated at Sophia University where he received a PhD in 1996. In addition, he was trained at the C. G. Jung Institute of Zurich and obtained his diploma in 2001. (The title of his diploma thesis was "The Logic of the Soul: Neurosis of Jung's Psychology and its Conceptual Constitution.") He is the author of the following papers in English: "On the Logic of Japanese Ophiolatry: Can the imaginal or symbolical always be psychological?" *Archives of Sandplay Therapy*, 13(1), 89–108, 2000; "The Alchemical Images and Logic in Analytical Psychology," *Harvest* 47(1), 7–30, 2001; "Is it True that Dreams do not Conceal but Teach?" *Harvest* 48(1), 22–42, 2002; "On Dissociation as a Psychological Phenomenon," *Psychologia 2008*, 51(4), 239–257, 2009; "On Some Features of Obsessive Symptoms that Patients with High-Functioning Pervasive Developmental Disorder Develop during Puberty," *Archives of Sandplay Therapy* 25(2), 75–90, 2012.

FOREWORD

"The psychological difference"

David L. Miller

Reflections on Psychology as the Discipline of Interiority

In the autumn semesters of 2001, 2002, and 2003, I taught a course called "Post-Jungian and Archetypal Theories of Myth" at Pacifica Graduate Institute. It featured the work of Adolf Guggenbühl-Craig, James Hillman and Wolfgang Giegerich, and it also included the writings of Paul Kugler on language, Stanton Marlan on shadow and Ronald Schenk on play. The course went well, I thought, with the exception of the session on Wolfgang Giegerich's then recently published book, *The Soul's Logical Life*.[1] The students seemed perplexed and I thought resistant in spite of my best pedagogical attempts. It was likely one of the murkier moments of my almost fifty years of teaching. In response to their perplexity, some of the students from the 2003 class organized a weekend seminar at El Capitan Canyon park north of Santa Barbara to be held the following June. They invited the author of our course's text to come from Germany to California in order to explain to them what I had not. Twenty-nine doctoral students attended this most remarkable occasion, to which Greg Mogenson and I were invited to be respondents. The participants were as open and reflective as they had seemed perplexed and resistant earlier. The proceedings were published in 2005 as the book *Dialectics and Analytical Psychology*.[2] Besides *Soul's Logical Life*, this book represents one of the earliest works in English on "psychology as a discipline of interiority," which is the present book's theme. I contributed an "Introduction" to the earlier volume, just as I am now offering a foreword to the current work.

---

1   Wolfgang Giegerich, *The Soul's Logical Life: Towards a Rigorous Notion of Psychology* (Frankfurt am Main; New York: Peter Lang, 1998).
2   Wolfgang Giegerich, David L. Miller and Greg Mogenson, *Dialectics and Analytical Psychology: The El Capitan Canyon Seminar* (New Orleans, LA: Spring Journal, Inc., 2005).

In the "Introduction" to the 2005 book I made a comment that I did not then explain. But now, ten years later, I have an opportunity to say what I meant by the somewhat cryptic language that I used. I was speaking about what seemed to me to be a "next stage" in Jungian psychology, and the unclear allusion occurs with the word "wave" in the following sentence: "If James Hillman's work on 'archetypal psychology' represents, after Jung himself, second wave Jungianism, the work of Wolfgang Giegerich may well indicate third wave Jungian thinking."[3] Though I did not mention it at the time of the earlier book introduction, I had in mind a category that has been used in tracing the history of the feminist movement, namely, "third wave feminism."

Rebecca Walker is credited with originating this phrase in 1992.[4] Rebecca Walker is the daughter of Alice Walker, author of *The Color Purple,* and, like her mother, she is a writer. Since 1992, the phrase has been adopted by many who theorize post-modern feminism. The idea is that first wave feminism originated during the end of the nineteenth century and continued until 1919 when women in the United States were given the right to vote. The liberation of women in first wave feminism had mainly to do with suffrage. Second wave feminism noted that there is more to liberate than simply voting rights and that the logic of first wave feminism had not been extended far enough. So from the 1960s to the 1980s a new thrust in feminism focused on politicized personal lives, sexist structures of power in the workplace, and other issues of equality from economic to reproductive matters, and a central theme was a common female identity. But again the logic was not followed through completely, since it was noted that a feminine essentialism (a putative common female identity) dominated second wave feminism and that diversity of perspective was lacking a necessary expression. Therefore, third wave feminism from the 1990s to the present began to stress diversity and anti-essentialism (no single way of being a woman), globalism, anti-upper-middle-class-white values, queer theory, women of color consciousness, post-colonial theory, transnationalism, ecofeminism, abolishing gender-role expectation, ambiguity and division about pornography, sex work, and prostitution, and so on. All three waves are, to be sure, about women, but all of the waves are also radically different, just as a surfer at the beach knows full well that riding a wave is all about water, but that when choosing a wave to ride all options are by no means the same.

---

3   David L. Miller, "Introduction," in *Dialectics and Analytical Psychology,* x. I repeated the use of the "wave"-metaphor in the "Introduction" to the *Spring* journal issue on "Philosophy and Psychology." See *Spring* 77 (2007): 6: "If Jung and Hillman may be thought of as first and second wave Jungian thought, Giegerich's work may be thought of as third wave Jungianism." Giegerich responded to this second use in an essay "Progress of Psychology?" (*The Soul Always Thinks (Collected English Papers, Vol. IV)* (New Orleans, LA: Spring Journal, Inc., 2010), 575): "David L. Miller … diagnosed an instance of a kind of progress in psychology…. If [his] view is correct …, would it contradict my thesis in this paper that there cannot be any progress in psychology? By no means. Because in the cases mentioned [Jung, Hillman and Giegerich] the psychological position that has been overcome by the later move nevertheless continues to flourish undisturbed side by side with the further developments. Its having been overcome does not outclass it."

4   "Third Wave Feminism," in: https://en.wikipedia.org/wiki/Third-wave_feminism, accessed 12/11/15.

When I wrote the earlier introduction ten years ago, I was thinking of the movement of Jungian theorizing in analogy to that of feminism. Jung, Hillman, and Giegerich are together in stressing that an authentic depth psychology (*psyche*) is about soul and not about the personal ego, but these thinkers are also different.[5] Just as Jung pushes off from Freud on issues of sexuality, Hillman pushes off from Jung on the nature of archetypes, and Giegerich pushes off from Hillman on the thematic of image and imagination.[6] This is what this book is about: numerous authors pushing off from Giegerich concerning his notion of psychology as the discipline of interiority.

One may wonder why in psychology "pushing off" is crucial, why various waves are necessary, why different theorizings are important, a variety, indeed, that the reader will meet while reading this book. "Pushing off" is crucial in order to keep a perspective from turning into a belief-system.[7] "Believing or disbelieving is not of fundamental importance" to an authentic depth psychology.[8] Psychology as the Discipline of Interiority is not a belief. If it were a part of a belief system, then Alfred North Whitehead's comment about European philosophy would be apt. Whitehead wrote that occidental philosophy is merely a "series of footnotes to

5   For example, see: Wolfgang Giegerich, *Soul's Logical Life*, 33 ("Psychology has to be about the life of soul") and 38 ("The subject matter of psychology, the soul, is … not 'empirical,' it is not a 'transcendent mystery,' it is the dialectical logical *life* playing between the soul's opposites"); Wolfgang Giegerich, *What is Soul?* (New Orleans, LA: Spring Journal, Inc., 2012), 5–26, ("psychology with soul").

6   See Chapter 1 by Wolfgang Giegerich, where the dynamic (creating a wave!) of Jung pushing off from Freud is noted.

> Psychology constitutes itself by pushing off from its one (the "Freud") side, because only in this way can it come truly into its own, to its "main concern". It establishes, and operates with, a fundamental difference. This difference (here exemplified by the Freud–Jung opposition) is indispensable for psychology—for a psychology in the tradition of C. G. Jung, a "psychology *with* soul" – and because it is indispensable (indeed its constitutive principle), we call it *the psychological difference.*"
>
> (See p. 17.)

In his chapter Giegerich uses the phrase "push off" and "pushing off" twelve times. This is by no means incidental. It is an important aspect of the logic of "psychological difference" as shown throughout the present book.

7   See my argument concerning the psychological danger of belief, in David L. Miller, "Jung's Warning about Faith: The Psychological Danger of Belief," in *Imagining Psychological Life: Philosophical, Psychological and Poetic Reflections*, ed. M. P. Sipiora (Pittsburgh: Trivium Publications, 2014), 99–106. Cf. Jung's comment in the *Red Book*: "It is [psychologically] dangerous to believe too much" (*The Red Book*, ed. S. Shamdasani [New York: Norton, 2009], 335f.).

8   Wolfgang Giegerich, "The Psychologist as Repentance Preacher," *Spring 82* (2009): 210; cf. Wolfgang Giegerich, *What is Soul?*, 122; and *The Soul Always Thinks*, 48 ("… I am here not criticizing the theory of archetypes as such. What I criticize is the *belief* in this theory, one's having become identical with it so that one routinely *envelops* in it any object of study as if in its self-evident backdrop. It is the use of the archetypal theory and the theory of the Gods as an *ideology*."); and cf. 28, 49f., 71, 208, 473f., and 578.

Plato."[9] So turning Jungian psychology into a belief-system would be merely a series of footnotes to Jung, Hillman, or Giegerich.

The University of Chicago historian of religions, Jonathan Z. Smith, referred to this footnoting as "paraphrase" or "show-and-tell." Smith addressed an international gathering of professors of religion in Anaheim, California, in 1989, and he said: "the most important function of theory … is to force an answer to that most blunt of all questions: 'So what?' Too much of what we do … may be placed somewhere between show-and-tell and paraphrase."[10] Much Jungian writing is paraphrase of Jung or show-and-tell examples intending to confirm the truth of what Jung thought and wrote. It does not "push off," like one wave does from another. It does not make waves, as did Jung and Hillman and (now) Giegerich. It does not do what Jung did. It does not think the soul forward.

The reason that waving is important to Psychology as the Discipline of Interiority is indicated by the Zen-like concept of "eachness," which occurs often in the writing that follows in this work. Psychology, if it is a discipline of interiority, privileges the soul-truth that appears in particular moments of individual and collective history. A clinician cannot possibly know who or what is going to walk through the door as the patient comes in for a session. (For that matter, a clinician cannot possibly know who or what is going to walk through the door as she or he enters the room.) What appears in the transference and counter-transference is not predictable according to a set of abstract psychological theories taken as beliefs. What happens in its suchness and eachness must be sensed and honored. And for this reason and for the reason of its unpredictability, the clinician needs all of the theories (all of the waves!) that she or he can get in order to be appropriately connected to the phenomenological eachness of the soul-situation at hand. James Hillman—with help from William James—already in 1981 had insisted on this notion. He wrote, "Eachness: that is the place I share with [William] James—and with Jung, for what else is individuation but a particularization of the soul. For James, eachness is not so much achieved through an individuation process as it is already there 'just as it seems to be.'"[11]

Wolfgang Giegerich continues the Zen-ish notion, but differently and differentiated from Hillman's notion of psychological polytheism.[12] In 2012, Giegerich was clear about the idea of eachness:

9   Alfred North Whitehead, *Process and Reality* (New York, NY: Free Press, 1979), 39.

10 Jonathan Z. Smith, "Connections," *Journal of the American Academy of Religion*, 58:1 (Spring 1990): 12; and, *On Teaching Religion* (New York, NY: Oxford University Press, 2013), 58f.

11 "Psychology: Monotheistic or Polytheistic?" in David L. Miller, *The New Polytheism* (Dallas, TX: Spring Publications, 1981), 133f. This is an expanded version of an article with the same title published in 1971 in the journal *Spring 1971*: 193ff., but the reference to James and "eachness" does not occur in the earlier version. Hillman had addressed the same problematic in his Eranos lecture in 1976: "Egalitarian Typologies *versus* the Perception of the Unique," *Eranos 45–1976* (Leiden: E. J. Brill, 1980), 221–280.

12 See Wolfgang Giegerich's differentiation of the notion of "eachness" from that of "polytheism," in: "Comment on James Hillman's 'Psychology: Monotheistic or

Concerning the daily work in the consulting room, what I pointed out here [in the book *What is Soul?*] is not to be taken abstractly as the one and only recipe for the therapies of cases of neurosis ... There may be certain phenomena, for example, individual dreams, which need an imaginal approach ... There are many different situations in each actual therapy.... The question always is what this individual phenomenon or situation here and now needs. Eachness. This is why we need to discern the spirits, learn to know when it is time for the one and when for the other approach. For this the feeling function is required, an "instinct," as it were, that lets us sense what the soul needs: whether it wants us in this specific instance to resistancelessly follow it into its depth or whether what it presents us with it presents for the sole purpose that conversely we have something to push off from.[13]

Nothing could be clearer. Depth psychology as a discipline of interiority is attentive, not to ego, but to soul and soul-phenomena. The last sentence of Wolfgang Giegerich's essay in the present volume makes this plain. He writes:

If and where psychology nevertheless insists on there having to be a present reality or immediate presence—as, for example, in the form of peak experiences, "high" feelings, the emotion of numinosity, the veneration of "the imaginal," the presence of "the sacred," "the Gods," "Angels," or the discovery of "one's personal myth"—there it [analytic theory or therapy] would turn into kitsch, and soul into a consumer good for the gratification of the greedy ego.[14]

Yes, of course! But just here is a potential irony and a possible seduction. Here there can be a breaking of the wave.

The reflections of the authors of this volume may be compelling to a reader. One may find the arguments persuasive and may even begin to believe them! That would of course be a step in the direction of treating Psychology as a Discipline of Interiority as a belief-system, counter to its own view of itself. This is a basic difficulty and conundrum for a depth psychology that focuses on soul rather than ego.

Polytheistic?" in: *Soul-Violence (Collected English Papers, Vol. III)* (New Orleans, LA: Spring Journal, Inc., 2008), 339–352, which is a response to Hillman's earlier 1971 version (see footnote 10, above), but includes a 2007 "Postscript" that addresses the difference in what would become Hillman's notion of "eachness" and Giegerich's later notion of "eachness" (see especially 350f: "In contrast to all abstract, scientist, and personalistic approaches to psychology" a psychology "with soul ... pleads for our coming down from the height of comprehensive theories that subsume the individual phenomena under some overall scheme ... down to the humility of a wholehearted dedication to psychological phenomena in their eachness").

13 Wolfgang Giegerich, *What is Soul?*, 334f.; Cf. *Soul-Violence*, 73f, 350: *The Flight into the Unconscious, (Collected English Papers, Vol. V)* (New Orleans, LA: Spring Journal, Inc., 2013), xiii, 132, 395, and 397.

14 This book, 41–42.

In the chapter that follows in this book, Wolfgang Giegerich makes the case that soul and soul-work happen for soul's sake, not "for our [ego's] benefit, our understanding, our self-knowledge."[15] This goes with viewing psychology as the discipline of interiority. But then Giegerich notes that "*we* [egos] may, through our participation in it [soul work], also find our deepest satisfaction, because in the deepest sense we exist not as organism, but as soul or *Geist*."[16] In an earlier work, Giegerich had noted that "it is of course possible that the event of a successful truly psychological interpretation creates in the person [ego] having performed it a feeling of being deeply moved or an emotion of joy and thus a 'spark.'"[17] When soul-work or soul-perspective produces ego-satisfaction, i.e., when it is clinically and thera-peutically "successful," it risks self-destructing, like a wave defining itself in the moment of its breaking.[18] The danger is in witlessly and unwittingly side-slipping or back-sliding from a soul psychology into an ego-ology.

But Giegerich attends thoughtfully to the risk, noting that in spite of the apparent irony there is no real paradox. He says about the feeling of "being deeply moved" or of experiencing "joy" that such a phenomenon "is a psychic event *in view of* and *occasioned by* an actual happening of psychology, which *itself*, however, remains averted, averted even from the subject doing psychology."[19] Here Gie-gerich is observing, as this book's title puts it, "the psychological difference" between ontological and ontic, formal and material, syntactic and semantic, and soul and ego.

Attending to what the authors participating in a discipline of interiority in this book refer to as "the psychological difference" is crucial. Riding waves requires hard work and constant attention lest one lose one's balance.

---

15 This book, 34.
16 This book, 34.
17 Giegerich, *What is Soul?*, 86n53.
18 This image is taken from a poem, *Self-portrait in a Convex Mirror*, by John Ashbery. The poem's theme is the *kenosis* of soul-work and it trades on a painting by Parmigianino. See the discussion of this in Harold Bloom, "The Breaking of Form," *Deconstruction and Criticism* (New York, NY: Seabury Press, 1979), 30. The relevant lines from the poem are: "They seemed strange because we couldn't actually see them,/And we realize this only at a point where they lapse/Like a wave breaking on a rock, giving up/Its shape in a gesture which expresses that shape."
19 Giegerich, *What is Soul?*, 86n53.

PREFACE

> Lacking strength, Beauty hates the Understanding for asking of her what it cannot do. But the life of Spirit is not the life that shrinks from death and keeps itself untouched by devastation, but rather the life that endures it and maintains itself in it. It wins its truth only when, in utter dismemberment, it finds itself.
>
> (G.F.W. Hegel, "Preface" to Phenomenology of Spirit[1])

For Jungian scholar and analyst Wolfgang Giegerich, modern psychology must be willing to follow and consciously accompany the life of the soul into the wild, relentless even in the face of devastation or (ego) death. Psychology must endure and maintain itself in this same place, and ultimately find for itself its truth in its own utter dismemberment. Psychology as the Discipline of Interiority throws down the gauntlet to Analytical and Archetypal Psychology to continue the thought originating with Jung's constituting insight that seems to have been forgotten: psyche—or soul—both creates and at the same time investigates it*self.* There *is* nothing else.

In 1994, James Hillman described Wolfgang Giegerich's work as "the most important Jungian thought now going on—maybe the only consistent Jungian thought at all,"[2] signaling Giegerich as a true equal and (ensuing) respected adversary. In the twenty years since, Giegerich's work has established itself as a legitimate and celebrated—albeit at times provocative and incendiary—theoretical approach within the Jungian and post-Jungian tradition.[3] Considered by many to be a new "wave" of Analytical Psychology, the beginnings of this movement arose out of

1   G.W.F. Hegel, *Phenomenology of Spirit*, A.V. Miller, trans. (Oxford: Oxford University Press, 1977), § 32

2   James Hillman, "Once More into the Fray: A Response to Wolfgang Giegerich's 'Killings'." *Spring 56* (1994): 1.

3   Giegerich's dialectical psychology is also emerging as relevant to other traditions, including philosophy, ecology, and critical theory.

Giegerich's landmark book, *The Soul's Logical Life*, in 1998. Here, he questioned and critiqued the fundamental identity and structure of Analytical and Archetypal Psychology, arguing for a psychology based in "thought." In the course of his analytical career, Giegerich amassed a total of six volumes of collected essays, four books, and numerous articles.[4] His more recent work, *What is Soul?* (2012), further refines his definition of psychology, and his latest book, *Neurosis: The Logic of a Metaphysical Illness* (2013), radically redefines neurosis from within his dialectical perspective. In all, Giegerich has opened up a new dimension of psychology that re-establishes its rootedness in philosophical history and the soul from which it comes. Psychology as the Discipline of Interiority "completes" the psychology originating in Jung that was further developed by Hillman, resulting in a progressive psychology that has truly come home to itself in thought.

There is no doubt that the work of Giegerich has been met with deep resistance in the wider Jungian community. Responses to his work have ranged from thoughtful criticisms to intense emotional reactions to outright attacks on his character. Many times, we (the editors) have noticed that the critiques of Giegerich's work are based on an incomplete or faulty understanding of his theory, e.g., the tendency to collapse the "psychological" into the "psychic," wherein "thought" gets conflated with the "thinking function," or when Giegerich's focus on the soul is misunderstood as a lack of care for the individual.[5] Such criticisms ultimately fall short because they stand *outside* rather than from within the definition of psychology that Giegerich articulates. The essays presented in this book do not typically engage in evaluative commentary concerning the validity of Giegerich's psychology from the outside. They are written instead from a point of view of already having fully entered into psychology defined as the discipline of interiority. We feel the insights offered from such a perspective are important and valuable in their own right and serve to deepen and further the study of psychology.

From within what Giegerich calls the "human all-too-human" perspective, we imagine our attitude towards Psychology as a Discipline of Interiority as similar to that of working with a patient, except in this case, the patient is soul. When we stand back and look at the history of Analytical Psychology and the various waves that have emerged, we recognize that right now, psychology is in a new wave. Just as when a particular movement occurs in a patient, even if at times it may seem

4   This describes only Giegerich's works in English.
5   In "Giegerich's Response to Mogenson's Critique," Giegerich writes,

> This difference of the psychological versus the ordinary consciousness sense of "individual" is essential. My whole argument is a psychological one. I am not speaking from the point of view of ordinary reality. This is to say that I attack the *psychological idea* of the individual *as focus and purpose*, not the positive reality called individual. In a way I am trying to return (or advance?) to the truth of alchemy: that what counts is the transformation of the prime matter, not my own; and only to the extent that I dedicate myself to the prime matter's and not my own individuation or transformation process can I, too, experience *my* "redemption."
> (http://ispdi.org/images/stories/PDFdocuments/G_REPLY.pdf. Accessed March 28, 2016)

somewhat destructive, possibly even carrying a shadow of its own, the patient must be contained and supported to allow for change, development, and transformation. Our attitude towards Psychology as the Discipline of Interiority is thus not one of defense. For us, the question of whether or not we *agree* with psychology as the discipline of interiority does not really matter, just as whether or not we agree with our patient's movement does not matter. Our goal is to think from within this psychological perspective, understand it as Giegerich has articulated it, and attempt to explore phenomena from within this perspective so as not to stop the wave from forming altogether. After all, Giegerich's book, *Neurosis: The Logic of a Metaphysical Illness*, was published only three years ago; there is still much work to be done to fully understand Giegerich's texts as well as the possible implications of what it would mean to *think* psychologically.

Thus, we might imagine ourselves as surfers—seeing the wave, judging and timing its place and direction, catching it as it breaks, and riding it all the way to its end. Of course, we recognize that this wave may just not appeal to other individuals, as each wave looks very different to each surfer. But this is the wave we have chosen to ride. From the psychological perspective, however, one could also ask here "Is it I who have chosen the wave, or has the wave not chosen me? Are we really talking about waves, or is it, better yet, not the water comprising *all* waves about which Psychology as the Discipline of Interiority is speaking?" It is with this question that the book begins.

Why This Book?

Throughout our graduate studies, doctoral research, and clinical work, we found ourselves immersed in the fascinating fields of psychology and philosophy, from psychoanalytic, Jungian, and archetypal psychology, to phenomenology, critical theory, and other modern philosophies. When in the later course of our studies we encountered the work of Wolfgang Giegerich, something rather shocking dawned on us that until then had been completely obscured: we had been studying psychology, writing about psychology, and applying psychological concepts in our consulting rooms, but all the while we were not *thinking* psychologically.

To think *psychologically* is truly an *opus contra naturam* and must be consciously entered into, learned, and practiced. As Giegerich wrote back in 1998,

> Apart from a comprehensive knowledge about the phenomenology of the soul's life as manifested in the history of mankind, the training of candidates should be a differentiation of their mind: mind processing! The mind needs to learn to easily make the complex logical, dialectical movements that are required if an understanding is to be truly psychological and if the logical level of soul is to be reached at all. It needs to acquire truly psychological categories and forms of thought, and thorough practice in working with them.[6]

6   Wolfgang Giegerich, *The Soul's Logical Life: Towards a Rigorous Notion of Psychology* (Frankfurt am Main; New York: Peter Lang, 1998), 277.

The ability to make complex, dialectical movements and acquire truly psychological categories and forms of thought was what we were missing. The most important question, "How, through the subject matter at hand, is the soul speaking about *itself?*" went unasked.

For us, the process (ever ongoing) of answering this question has been exciting, enriching, and liberating. At the same time it has been profoundly difficult, at times disorienting, and even painful! Answering this question means surrendering one's subjective, egoic position in order to make room for the psychological perspective. Giegerich writes,

> A real understanding presupposes a kind of love, one's abandon of one's own subjectivity; not love as sentiment or emotion, but logical love. If we have not succeeded in (at least experimentally) giving ourselves over to the inspiring core of the work we are examining, we will not even be able to criticize it.[7]

As echoed in the Prayer of St. Francis, "Make me an instrument of your peace," Psychology as the Discipline of Interiority relegates the human being to mere instrument and mouthpiece—the very vessel through which the logical life of the soul might be witnessed and spoken—thus granting the soul its proper place and reality.

We realize this book is a beginning. Its dialectical approach is challenging on many levels. There is most certainly "an entrance problem."[8] However, we feel Jungian analysts, clinicians, scholars, and writers would do well to take Giegerich seriously, as his thought has profoundly enriched our work with patients insofar as our "feeling" has become more refined and deepened our capacity to meet patients *where they are.* His vast body of work has earned its place with the transformational writers in the field of psychology and deserves to be taken up with dedication, openness, and intellectual rigor. We must work to familiarize ourselves with the writings of Giegerich, just as we would with Freud, Jung, or Hillman. We must wrestle with the concepts in an undefended manner, give ourselves over to them, learn how to think dialectically, and work psychologically. Analytical theory requires *critical* self-reflection; to rise above itself it must display a willingness to "cut into its own flesh," to undergo a dissolution, a self-sublation, and allow itself to be utterly dismembered so as to find itself anew. As psychologists in search of soul, we must allow ourselves to be reached by the interiority of these ideas, to both comprehend them and be comprehended by them, and thus be transformed by them. *We can no longer afford to let our thinking miss the dialectic of the soul's life.*

Psychology as the Discipline of Interiority: "The Psychological Difference" in the work of Wolfgang Giegerich is our "passionately attempted forward movement"[9] to share the

---

7   Giegerich, *Soul's Logical Life*, 89.
8   See Chapter 1, "No Admission!: The Entrance into Psychology and the Style of Psychological Discourse," in Giegerich, *Soul's Logical Life*, 13–38.
9   Wolfgang Giegerich, David L. Miller and Greg Mogenson, *Dialectics & Analytical Psychology: The El Capitan Canyon Seminar* (New Orleans, LA: Spring Journal, Inc., 2005), 16.

ways in which Psychology as the Discipline of Interiority has been taken up by various scholars and clinicians. In appreciation for those who follow in whole-hearted accompaniment the life of the soul, we wish to thank Dr. David Miller, Watson-Ledden Professor of Religion, Emeritus, at Syracuse University and long-standing influential voice in the field of Analytical Psychology, for his contribution to this work as well as his inspiration, support, and friendship. We would also like to thank Greg Mogenson, Jungian analyst and series editor of Dr. Wolfgang Giegerich's *Collected English Papers*, for his leadership in the field of psychological studies as well as his contributions, guidance, and encouragement throughout this project. Our gratitude extends to the distinguished contributing authors of this book. We thank them for their participation and intelligent scholarship, and for sharing the ways in which true psychological thinking is unfolding in their own work. Finally, we wish to extend our heartfelt gratitude to Dr. Giegerich for his generous and original contribution to this effort. His lifelong work has not only provided the revolutionary change of consciousness that is needed in the study of psychology, but it also has changed us.

INTRODUCTION

Jennifer M. Sandoval and John C. Knapp

In order to do psychology, a change of consciousness is needed.[1]

Psychology as the Discipline of Interiority originates from the body of thought developed by Jungian scholar and analyst Wolfgang Giegerich over the course of more than three decades. While the overall work of C. G. Jung is foundational to his thinking, Giegerich's rigorous and dialectical application of analytical psychology to *itself* identified and distilled Jung's most advanced, extraordinary, and subtle insights, forming a radical new basis from which to ground a modern psychology. In this, Psychology as the Discipline of Interiority extends beyond the boundaries of Analytical Psychology into philosophy, Hegelian dialectics, and the abstract spirit of the soul in contemporary phenomena such as mass media, technology, digital communications, nuclear warfare, and sophisticated neuroses. With this psychology, Giegerich has laid the remarkable groundwork that makes possible the "catapulting [of] consciousness to a higher stage and status of itself,"[2] opening up the field of psychology as the study of the soul in the 21st century.

In 2012, the International Society for Psychology as the Discipline of Interiority (ISPDI) was formed in order to provide a more formal home and community within which the work of psychology might proceed. Many of the essays contained within this book originated from papers presented at ISPDI conferences. This volume reflects the current thinking of this community of scholars as well as the ongoing maturation of Giegerich's work as it has developed within the wider psychological community. We hope this book makes the complexity, depth, and

1 Wolfgang Giegerich, *Neurosis: The Logic of a Metaphysical Illness* (New Orleans, LA: Spring Journal, Inc., 2013), 3.
2 Wolfgang Giegerich, *What is Soul?* (New Orleans, LA: Spring Journal, Inc., 2012), 321.

innovativeness of such "thought" accessible to scholars, practitioners, and students, and further elevates psychology to its true discipline as the study of soul.

An introduction, negated.

In the attempt to "introduce" Psychology as the Discipline of Interiority, we immediately arrive at what is commonly referred to as the "entrance problem" of psychology,[3] in which a seeming contradiction surfaces, namely, that one must already have arrived at the psychological level in order to enter it. This apparent contradiction speaks to the dialectical nature of psychological thinking in that a truly dialectical "introduction" would itself also be *at the same moment* psychology's conclusion, or "absolute negativity." Already, we are thrown into the language of which we, as ego personalities, are unfamiliar, serving as the initial and very first negation that might drastically alter our perspective. We come to the realization that we do not know what psychology itself is; we are fundamentally *outside* psychology as we are introduced to it. As challenging as this dialectical process is, though, we proceed, as there is no other route by which one might reach psychology proper. To further elucidate this dialectic, then, let us explore the three "moments" of psychology as the discipline of interiority—*psychology, discipline*, and *interiority*—as individual concepts from within the psychological perspective. This might serve to further explicate the dialectical process that is psychology itself and better "introduce" Psychology as the Discipline of Interiority and the essays contained within this book.

Psychology

Psychology defined as a discipline of interiority is decidedly *not* ordinary psychology. It does not primarily concern itself with the "scientific study of the human mind and its functions."[4] While this notion of psychology does not *exclude* such aspects, its main concern lies with that which is over and above ordinary psychology, or the very logic giving rise to consciousness itself—what Wolfgang Giegerich calls "soul." Psychology is thereby defined as a psychology with soul,[5] and as such distinct from other psychologies. In his book, *What is Soul?*, Giegerich observes:

> Academic psychology and most schools of psychotherapy do not use, or rather systematically avoid, the concept soul. One talks instead, for example, about "the psyche," about the "behavior of the organism," or about "what goes on inside people" as "the subjective aspect of human life," but not about the

3   Wolfgang Giegerich, *The Soul's Logical Life: Towards a Rigorous Notion of Psychology* (Frankfurt am Main; New York: P. Lang, 1998), 23.
4   www.merriam-webster.com/dictionary/psychology. Accessed on March 28, 2016.
5   Jung describes his psychology as a "'psychology with soul' that is, a psychology [*Seelenlehre*] based on the hypothesis of an autonomous mind [*Geist*]" (*CW* 8 § 661, transl. modif. by Giegerich).

soul... [I]t is a unique feature of Jungian psychology that it makes serious use of the term soul.[6]

However, soul is here quite different than the traditional notion often found in analytical literature, as psychologically "the soul" does not "exist" as a static entity. It is *not*, for example, the substantive, *a-priori*, "feminine," benevolent, personal, or *for-us* "soul" that may appear in Jungian, transpersonal, or New Age psychologies. The soul is expressly *not* substantiated, *not* given, *not* imbued with human characteristics, and certainly not for us. "Where the soul does not stir, where it does not produce (feelings, ideas, symptoms, dreams, works of art or culture...), *there simply is no soul*."[7] Giegerich writes, "The soul must not be positivized. It does not exist. But this does not at all mean that it is simply nothing."[8]

At the same moment, the soul does exist! A joke may aid in illustrating the (logically) negative nature of soul: a German worker gets a job in Siberia during the reign of Stalinism. Aware that all correspondence will inevitably be read by censors, he tells his friends: "Let's establish a code: if a letter you receive from me is written in ordinary blue ink, it is true; if it is written in red ink, it is false." After a month, his friends get the first letter, written in blue ink: "Everything is wonderful here! Stores are full, food is abundant, apartments are large and properly heated, movie theaters show films from the West, there are many beautiful people ready for an affair—the only thing unavailable is red ink."

How does this joke relate to the soul as absolutely negative? Let us consider the ordinary blue ink as the language and form of daily life, of things in their appearing or semantic form. The red ink would then signify the simple negation of those forms, but still in the same language and on the same semantic level. The knowledge that the red ink is *missing* however *negates* the presence of the red ink, thus serving to convey the blue ink in its absolutely negated form—as the missing red ink. In other words, the knowledge that the red ink is missing is able to convey the *real* truth of the blue ink (as *untruth* − not everything is wonderful in Siberia!).

Psychologically speaking, the ego writes in blue ink and insists that what it writes is true. Otherwise, it would simply be written in red ink. It can only conceive of a simple negation, or red ink, for it does not discern the *psychological* difference. While everything the soul writes has to be written in blue ink, *psychology knows that the red ink is missing*. A true psychology, then, *thinks as* the missing red ink. In this, the missing red ink in our joke signifies the absolutely negative status of soul as *departed*, or *absent*; not present, but certainly not *nothing*! The soul's *presence as absence* is signified by the knowledge that red ink is missing, indicating the logical form of soul as *thought*. Such knowing allows us to comprehend the truth in its essence, absolved from its own *literal* (blue ink) truth. Because soul exists as syntax, or the *form* of form, it is "invisible" and "shows" itself only indirectly, on the

---

6   Giegerich, *What is Soul?*, 5–6.
7   Giegerich, *What is Soul?*, 41.
8   Giegerich, *What is Soul?*, 22.

semantic level as cultural expressions such as art, literature, media and the internet, nuclear arsenals, capitalism, political movements, etc., i.e., all written in "blue ink" by the objective psyche as its self-expression in the world. But these are mere expressions, not soul itself. Soul, as absolutely negative, is not a substance but pure *process* and can only live for us as "missing."

This is why from a psychological perspective we cannot refer to psychology as a substantial entity, such as "Psychology as the Discipline of Interiority", as the "proper noun," or the "branch" of psychology developed by the man named "Wolfgang Giegerich." Psychology as the discipline of interiority cannot be reduced to an acronym either, i.e., "PDI," because psychology must always strive to be an investigation, articulation, and practice of psychology itself. If it is to *live as the missing red ink*, soul can only exist as *living* psychology and not as static entity. Proper nouns or abbreviations, in this sense, would serve as stopgaps for fully thinking the soul and further deaden the soul to a mere object as opposed to active process, or absolute negativity.[9]

While we cannot hope to fully define what the soul is here (after all, Giegerich wrote an entire book devoted to that task!), to do psychology one must let go of the concept of soul as empirically graspable, for to reach the absolutely negative soul, the substantial notion of soul must be allowed a true negation, wherein its absence bears witness to the soul's reality, as if waiting for us to *make* it.

Discipline

An essential guiding principle of psychology as stated by Jung is, "Above all, don't let anything from outside, that does not belong, get into it, for the fantasy-image has 'everything it needs' [*omne quo indiget*] within itself."[10] Psychology as a *discipline* speaks to the commitment of the psychologist to "eachness" in staying with and lingering with the fantasy image, dream, symptom, problem, situation, text— whatever phenomenon is in the alchemical retort—and wholeheartedly giving herself over and listening to what it conveys in its own context and on its own terms such that it becomes her entire *world*. Only in leaving behind one's ego personality, undergoing a relentless exposure to the unknown in its vastness and unpredictability and fully "entering the retort" with the subject matter at hand can one hope to see the phenomenon psychologically and enter into its infinite interiority.

The experience of parting with one's ego-personality is a requirement of doing psychology and is reflected in the word *discipline*. True to its namesake, psychology as the discipline of interiority speaks to the degree of effort and rigorous thinking necessary to arrive at psychology proper. Such thought entails a painstaking "labor

9   We would like to thank Dr. Giegerich for awakening us to this idea in our email exchange with him, as originally we had been blind to what he called the "stopgap" nature of the "PDI" acronym.
10 C. G. Jung, *CW 14*, § 749.

of the concept," an effort that may even include a degree of suffering (in the way of *mortificatio* or *putrefactio*) resembling the "punishment" associated with discipline as one suffers the logical death, or loss of the semantic or substantive reality, required to reach the syntax of true psychology. Reaching the soul level entails the relinquishment of the subjective ego-personality and total surrender to the objective psyche, an *opus contra naturam* akin to "cutting into one's own flesh," so to speak.

Thinking here is a crucial aspect of discipline and is distinct from Jung's "thinking function." Giegerich states:

> It cannot be stressed enough: thought is not a "function," even though what Jung called the "thinking function" is of course one moment in developed, explicit thought. Thought is ... the *quinta essentia* of, and beyond, all four functions. It is the breakthrough ... to the entirely different *level* of logic or the Notion. ... Basically, thought is the soul's (or "the whole man's") openness to what *is*, the capacity to express and respond to the *truth* of the age. It is what allows the human being to enter Actaion's wilderness, to extend into the realm of origins and pre-existence. What is meant by thought in this context is, therefore, not abstract, but living thought, or better: logical movement, logical life.[11]

Returning to the notion of soul, it is our *active* thinking that grants access to the soul level of consciousness. "[Soul] is only in the doing: in the act or process of awareness, feeling appreciation, thinking comprehension."[12] The soul, and psychology, is not a given. Rather, psychology and soul must be created over and over again, each time anew, in and through a discipline that is willing to suffer and surrender to the logical death that is to be died at any given moment.

That the psychologist would freely take up the difficult and demanding discipline of psychology reflects the devotion inherent to discipline insofar as a "disciple" is one who devotedly seeks knowledge or *truth*.[13] Any psychological discussion on the notion of discipline, then, would simultaneously include a discussion on truth, as discipline is ultimately aimed towards achieving or reaching a specific "goal"—whether that goal be knowledge, or simply the "excellence" of the craft one practices. In the case of psychology, truth occurs as a consequence of discipline, as it is inherent, or internal, to the very notion of discipline. Truth might be here linked to the profound *freedom* which occurs as a result of disciplined practice.

A helpful way of elaborating upon the dialectic of discipline and truth might be to compare this dialectic to that between imprisonment and freedom. It is common to think of imprisonment and freedom as being inherently opposite of and indeed

---

11 Giegerich, *Soul's Logical Life*, 125.
12 Giegerich, *What is Soul?*, 50.
13 The "inexplicable" desire of the psychologist to undergo such a difficult experience is discussed briefly in Chapter 6 of this volume.

divorced from one another, especially when the notion of freedom is so frequently reduced to mere *human* freedom, i.e., as the capacity to choose based upon being un-encumbered. In a heavily consumerist society and free world, the un-encumberedness of freedom is only more exaggerated, where the idea of freedom occurs solely as a positivistic notion of "freedom-as-literal." For a psychological, or dialectical, interpretation, however, this idea of freedom must be re-leased so that we might arrive at *psychological* freedom, wherein freedom would be inherently tied to the notion of imprisonment. Plato's Cave Allegory is a good example of this dialectic, wherein the allegory, when taken as a whole—as one *single* thought—speaks to the necessity of imprisonment in the quest for the world of the Sun, or Truth. There are not two worlds—the world inside the cave and the world outside the cave—but one world: the world of thought. Just as "Mercurius can only be freed from his imprisonment in the bottle *within* his absolute imprisonment,"[14] so too can psychology only be practiced within the discipline of its very own logic.

Interiority

If one can speak of an "introduction" to psychology as related to the "entrance problem," one might speak of a "conclusion" as related to "interiority." In order to elucidate this point, let us remember that psychology's constituting insight is that the psyche or soul both *creates* and at the same time *investigates* it*self*. Giegerich notes, "As opposed to all sciences, psychology does not and cannot have an Archimedean point outside of itself (which is its singular distinction and the reason why it is in a logically higher status of consciousness than the sciences)."[15] To work and think psychologically then is like trying to build a boat while you are already out on the water. As Greg Mogenson describes:

> Whereas actual sailing vessels are built in shipyards, only subsequently to be launched into the sea ... psychology ... is different. The ship that it *is* has to build itself at sea, from what looms up or bobs up from behind the scenes of whatever the matter of interest may be that it finds itself submerged in on each interpretative occasion.[16]

No objective external vantage point means that any true observation of psychological subject matter must occur from *within* the subject matter, via the *interiorization* of the subject matter into *itself*. "*If* there is to be psychology at all," writes Giegerich, "it has to recover the world of outside facts as already reflected, sublated, ones within its own Notion of soul, and not somewhere out there."[17] Psychology must "turn, not just introspectively to the literal 'inside,' but to the same outside facts

---

14   Wolfgang Giegerich, "Closure and Setting Free," *Spring: A Journal of Archetype and Culture*, 74 (2006): 59.
15   Giegerich, *Soul's Logical Life*, 95.
16   See Greg Mogenson's "Afterword" in this volume, 198.
17   Giegerich, *Soul's Logical Life*, 96.

that all the different sciences turn to, but *via itself, via its own center, its own internal Notion.*"[18] This is what makes psychology exist not only as "introduction" but also as its own "conclusion."

This inward turn or *interiority* is not interiority in a traditional sense. It is *not* the interiority that might be used by a phenomenologist to describe the "things themselves," for example, as in a rich phenomenological description or amplification of a particular phenomenon; this would only be interiority on the horizontal, or semantic level of appearance, and not on what Giegerich describes as the vertical or syntactical level of the soul. Nor is interiority that part of the human person that resides "inside"—as in when one refers to the psychodynamic life of the human being; this has still not transgressed the horizontal plane at which psychic life occurs. Interiority, rather, uroborically refers to the interior life of the soul *as such*—the inner Truth of psychology as it becomes conscious of *itself*, wherein the soul "is not the (literal, in itself external) inwardness in man, not traditional psychology's 'the unconscious,' but [the soul's] inwardness in itself, absolute interiority."[19] The infinite interiority of the soul is reached through a *logical* act, that of the dialectical *negation* of externality as such, or the *dialectical interiorization* into absolute negativity.

Slavoj Zizek likes to re-tell a wonderful dialectical joke in Lubitsch's *Ninotchka*: The hero visits a cafe and orders coffee without cream; the waiter replies: "Sorry, but we have run out of cream. Can I bring you coffee without milk?"

The beauty of this joke is that it offers a hint of the "hidden" meanings exposed through dialectical thought. We suddenly realize that coffee without cream is not the same as coffee without milk; the dialectic reveals the particular lack (negation) to function as a *positive* feature that further differentiates our cup of coffee. The dialectical logic also hints at another reality of the hero's coffee without cream: it is not the same as coffee without milk on the one hand, and yet of course coffee without cream *is* the same as coffee without milk on the other. Thus the waiter has shown, through dialectical thought, the hero's coffee as the "unity" of the union of coffee without cream with its difference—coffee without milk—to reveal *precisely* a further determination of meaning in the hero's request![20] Notice how this deeper logical structure cannot be *imagined*, as the imagination gets trapped by variations of coffee with or without dairy products, but that the dialectic *can* be completed in *thought*. Giegerich echoes this:

> The moment we become conscious of a contradiction (a contradiction not due to faulty thinking but inherent in the structure of an idea), the imagining and pictorially thinking mind comes to the end of its wits. It is the moment where thought, dialectical thinking, has to take over. The moment when the soul has moved from semantics to syntax, from the fish swimming in the

18   Giegerich, *Soul's Logical Life*, 96.
19   Giegerich, *What is Soul?*, 333.
20   Note that coffee-*with*-cream and coffee-*with*-milk both exist as sublated (negated) moments within our hero's coffee *as* coffee-without-cream and (not) coffee-without-milk.

waters to the waters themselves, from content to logical form, there is no way around thought.[21]

Psychology, or the study of the soul, requires thought because the soul is not a substantial "thing" that *can* be imagined. Rather, soul is pure methodology, sheer fluidity, dialectical liquidity, or the *absolute negativity* from which substantiality issues. Thus, psychology finds its ultimate truth in the psychologist's ability to *think*.

Part I: "The psychological difference" in theory

This book explores one of the most crucial concepts of psychology, and one on which the entirety of a "true" psychology rests, in the idea of *the psychological difference*. While the psychological difference is a rather complex notion, it can be most simply defined by nature of its two parts—the psychic and psychological—and the recognition of the difference between these two dimensions. While psychic life includes all those aspects of the human organism such as one's biology, emotions, feelings, thoughts, instincts, and fantasies, psychological life, on the other hand, is about the inner life of the soul, or the question of what, in fact, psychology is. Giegerich notes:

> True psychology depends on the awareness of what I call the "psychological difference" (a kind of analogy to Heidegger's "ontological difference"). It is the difference that runs through the meaning of the word psychology itself and divides "psychology" as the account of the psychologies that people have (personalistic psychology) from "psychology" as description of the life of the soul.[22]

With the idea of the psychological difference, psychology is able to know itself in the modern world, free from those anthropomorphic or personalistic biases which would fail to recognize the difference between man and soul.

The essays in part one reflect upon and apply the *logic* of psychology, often further differentiating it from traditional analytical and archetypal theory. Following the idea that "psychology must be applied to itself and not only to patients or cultural phenomena like myths and fairy tales,"[23] Psychology as the Discipline of Interiority employs a dialectical method of inquiry and analysis, being an inherent theoretical, speculative, and *critical* psychology.[24] For in allowing the underlying thought process

21 Wolfgang Giegerich, *Dreaming the Myth Onwards: C. G. Jung on Christianity and on Hegel: Part 2 of the Flight Into the Unconscious (Collected English Papers, Vol. VI)* (New Orleans, LA: Spring Journal, Inc., 2014), 67.
22 Giegerich, *Soul's Logical Life*, 124.
23 Wolfgang Giegerich, *The Flight Into the Unconscious: An Analysis of C. G. Jung's Psychology Project (Collected English Papers, Vol. V)* (New Orleans, LA: Spring Journal, Inc., 2013), 1.
24

> Psychology is no more than one of the possible methodological approaches to what happens and has given up any claim to being or striving for true knowing. Psychology is merely one of the things one can do if one is so inclined. Although the sense of truth is still vital to it, this sense of truth, or its truth itself, is merely internal

of the subject matter at hand to reach its logical conclusion, psychological thinking must inevitably *negate* those ideas it encounters that have failed to further develop, or, having been reified and concretized, become "frozen" in their tracks. The *ego* experience of such negation is predictably a threatening or caustic one of criticism, invalidation, or rejection.[25] Yet in identifying and negating fixed or stagnant ideas, consciousness can further itself, in effect "pushing off" from its position into ever deepening knowledge of itself.

It may help here to recognize that with a true negation, that which is negated is not fully lost but rather *sublated*,[26] having "fulfilled" its function as an integral moment of the logical life of which it is a part, such as the blossom gives way to the fruit. As Hegel explains:

> The bud disappears when the blossom breaks through, and we might say that the former is refuted by the latter; in the same way when the fruit comes, the blossom may be explained to be a false form of the plant's existence, for the fruit appears as its true nature in place of the blossom. The ceaseless activity of their own inherent nature makes these stages moments of an organic unity, where they not merely do not contradict one another, but where one is as necessary as the other; and constitutes thereby the life of the whole.[27]

The essays that follow, in "thinking" the inner logic of psychology, are written in an academic spirit of inclusivity, respect, and recognition of the value and indeed *necessity for the soul* of those ideas from which they push off, so as to constitute psychologically "the life of the whole." At the same time, for the blossom to become fruit, it must undergo a fundamental transformation, and the essays also begin where this transformation occurs. In the case of fruit, this happens, of course, by nature of pollination. Just as when pollination occurs, a wholly new life is created and established that must now live itself further and unfold from within its own new nature, so too is psychology *born* psychology and must unfold according to its new logic.

> to it as a methodological guiding principle and aim. Its validity remains enclosed within itself. It does not extend out beyond itself.
>
> (Giegerich, *What is Soul?*, 288)

25 Giegerich is highly critical of Jungians who fail to recognize the primary insight of Jungian psychology, that psychology is unique in that it has no objective Archimedean point from which to view itself. Thus any external reflection of psychological ideas or concepts is unpsychological and often includes the additional failure of excluding *itself* in its analysis. Any attempt to view a phenomenon externally (from the fantasy of an Archimedean point) is patently unpsychological.

26 "The concept of sublation implies that kind of overcoming or superseding that is at the same time a retention of what is being superseded" (Giegerich, *Soul's Logical Life*, 193). To "sublimate" is distinct in that it primarily refers to the more appropriate re-direction of libido, thus lacking the *distillation* quality of sublation.

27 Georg W. Friedrich Hegel, *The Phenomenology of Mind: Volume 1* (New York, NY: Cosimo Inc., 2005), 62.

Part II: "The psychological difference" in contemporary life

With the notion of the psychological difference comes the recognition that the soul is fundamentally *historical,* i.e. the soul changes and develops through time as it gains further self-determination and self-awareness. Currently, the soul's historical form reflects the highly distilled and abstract thinking of the 21st century, expressing itself in today's world through what may seem to be the very soulless phenomena of high tech, digital communications, climate change, money markets, nuclear weapons, genocide, and mass media, for example. However, psychology recognizes such phenomena as expressions of soul. Giegerich states, "[Ours] is a world of steel-and-glass architecture, asphalt streets, airplanes and spacecraft, electronics, computer tomography, shopping malls, etc. Tremendous changes have occurred since the days of mythological man: they are the assignment, we have to do our homework."[28]

Where other psychologies do not recognize the soul in this, its now modern form, even pitting the soul *against* such "traumas of the Real" in an effort to save it, they do not practice or exist as *true* psychology. True psychology, bearing in mind the psychological difference, *recognizes modern reality as a legitimate expression of the soul,* studying it to better comprehend the unfolding of the soul's logical life.[29] Giegerich writes:

> Neither the ancient tools for making the soul's plight visible and for thinking about and dealing with it, namely myths, symbols, divine images, rituals, oracles, visions and the like, nor the modern tools (empathy, hermeneutic under-standing, subjective confession, free association, dream interpretation, analysis of transference, etc.) are capable of really catching sight of where the soul is today. The psychological mind has to acquire for itself a (psychological) ... level of abstract thinking. Otherwise ... this mind is like somebody who looks inside his radio for a little man speaking the news, because he has no notion of radio waves; and who has no notion of radio waves because his idea of reality is confined to what human eyes can see and human hands can touch and because he refuses to allow his idea of reality to undergo a revolution.[30]

28   Wolfgang Giegerich, *Soul Always Thinks,* 70.
29

> If you start out with the idea of the objective psyche, you do not have to work at re-ensouling anything, because the soul is already there to begin with, and it is usually where it is least expected and least wanted. This is why I want to mine the objective phenomena (for example, the phenomena of Globalization, Profit Max-imation, etc.) for soul ... Instead of responding in the sense of a *compensatory* rela-tionship between psyche and the traumas of the Real, I want to listen to what the real process is telling me; I want to be taught by the Real how I have to think, I want to be put into my place, maybe even "baptized" by it. This is how *I* am trying to lay my "infinitesimal grain in the scales of humanity's soul."
>   ("Giegerich's Response to Mogenson's Critique." Accessed on March 26, 2016, http://ispdi.org/images/stories/PDFdocuments/G_REPLY.pdf)

30   Giegerich, *Soul's Logical Life,* 31.

Where ordinary psychology is guided by a personalistic focus on the individual, perhaps even in an attempt to save or re-ensoul the world, it fails to engage with the abstract complexity of contemporary phenomena; it is not relating to the soul of the Real and thus cannot comprehend the modern soul in its actual condition. In this, it fails to catch sight of and *misses* the guise of the modern soul in its distilled, negative, and abstract form altogether. A true psychology, however, operates on the same logical level as the absolutely negative soul of modernity, establishing a rigorous "thinking" that is intellectually on par with the sophisticated spirit present within contemporary cultural phenomena.

In contemporary life, the soul knows itself directly as spirit or concept. This historical transformation constitutes a dialectical movement, or *telos*—a labor of ever greater self-refinement and distillation similar to that found in the alchemist's quest for the treasured *lapis*.[31] Having emerged from the waters of "Meaning,"[32] the soul, Giegerich suggests, has emancipated itself from *itself* and now operates on the level of pure syntax, or logic. He notes:

> Now that the soul has been born out of nature, that it has—logically, psychologically—left nature, substance, and content fundamentally behind itself, now that man has been able to go to the moon and, via satellites, essentially looks down upon the Earth from outer space, now that he manipulates the innermost constitution and workings of nature itself (nuclear power plants, nanotechnology, genetic engineering) and lives and thinks on a very abstract level of functions, logical relationships, structural forms, now mythic imagination has fundamentally become incapable of expressing the soul.[33]

In modernity, the soul has left behind its mythic imagining and now reflects its current logical form in abstract contemporary phenomena; we might here imagine the soul's imaginal roots as the blossom having given way to the "fruit" of modern life, where man has fully disrobed from his mythical garment and revels in his autonomy. "The freedom from soul is total today," writes Giegerich, *"with one single exception: neurosis."*[34]

In his book *Neurosis: The Logic of a Metaphysical Illness*, Giegerich lays out a rigorous and comprehensive blueprint for the underlying *logic* of neurosis, having implications for both the psychic and psychological level. On the psychic level, Giegerich radically diverges from the conventional Jungian perspective that interprets neurotic symptoms as meaningful[35] or helpful.[36] Instead,

---

31 The soul's *opus magnum* and *opus parvum* in alchemy reflect the soul's psychological difference.

32 Wolfgang Giegerich, "The End of Meaning and the Birth of Man. An essay about the state reached in the history of consciousness and an analysis of C. G. Jung's psychology project," in *The Soul Always Thinks*, 189–283.

33 Giegerich, *What is Soul?*, 151–152.

34 Giegerich, *What is Soul?*, 330.

35 "Neurosis is intimately bound up with the problem of our time and really represents an unsuccessful attempt on the part of the individual to solve the general problem in his own person" (Jung, *CW* 7, § 18).

36 Referring to neurosis, Jung writes, *"Not it is what is cured, rather it cures us. A human being is ill but the illness is nature's attempt to heal him"* in *CW* 10, § 361.

[neurosis] is the soul's free decision to refuse its real truth, a truth which in the case of the modern soul is its emptiness or absence, i.e., its negativity, and instead to insist on "The Absolute" as an artificial substitute for the lost metaphysics of two or three hundred years ago.

As such, neurosis is not a *morbus sacer* as it was for Jung, but merely "a manifestation and product of the *sick* soul," with no redeeming value.[37]

On the psychological side, however, neurosis is purposive and necessary for the soul's becoming conscious of itself. "[T]he invention of neurosis as a cultural phenomenon during the 19th century ... happened for the sole purpose of forcing itself (the soul) to explicitly emancipate itself from itself."[38] Giegerich continues,

> It [the soul] has to actively, systematically, in full detail and in full awareness *work off* its own fascination and infatuation with the metaphysical, the mythic, the numinous, and the suggestive power of the imaginal—*through* pulling itself out of its neurosis, *really* stepping out of it and leaving it behind as the nothing that it is.[39]

In this sense, modern neurosis can be seen as an alchemical acid bath for the soul, by which semantic content is burned off and dissolved.

At the same time that neurosis emerged in the 19th century, so too did the institution of psychotherapy.[40] The reader may recall the four stages of therapy described by Jung as confession, instruction, education, and transformation. In the initial stages, patients are often in need of "down-to-earth help, such as real human attention, sympathy, and understanding; an *honest* face-to-face encounter with another human being; guidance through personal crisis or difficult life situations"[41] as opposed to dispensing with psychic ego concerns for the sake of the psychological work of soul-making. However, when it comes to the soul, only in this final category, that of *transformation*, "would [one] reach the precincts of psychology proper."[42] Giegerich, in speaking of the psychological difference and its relevance to his clinical work, states:

> Especially important is for me the respect for the psychological difference. I try to be present in the sessions as the concrete ordinary person that I am (human, all-too-human) and to also see the ordinary human being in my patient ... But despite this acknowledgement of the human level, this is ... not my focus.

---

37 "Neurosis ... is simply sick, a terrible aberration, and a dead end.... [I]t certainly does not cure us," in Giegerich, *What is Soul?*, 160.
38 *What is Soul?*, 331.
39 *What is Soul?*, 332.
40 Giegerich suggests that neurosis and psychology are equiprimordial. See Giegerich, *Neurosis*, 101.
41 Giegerich, *What is Soul?*, 316.
42 Giegerich, *What is Soul?*, 316.

The focus is the soul, the psychology of the situation, the soul level. What does the soul, the objective psyche, want?[43]

The clinical practice of psychotherapy is a soul phenomenon, yet only to the extent that it is oriented toward the objective soul (i.e., over and above the subjective ego). While human consciousness is the place in and through which the soul works, a psychological perspective recognizes that the soul "does not speak about us and ... has no interest in us and our well-being."[44] This in no way suggests human beings are inconsequential to the soul's life. Giegerich writes,

> [A]s the place in and through which [soul] can realize itself, we are ... needed, even indispensable for it, and if we let it find its "eternal recreation" and fulfilment, then even we may, through our participation in it, also find our deepest satisfaction, because in the deepest sense we exist not as organism, but as soul or *Geist*.[45]

The essays in this book attempt to follow the life of *Geist*, keeping before them the foundational questions that guide any true psychological inquiry: *What is the soul saying about itself? What does the soul want?*

---

43 With regards to the psychological difference and psychotherapy, Giegerich also notes,

> The psychological difference ('render unto Caesar the things that are Caesar's and to God the things that are God's') helps to avoid the two dangers that go along with a therapeutic approach unaware of the difference, first, the danger of becoming personalistic and positivistic as often in developmental psychology, and secondly, the danger of mystification (unnecessarily inflating the patient's life and experiences with mythic importance; seeing the patient's process as his 'individuation' in the loaded Jungian sense; operating with the search for wholeness and meanings, etc.)
>
>   (in Ann Casement, "The Interiorizing Movement of Logical Life: Reflections on Wolfgang Giegerich," *The Journal of Analytical Psychology*, 56(4) (2011): 540)

It should further be noted that the inability to recognize the soul's contemporary logical status can oftentimes result in its being "acted out" clinically by labeling all moments of its elevated status as inflated, or narcissistic.

44 Giegerich, *What is Soul?*, 45.

45 See Wolfgang Giegerich's, "'*Geist*' or: What gives Jungian psychology its absolute uniqueness and is the source of its true life," Chapter 1 in this volume.

PART I

"The psychological difference" in theory

1

"GEIST" OR: WHAT GIVES JUNGIAN PSYCHOLOGY ITS ABSOLUTE UNIQUENESS AND IS THE SOURCE OF ITS TRUE LIFE

Wolfgang Giegerich

At the end of his chapter on Sigmund Freud in his *Memories, Dreams, Reflections* Jung states

> It is a widespread error to imagine that I do not see the value of sexuality. On the contrary, it plays a large part in my psychology as an essential—though not the sole—expression of psychic wholeness. But my main concern has been to investigate, over and above its personal significance and biological function, its spiritual aspect and its numinous meaning, and thus to explain what Freud was so fascinated by but was unable to grasp.[1]

He adds by way of corroboration that the works in which his thoughts on this subject are contained are "The Psychology of the Transference"[2] and the *Mysterium Coniunctionis*,[3] both studies of his late period. A difficulty posed for us by this quote lies in the translation. By saying this I do not refer to the inaccuracies or mistakes it contains, because in this particular case they do not really change the basic meaning that Jung wants to convey. The serious problem is caused by the translation, "*ihre geistige Seite*" as "its spiritual aspect". Although not a mistake ("*geistig*" is really untranslatable), it is nevertheless misleading. We encounter the same problem a few pages earlier in the same chapter where Jung discusses Freud's attitude toward sexuality in more detail. I quote only the following passage:

> Although, for Freud, sexuality was undoubtedly a *numinosum*, his terminology and theory seemed to define it exclusively as a biological function. It was only

1   Jung, *MDR*, 168.
2   Jung, *CW* 16.
3   Jung, *CW* 14.

the emotionality with which he spoke of it that revealed the deeper elements reverberating within him. Basically, he wanted to teach—or so at least it seemed to me—that, regarded from within, sexuality included spirituality and had an intrinsic meaning. But his concretistic terminology was too narrow to express this idea.[4]

Jung's text reads, "*daß, von innen her betrachtet, Sexualität auch Geistigkeit umfasse, oder Sinn enthalte*" (that regarded from within, sexuality also comprehends *Geistigkeit*, or contains meaning). "It comprehends *Geistigkeit*" is equivalent to "its *geistig* side" ("side", rather than "aspect") in the first quote. "Spirituality" does not capture the particular meaning of *Geistigkeit*. Both "spiritual" in the former quote and "spirituality" in the latter are a stopgap solution for the rendering of a not really translatable word. This is not merely a translation problem and not only locally relevant for these particular passages about sexuality. What Jung says here illustrates, by way of this one example of sexuality, his general approach and "main concern". The understanding of Jung's entire psychology is at stake.

1 Difference

Before we turn to the question of what Jung's words *geistig* and *Geistigkeit* mean and what precise aspect of the reality of sexuality is Jung's foremost focus according to his statement, his statement's logical form alone tells us that Jung operates here with a crucial distinction: between Freud and himself. Already in 1929 he had written about the "opposition" between the two, about "The Freud–Jung Antithesis".[5] We do well to comprehend such conceptions as more than merely descriptive historical accounts. Other than historians, as psychologists we are on principle not interested in facts as such; just as in dreams we do not comprehend the figures in them (e.g., the dreamer's mother or father, the figure of family doctor, his girl friend) on the "object level" as the people they are outside the dream, in external social reality, but rather as personifications of the dreamer's or the soul's own different internal tendencies or "voices", so we can also conceive of the figure of "Freud" in Jung's autobiographical narrative as an *internal* other.[6] As much as this text is ostensibly about Freud and Jung and the difference between them, the difference has its ground not simply in Jung's empirical observation of facts "out there".

　We are all the more justified in reading the text in this way because Jung himself prefaced his *Memories, Dreams, Reflections* as a whole with the express comment that

---

4　Jung, *MDR*, 152.
5　"Der Gegensatz Freud und Jung", see C. G. Jung, *Gesammelte Werke*, Band 4 (Zurich and Stuttgart: (Rascher) now Olten and Freiburg i.Br.: Walter-Verlag, 1958), 383 ff. In *CW* 4, 333 ff. it is translated a bit more meekly as "Freud and Jung: Contrasts".
6　With this focus, the focus of a psychological (rather than historical) reading on psychology's needs, we are at the same time freed of the entire question of whether Jung's description of Freud is factually correct and a fair assessment or whether it is not perhaps based on misunderstandings and misconstruals.

"I have now undertaken … to tell the myth of my life. I can however … only 'tell stories.' Whether they are true is not the problem. The only question is whether it is *my* fable, *my* truth".[7] Jung conceives his autobiographical narrative not as factual historical account, but as the self-display and unfolding, in story form, of the inner logic of his life, *his* life.

By the same token, when Jung ostensibly shows in these passages what "*his* main concern" is, we have to understand that in a deeper sense he describes *psychology*'s "main concern" (as he sees it). By referring to the contrast between "Freud" and "Jung" his topic is of course his deepest needs *as psychologist* (rather than as private personality) and that means the essential *theoretical* needs of psychology itself. The personal names are abbreviations for different conceptions of the ultimate task and purpose of psychology. And the fact that "this main concern" needs to be articulated by means of the "Freud"–"Jung" *antithesis* in our passages has the function of suggesting that psychology's "main concern" can only be described as a fundamental contrast to its (internal) Other. Psychology constitutes itself by pushing off from its one (the "Freud") side, because only in this way can it come truly into its own, to its "main concern". It establishes, and operates with, a fundamental difference. This difference (here exemplified by the Freud–Jung opposition) is indispensable for psychology—for a psychology in the tradition of C. G. Jung, a "psychology *with* soul"—and because it is indispensable (indeed its constitutive principle), we call it *the psychological difference*.

Freud too knew and worked with opposites, e.g., conscious—unconscious, *eros*—*thanatos*, etc. But for intrinsic reasons his psychology did not need to be set off against Jung's (or any other psychology) in order to push off from it and come home to itself, the way Jung's psychology *within itself* pushed off from Freudian psychoanalysis and furthermore from consulting room and personalistic psychology as such. Freud's psychology was not structured by and did not operate with the psychological difference. The opposites just mentioned are pairs on the same level, alternatives, even mutually exclusive. Each side of any of those pairs of opposites is defined as simply being what the other side is not. Of course, Freud had in a certain sense also pushed off from the previous types of psychology that did not work with the concept of the unconscious. He established his mode of dream interpretation clearly in contrast to former traditional ideas about dreams. However, *this* kind of "pushing off" was something very different because the earlier theories remained external to and logically irrelevant for psychoanalysis. The latter did not need them in order to come into its own by pushing off from them as from its own internal other. Similarly, Alfred Adler did not need a "Freud–Adler" antithesis for his thought's coming into its own, although literally he, too, had developed his psychology in open contrast to Freud.

The psychological difference that we discover at work in Jung's cited passages is characterized by a completely different form of relation between the opposites and a different form of pushing off. Jung's psychology has within itself the fantasy of

---

7   Jung, *MDR*, 3, transl. modif.

being the *negation* of the Freudian position and this fantasy is, so to speak, its foundation myth. We see this logic of negation also in another instance of the psychological difference in Jung, namely in his crucial distinction between the "personal" and the "collective" unconscious. His psychology does not simply reject (what Jung sees as) the Freudian "personal unconscious". In order to be able to believe in the "collective unconscious" and the *Geistigkeit* of sexuality Jung does not deny or simply turn his back on the "biological function" and "personal significance" side of sexuality exclusively seen by (Jung's) "Freud". No, both "Freudian" tenets are fully confirmed and accepted by Jung's psychology and even interiorized into it as referring to an integral part of the complete reality of the human psyche. In other words, there is not a splitting them off and keeping them outside. Jung does not, as Adler did, *replace* Freud's psychology by his own. On the contrary, the Freudian tenets mentioned are precisely integrated into Jung's psychology—but integrated only as *sublated* realities from which to push off to the standpoint of the "collective unconscious" or to that of the "*geistig* side". This means three things:

1. The relation between the opposite sides of the psychological difference is hierarchical or vertical rather than a horizontal relation of alternatives on the same level (the way we speak, for example, of the political left and right). Jung says unambiguously, in the first passage cited, that his "main concern has been to investigate, *over and above* its [sexuality's] personal significance and biological function, its spiritual aspect and its numinous meaning" (my emphasis). "Over and above"[8] indicates that its personal significance and biological function are still seen and appreciated as valid, but they are reduced to a sublated moment within psychology proper.
2. Psychology's pushing off from, and thus its negating and sublating, the one side are not directed at an external, foreign element. They happen fundamentally within *itself*. The "Freud" from whom Jung pushes off is internal to Jung's own thinking. His pushing off from him is a strictly internal relation and internal logical move; what it pushes off from is not cast outside, not exiled. Psychology within itself negates it as *its own* basis; it sublates an integrated and acknowledged element of itself, and *within itself* rises above this basis to its own true home. With another metaphor, this rising above or negating the prevailing initial standpoint, and thus the beginning of true psychology, is in our second quote represented by Jung as a radical shift from an external view to one's "regard[ing] [the phenomenon] *from within*", or, to say it with a phrase from a late letter of Jung's, as our "changing our point of view and looking at it from the *other* side, i.e., not from outside but *from inside*".[9] Psychology has to be the discipline of interiority. In yet other and

8   With equal right Jung could have said "under and beneath", which shows that the spatial metaphor is used to express a *logical* and not a spatial difference.
9   Letter to Earl of Sandwich, 10 August 1960, my italics in C. G. Jung, *Letters, Vol. 2: 1951–1961*, ed. Gerhard Adler, trans. R. F. C. Hull (Princeton, NJ: Princeton University Press, 1975), 580.

more succinct conceptual terms, the psychological difference is the difference between seeing a phenomenon "from the point of view of the ego" versus seeing the same phenomenon "from the point of view of the soul"[10] which shows once more why I speak of the *psychological* difference.

3.   *To* what it pushes off and rises up, cannot be obtained without this *negation* of its own internal basis. It comes into being only through this act of pushing off from the other "side" or through the shift to the "from inside" standpoint. The *"geistig* side" and what Jung calls the "collective unconscious" are not always already naturally and factually given, in the same sense that the biological function of sexuality, to stay with this example, is an empirical positive fact. But the *"geistig* side" and along with it true *psychology* not only come about through negation, they are also in themselves in the status of absolute negativity. This means that there simply and honestly *is* nothing to be seen and therefore also nothing to be "grasped" *for* a strictly empiricist, positivistic approach, or "from outside", or "from the point of view of the ego" (even if the investigating psychologist is as intelligent and gifted as Freud and, what is more, even if unconsciously he should be personally deeply fascinated by this "nothing"). Furthermore, the *geistig* side's and psychology's absolute negativity means that they need to be "made": soul-*making.*[11] *If* there *is* to be psychology, then one has to *rise* to that "over and above" level and by rising to it *create* it for the first time since it is not positively given, not always already "there" and merely waiting to be discovered. This is the predicament *and* distinction of psychology. It is what gives Jungian psychology its uniqueness. (Jung's) "Freud" did not rise to this level, did not regard things *from inside,* did not enter true psychology. We could also say: he did not perform the psychological difference. He stayed on the obvious, naturalistic or positivistic level of the personal and biological, that is to say, the level of "the *psychic*" (in contrast to "the *psychological*") and consequently also did not break through what for Jung was the narrowness of "his concretistic terminology and theory".

2 "Numinous meaning"

2.1 The cold objectivity of substantial contents

If the *"geistig* side" is first created in the act of our rising to it, it seems to be something entirely subjective. But this is contradicted by the fact that the difference between Freud and Jung is primarily described as not merely a subjective one of the psychologists' different perspectives, their different ways of viewing. The way Jung describes it, it is ultimately a difference that goes right through the *reality* which is to be assessed and comprehended, i.e., right through the phenomenon of

10 Jung, *MDR*, 314, transl. modif.
11 Whereas soul needs to be made, psyche, as rooted in the human animal, is something natural and positively given.

sexuality itself. According to Jung's presentation here it is sexuality itself that is divided into two halves, as it were; *it* has two "sides": on the one hand, *ihre geistige Seite* and, on the other hand, the "side" of its personal significance and biological function. The difference is objective, it has its ground in the real itself (which is why I pointed out above that I prefer the translation "side" over "aspect", since the latter word inevitably implies a viewing subject and what is seen from its point of view). One might therefore almost feel tempted to say that the difference is "ontological". Sexuality, this is obviously Jung's underlying claim, *has* this "side" (just as it also has the other personal-significance and biological-function side). It has both sides the way a 24-hour period consists not only of day but also of night (or vice versa), or the way that a word has a meaning side in addition to its sound side, and the way we all, in addition to our conscious personality, carry a "shadow" within ourselves.

Likewise, when Jung says that sexuality "has an intrinsic meaning" or when he speaks of "its numinous meaning" he does not want to say that sexuality is something *meaningful*, in other words, a source of meaning (for us),[12] because this would make it, the "other side", precisely part of the "first side", the personal significance side. What he suggests is something else, namely that it objectively *contains* a meaning that is one of the essential integral features making up the total reality of the phenomenon of sexuality.[13] This meaning is part of its nature much like vitamins are contained in certain fruits, or nitrogen in the air. Those fruits contain the vitamins regardless of whether we eat them and benefit from those vitamins or not. In the same way, this meaning, according to Jung, is objectively inherent in sexuality, even if it is not seen or felt. A complete description of the make-up or logical constitution of sexuality, this is Jung's thesis, must include, and do justice to, its meaning quality.

However, whereas vitamins are special ingredients or components *in* fruits, separable from other chemical components, and have an important nutritional *function* for us, meaning is, according to this thesis, not really an ingredient, but the logical *character* or *nature* of the phenomenon of sexuality *as a whole*. Sexuality has— for Jung and *if* seen "from within"—an inherent *meaning structure*; it is itself a meaning phenomenon the way words, or paintings, or novels are meaning phenomena, in contrast to stones, trees, sunshine. The latter simply are what they are; they represent themselves as what they are. Not so a word, say, "table". It does not represent *itself*, not represent itself as what it is, namely, a sequence of sounds or letters. A word is not content and satisfied with representing itself. Rather, it is only what it is by pointing away from itself to the idea, image or reality that it *means*. It points to the meaning by negating itself, having, as it were, the internal logic of, "*it* (the meaning) must increase, but I (the combination of sounds) must

---

12 On the problem of the meaning of "meaning" in Jungian psychology see my "A Serious Misunderstanding: Synchronicity and the Generation of Meaning", *Journal of Analytical Psychology* 57 (2012): 500–511.

13 Needless to say, "sexuality" in Jung's text always refers to the phenomenon of *human* sexuality.

decrease". The meaning structure is essentially an "about structure". A tree is not "about" anything, does not point away from itself. It does not even point to itself: it simply *is*, it presents itself.

But this fact that a word or a novel has a meaning structure obviously does not also mean that it has the function of "providing" Meaning (with a capital M) to us ("meaning" in the subjective, experiential, or "quest of meaning" sense: making life, human existence as such meaningful). Even if we don't like it, find it boring or quite trivial, it nevertheless is a meaning phenomenon (in the lower-case sense of meaning). It would be ridiculous to try to find Meaning in the word "table", but just as ridiculous to deny that it is truly a meaning phenomenon. We could also say that the meaning we are concerned with here is not *functional* (not of "personal significance" for us), but describes the cold, sober, logical reality of all meaning phenomena.

The psychological difference goes right through the notion of numinosity itself. The psychological difference divides this term's two radically different, indeed even mutually exclusive senses:

- a person's being deeply stirred or even spell-bound by a *numinosum*, his subjective emotionality and fascination, i.e., the *effect* on the ego, on the one hand,
- and, on the other hand, "its [the phenomenon's] numinous meaning", i.e., its involving the *cognition* of a *numen*[14] (to put it into the old religious language), in other words, its *objective* substantial (Jung would say: "archetypal") *contents*, its psychological subject matter, the *prima materia*, which is in need of professional ("scientific", scholarly, or therapeutic) psychological investigation and explanation.

What now needs to be elucidated is how the "meaning" of sexuality referred to by Jung (its "*geistig* side") can on the one hand be something that must be created by our rising to the "over and above" level and how it can nevertheless, on the other hand, be an objective "side" of this phenomenon itself. Here it becomes indispensable to try to get a clearer idea of what *geistig, Geistigkeit* (and also *Geist*) in the present context mean and why the translation "spiritual(ity)" does not really capture their specific meaning.

One reason why spirituality (German *Spiritualität*), especially as used in present-day psychological circles, is inappropriate in Jung's statements and indeed misleading is that the idea of "spirituality" predominantly refers to or involves a human subject, its experience of or sensitivity and openness to things of the spirit, its deep attachment to religious values, its "spiritual" practices such as in transcendental meditation, yoga, Zen, or also, in a very general sense, its quest for meaning and its longing for transcendence or for "the sacred". But "*geistig*" and "*Geistigkeit*" in Jung's sentences

---

14 *Numen* in contrast to *numinosum* (which refers to how something is subjectively experienced).

are used in a strictly objective sense. We already know that in one way it of course makes a tremendous difference whether the *geistig* side is seen and adequately appreciated ("grasped") or not, and this is precisely the bone of contention between Jung and Freud. But in Jung's statement (about sexuality's *also* comprehending *Geistigkeit*) this is not the issue, and not implied. With this statement Jung merely makes a simple factual assertion about the reality of sexuality per se. His point is precisely that despite the fact that Freud was not able to *grasp* it this "*geistig* side" nevertheless exists.

2.2 "Grasping": the intellectual obligation and the rigorous process of understanding

No doubt, the quest of meaning is one important topic in Jung's psychology. But it is evident that in our two quotes it is not the "quest of meaning" Jung who is speaking. The one who speaks here is the psychologist Jung who considered himself a natural scientist (in his sense of the word); it is the psychological scholar and theoretician who considers it his (his psychology's) "main concern" to "investigate and explain [*zu erforschen und zu erklären*], over and above its personal significance and biological function," the *geistig* side of sexuality. (Of course, we must add, the *geistig* side not only of sexuality, which merely happens to be singled out here in Jung's discussion because it played an essential role in his strife with Freud, but of all psychologically relevant phenomena.) And the fact that, in Jung's eyes, for Freud sexuality was indeed a *numinosum*, and as such possessed very great personal significance, was precisely not enough. "The emotionality with which he [Freud] spoke of it" is, after all, simply that aspect of personal experiential significance "*over and above*" *which* that domain only begins which psychology is assigned to investigate. Anyone can be *fascinated* by something. This would be a subjective emotion and part of someone's personal psychic life. But psychologically that is neither here nor there. *Fascination and emotionality are just phenomena, "symptoms." They are not yet psychology.* What Jung demands of the psychologist is that he be able to "*grasp*" (i.e., comprehend) and "explain" (i.e., unfold, spell out in detail) the objective content of the reality in question (as Jung himself felt he had done in his late works, "The Psychology of the Transference" and *Mysterium Coniunctionis*). That this reality may in certain persons have given rise to subjective fascination is not relevant. Grasping, explaining, and the question of the right terminology, the right theoretical framework are what counts when it is a question of the *objective* psyche.

About Freud Jung states, concerning his one-sided view of sexuality: "Perhaps some inner experience of his own might have opened his eyes; but then his intellect would have reduced any such experience to 'mere sexuality' or 'psychosexuality'".[15] Again we see that it all depends on the *intellect*, on the "*terminology and theory*" (we

---

15   Jung, *MDR*, 153. Jung's idea of a "reduction to 'psychosexuality'" is a beautiful example of the psychological difference at work: "*psycho*sexuality" represents the merely "psychic", but misses out on the truly "psychological".

could also say: the entire mindset) and not on "some inner experience of his own"! Jung's example of *his* "Freud" shows us clearly that if it is a question of doing justice to the substantial *contents* of the soul's life, what is needed is not subjective emotion, not a state of fascination, not experienced numinosity. What counts is exclusively what the mind makes of it, to what degree and depth it is capable of apperceiving and comprehending it.

This is why we also have to criticize Jung for saying about Freud (at the end of the next sentence, after the one about the crucial importance of the intellect) that "he was a great man, and what is even more, a man touched and taken hold of in his innermost depth [*ein Ergriffener*]".[16] This "what is even more" does not make sense. Jung contradicts himself. The fact that (Jung's) Freud was not able in any way to grasp and give expression to the real content he had been touched by and taken hold of means that he had not been up to his own task, the very task specifically set for him by the soul. This deficiency so clearly described by Jung is apt to subtract from Freud's greatness—rather than raise him even above it, as Jung here suggests. The *greatness* of an artist or philosopher lies in no way in what he experienced in his private subjectivity and was deeply touched by, not in "the emotionality with which he spoke of it".[17] It lies exclusively in the degree of his power to grasp it in its depth and to authoritatively articulate it in a form that makes it accessible to mankind, to the *generality*. The great man is great because he produces a great *work*, gives *objectivity* to subjectively experienced feelings or ideas. To emotionally experience "the numinous" in one's inner is neither a psychological virtue nor a mark of distinction to be proud of, and being *unconsciously* in the grip of it least of all.

"In retrospect I can say that I alone logically pursued the two problems which most interested Freud: the problem of 'archaic vestiges,' and that of sexuality", Jung said in the same chapter.[18] What for us is noteworthy in this statement is not only that (according to his own assessment) he, Jung, pursued the questions that Freud was most interested in but for intellectual reasons[19] was unable to pursue, but also the converse: that while Freud was gripped by the numinosity of sexuality (even if unbeknownst to him), *Jung was not*. Sexuality was not a *numinosum* for him. He makes this very clear in the same chapter on Freud when he describes his overall reaction to the spirit of Freudian psychoanalysis.

16 Jung, *MDR*, 153, transl. modif. The translation of *MDR* has, "a man in the grip of his daimon". The point of the German word is, however, that it just talks about a person's subjective state without suggesting any agent that caused this state or being interested in who may have caused it. And the choice of "his daimon" as the causing agent is also an inappropriate fiction since what this context refers to is the *Ergriffenheit* by the (not grasped) "numinous meaning" of the real phenomenon of *sexuality*. On p. 168, *MDR* renders the adjective *ergriffen* much better with "deeply stirred".

17 Jung about Freud in Jung, *MDR*, 152.

18 Jung, *MDR*, 168. "I alone": the Jung of *MDR* has a clear awareness of the uniqueness of his psychology. And what makes it unique is not that he added new empirical observations and new insights (new semantic contents), but that he performed the syntactical move from the whole personalistic ("psychic") level to the fundamentally other level of true *psychology* (in Jung's quote referred to by means of the reference to the "collective unconscious" and to [the "*geistig* side" of] sexuality).

19 This must of course not be confused with a claim that Freud was not an "intelligent" man.

To me it was a profound disappointment that all the efforts of the probing mind had apparently succeeded in finding nothing more in the depths of the psyche than the all too familiar and "all-too-human" limitations. I had grown up in the country, among peasants, and what I was unable to learn in the stables I found out from the Rabelaisian wit and the untrammeled fantasies of our peasant folklore. Incest and perversions were no remarkable novelties to me, and did not call for any special explanation. Along with criminality, they formed part of the black lees that spoiled the taste of life by showing me only too plainly the ugliness and meaninglessness of human existence. That cabbages thrive in dung was something I had always taken for granted. In all honesty I could discover no helpful insight in such knowledge. "It's just that all of those people are city folks who know nothing about nature and the human stable," I thought, sick and tired of these ugly matters.[20]

Nothing numinous. Nothing remarkable. No fascination or *Ergriffenheit*. Only the "all too familiar and 'all-too-human'", "the human *stable*" (!), or even: only "sick and tired of these ugly matters". So much for the *numinosum* aspect. The other important aspect for us that comes out in this passage is that we get a clear idea of what Jung thought about the importance for psychology of the other, non-*geistig* side of the psychological difference, i.e., the personal significance and biological function side, and that indeed he decidedly pushed off from it. The experiential and behavioral reality of sexuality is described as being irrelevant for psychology: boring ("all too familiar"), not remarkable (not worthy of closer attention) and not calling for any special explanation—in contrast to what for Jung absolutely needed to be investigated and explained and what in fact got his in-depth attention in his late works: the *Geistigkeit* of the phenomenon.

In this connection it may be helpful to also call attention to a paragraph in *MDR* concerning Jung's Red Book in which he discusses that and why "I gave up this estheticizing tendency in good time, in favor of a rigorous process of *understanding* ... For me, reality meant scientific comprehension."[21] This shift is his pushing off to true psychology not from the "all-too-human", but from his own previous indulging in and celebrating numinous feelings through this estheticizing tendency, a celebration that in the following paragraph (unfortunately omitted in the English edition) he brands as "the tyranny of unconscious presuppositions": "In order to free oneself from the tyranny of unconscious presuppositions both are needed: fulfillment of the intellectual as well as the ethical obligation".[22] Freud was merely unconsciously (and thus honestly) gripped. But early Jung, the Jung of the Red Book, consciously indulged in mainly self-induced numinous feelings and images. But this is what mature Jung uncompromisingly distanced himself from—whereas

20 Jung, *MDR*, 166.
21 Jung, *MDR*, 188.
22 C. G. Jung, *Erinnerungen, Träume, Gedanken* (Zurich and Stuttgart: Rascher, 1967), 192, my transl.

many Jungians have succumbed again to the desire to indulge in the egoic cult of (mostly simulated[23]) numinous emotionality, *at the cost of* "its [whatever phenomenon's] numinous meaning" as the objective *prima materia* and "*geistig* side" that quite soberly needs to be made the subject of "scientific comprehension", of a "rigorous process of *understanding*" and "the efforts of the probing mind": intellectual—and hopefully truly intelligent, insightful—*work*, work on the contents of the objective *soul*.

To sum up this discussion about the numinous: By speaking of sexuality's numinous meaning Jung is precisely not referring to its possible fascination *effect upon the ego*. The term "numinous" is in this phrase roughly synonymous with what Jung elsewhere called "archetypal". It simply points to the contents[24] of the so-called "collective unconscious" in contradistinction to the "all too familiar and 'all-too-human'" that is the topic of personalistic psychology. The two phrases, "its *geistig* side" and "its numinous meaning" are also synonymous, but of course with slight difference of emphases.

Although what "*geistig*" means has by no means been sufficiently elucidated and will occupy us further in the next sections, I am ready—after all that we have heard about Jung's emphasis on grasping, intellect, scientific comprehension, rigorous process of understanding, intellectual obligation—to offer a better (even if far from ideal) translation instead of "its spiritual aspect". I suggest the wording, "its noetic side". "Noetic" brings with it the rich association with the Greek *Noys* (or *Nus*). Of course its drawback is that it is not a term of ordinary language the way "*geistig*" in German and "spiritual" in English are. But this word at least avoids the faulty ideas evoked by "spiritual" ("*spirituell*" in German) and points in the right direction. We could perhaps also have considered "intellective" as a possible translation. However, an uninformed reader might understand this (likewise unusual) word in the abstract sense of "intellectual" (as commonly used today), which would be misleading. The rarely used word "noetic" is free of this danger.

3 "Geistigkeit"

3.1 Overcoming the imagination. Its systematic blindness to the mind's syntactical form and to process and performance

The second reason for my critical rejection of "spiritual" and "spirituality" for *geistig* and *Geistigkeit* in Jung's sentences is that the very idea of "spirit" evokes

23 Whereas in (Jung's) Freud the fascination was a symptom (something that shows that the *soul* has been at work), in many Jungians it is a self-stylization, the work of the modern ego lusting after "high" feelings and self-affirmation. On the wider theme of simulation in psychology see the insightful paper by Michael Whan, "Fool's Gold: A Critique of Jungian Psychology's *Simulation* of Alchemy: Or, Tarrying with the Negative". See also his "Aurum Vulgi: Alchemy in Analysis, a Critique of a Simulated Phenomenon", *Alchemy and Psychotherapy*, ed. Dale Mathers (London, UK and New York, NY: Routledge, 2014), 170–183.

24 In order to fully present and unfold their internal logical complexity, these contents need book-length essays, as in the case of the "*geistig* side" of sexuality Jung's "The Psychology of Transference" and *Mysterium Coniunctionis* show.

wrong, far too lofty associations and mystifications. If one wants to grasp the specific meaning of German *Geist* in the sense that underlies the terms *geistig* and *Geistigkeit* as used in Jung's quotes (and only this particular sense of *Geist* is of concern here), then "spirit" and "spirituality" must be kept away (as also any sense of *pneuma*, the "pneumatic", and also the again different concept of "mind").

Concerning the term *Geist*, Jungian psychology and particularly archetypal psychology is haunted by views that have been pointedly articulated in James Hillman's (in its own way admirable) construal of the relation between "spirit" and "soul" in his essay, "Peaks and Vales".[25] A critical discussion of this paper will in the following allow us to develop a clearer idea of the very different reality of *Geist*. Without my wishing to repeat Hillman's argument here in detail, I can at least summarize a few of his essential ideas, namely, that he points out that through the decisions of Councils of the Early Church (Nicaea, 787; Constantinople, 869) the idea of human nature "devolved from a tripartite cosmos of spirit, soul, and body, to a dualism of spirit (or mind) and body (or matter)" and that consequently "that third place, the intermediate realm of psyche—which is also the realm of images and the power of imagination—" was exiled by "theological, spiritual men".[26] Long battles between spirit and soul, between abstractions and images, between iconoclasts and idolaters had been fought.[27] He claims that "By returning to image, Jung returned to the soul, reversing the historical process that in 787 had depotentiated images and in 869 had reduced soul to rational intellectual spirit. Jung said that his base is in a third place between the opposites spirit and matter: *esse in anima*."[28] Hillman then goes on in a section devoted to the opposition of "Soul and Spirit" to unfold the image of "peaks" as the imaginal place of the spirit and the image of "vales" as the locus of soul and soul-making.

My interest is not to raise the valid objection that the soul by no means disappeared from theology and Western thought. Until way into the 18th century people's and official theology's main religious concern was care for the immortal soul. To mention one example, is Dante's *Divina Commedia* concerned with either one of the only two realms left according to Hillman (with the "rational intellectual spirit", or, conversely, with the "body [or matter]"), and not much rather with soul? Nor do I want to go into the other necessary objection that as a matter of course Jung did not and could not possibly have reversed the historical process and returned something that had been lost (nobody can do that, probably not even

25   In James Hillman et al., *Puer Papers* (Irving, TX: Spring Publications, 1979), 54–74. I critiqued some aspects of the "peaks–vales" ("spirit–soul", "thought–image") opposition also in my "Afterword" in Wolfgang Giegerich, David L. Miller and Greg Mogenson, *Dialectics & Analytical Psychology: The El Capitan Canyon Seminar* (New Orleans, LA: Spring Journal, Inc., 2005), 107–112. But after what I wrote in the previous section of the present paper, it should be clear that I completely agree with Hillman's general attack in his "Peaks and Vales" paper on spirituality in the sense, for example, of Maslow's "peak experiences".

26   Hillman, *Puer Papers*, 54.

27   Hillman, *Puer Papers*, 55.

28   Hillman, *Puer Papers*, 56.

God, as Jung full-well knew: "We cannot turn the wheel backwards; we cannot go back to the symbolism that is gone"[29]). To want to attempt such a thing would be illusionary wishful thinking and nostalgia. I leave such possible objections about questions of fact aside and turn to psychologically more relevant ones.

It is Hillman who sets up and celebrates the dissociation between peaks and vales as being absolutely fundamental. It is he who tears apart (not "spirit" and "matter", but) "spirit" and "soul" and reduces (not soul, but) the *concept* of spirit to the extreme, and extremely emaciated, form of meaning nothing but "abstractions" and "rational intellectual spirit". Not spirit is the problem, but his narrow-minded, reductive concept of it, the interpretation he gives it, the straightjacket into which he forces it. *He* unwittingly practices the very abstractions that he ostensibly fights. What he does (and it is a doing, *his* doing!) contradicts his message. His own mind that is speaking here is a tough abstract intellect and, notwithstanding his *use* of images and his *plea* for the imaginal, is not really a soulful mind. Certainly, "peaks" and "vales" are images; but in Hillman's text they are precisely images *for abstractions*, if not used *as abstractions*. Inasmuch as image is construed in total opposition to thought, his own thinking is not imaginal in style, but an example of abstract thought.

Precisely by trying to "reconstitute"[30] "that third place" as an intermediate realm of psyche in between, he himself solidifies the split because this third in between inevitably functions as a wedge. This is why the recourse to "image" and "imagination" as the cure for "the malnourished root of Western psychological culture"[31] is its own trap and not at all the cure. The restoration of the realm of images is a cop-out because it "solves" the problem detected by Hillman only on the semantic or content level, the level of *what* is imagined,[32] while precisely reiterating and confirming it in the very style of his own thinking, in the syntax or logical form of consciousness. That third place has to stay "in between" and a "spatial" *intermediary*, when the real psychological task to be achieved would be to *actually perform* the *mediation* or the *mysterium coniunctionis*. Subsisting, substantiated realm—or act to be performed, that is here the question. The third *place* and the intermed*iary* are offered only as a remedy "out there", in *what* is imagined, in the "object" or the semantic content of the imagination (the imagination *about* the constitution of the soul). But the structure of the imagining mind itself, its own syntax or logical form, remains unaffected. It is inherent in the form of the imagination that it "*externalizes*", presents what it presents in spatial and temporal and sensuous forms and as objects, entities. It inevitably reifies and personifies. The imaging mind's own *logical constitution*, by contrast, is by definition out of reach for this mind. The imagination cannot reach and reflect and "cure" itself.

This irrevocable limitation of the image-approach promoted by Hillman (I say "irrevocable" because the limitation is rooted in its own logic) is highlighted when he emphasizes that "Images were venerated and adored all through the antique

---

29 Jung, *CW* 18, § 632.
30 Hillman, *Puer Papers*, 54.
31 Hillman, *Puer Papers*, 54.
32 We could also say that he merely "acted out" (on the intellectual level, in the imagination), but did not *erinnern*.

world"[33] and himself advocates the necessity of the notion of Gods (with capital G!) and of psychological polytheism for soul-making and imaginal psychology. That he does not favor "belief" in the Gods in a theological manner but takes them merely metaphorically[34] makes no difference. Whether this way or that, the notion of Gods comes with and confirms the fundamental *logical* structure of *otherness* and *externality*, even if the Gods are *semantically* imagined to be "within".[35] Due to its own otherness structure, the image-approach is systematically blind to the fundamental difference between "*intermediary* in between", on the one hand, and actual "*mediation*" (which mediates between the two extremes), on the other hand, between what is imagined as quasi-ontic "realm" in the middle of a "tripartite cosmos" and the real process and performance (actuosity) of mediation, between semantic content and syntactical form of mind.

This difference is ultimately the difference between two world-conditions, two eons of the world, which I will call here the "cosmological" one versus the "psychological" one (where "cosmological" refers to a focus on the "world", i.e., the object or the "what" of thought/imagination, whereas "psychological" refers to an interest in the subject, or "how"[36]). In the former, associated mainly with the ancient and archaic world (which is, however, one that Hillman, as we see here, attempts to revive), the soul innocently *directly* relates to the world and to experience as *what* is to be seen or imagined and explained, without being aware of the involvement of the subject in the experience. It is all "out there", in the cosmos, in what is imaged. The mind, in self-forgetfulness completely given over to what it sees in its imagination, only focuses upon its own contents: the semantic level.

The other world-condition, which fully came into its own five or six centuries ago, is characterized by the fact that this earlier innocence has been lost. The soul has become aware of *itself* and must take itself into account in all its experiences and semantic contents. It can no longer devote itself merely to the "what" but must also self-reflectingly be aware of the "how", the logical form of its experience as its own active, productive contribution to the experience.

The "Gods" in Hillman's theory guarantee the stance of passive receptivity and the innocence of self-forgetfulness, the stance of the *An-sich* (per se, in-itself). The images come and merely have to be carefully observed and attended to. Late Jung, by contrast, realized that, "So long as one simply looks at the pictures one is like the foolish Parsifal, who forgot to ask the vital question, because one does not become aware of *one's own* [the thinking or imagining mind's own] *participation*".[37]

---

33 Hillman, *Puer Papers*, 55.
34 I say "merely" despite Hillman's protest against any "merely metaphorical" in Hillman, *Puer Papers*, 59.
35 Hillman, *Puer Papers*, 72.
36 This term "psychological" as the opposite of "cosmological" is therefore completely different from that other one that is, e.g., evoked by "the psychological difference" and refers to the soul aspect in contrast to the "psychic" or "ego" aspect.
37 Jung, *CW* 14, § 753, transl. modif. Also, Cf. Jung, *CW* 10, § 498 where Jung, albeit in a completely different context, speaks of "man's intervention, that is, the indispensable participation of the psyche".

With his vertical peak–vale, up–down, tripartite versus two-realms fantasy, we see Hillman move within what I called the "cosmological" orientation. It is the ingenuous dedication to the object, to "how it *is*": whether *it*, the cosmos, is tripartite or dualistic. The image-approach is characterized by *systematic* self-forgetfulness.

However, despite being a form of the "cosmological" approach it is of course nevertheless *itself* a child of the "psychological" age (of the 20th century) and occurs within psychology! This means it comes too late and its message is belied by its own structure of consciousness (which may also explain the appearance of the emotion of hatred). Hillman tries to replay once more those battles of the bygone 8th and 9th centuries and today reverse their outcome, *at a time when* the issues of those Councils have long lost every actual relevance, a circumstance that turns his fight into a kind of shadow-boxing. These issues have lost their relevance because their final decisions have in the course of the centuries been fully integrated into the very structure of the soul and because the true psychological issue and battleground of today is a totally different one: namely, the "logical" relation between semantic contents and logical form, between *what* is experienced and the *syntax* of the experiencing consciousness.

3.2 "Geist": a structure, not a substance. The logic of self-production and self-knowing

This is where *"Geist"* comes in. *Geist*, as it occurs in Jung, is precisely not the extreme dissociated opposite of soul and image. It does not need to be fought with passionate hatred if soul is to have a chance. It is not what is only or predominantly to be found on peaks. It is not to be imaginatively associated with any *location* as such. It is not the tip of a "tripartite cosmos of spirit, soul, and body (or matter)", for, after all, Jung maintains that, "Sexuality is of the greatest importance as the expression of a chthonic spirit [*Geist*]".[38] As above so below; or heaven above, heaven below, alchemy tells us. For Jung the soul in its entirety (from the most sublime theological dogma to chthonic depth) is itself *geistig*. In Jung the place of the "cosmological" difference between peaks and vales is taken by the psychological difference between the personal (or biological), on the one hand, and the soul (the "*geistig* side") on the other, which, as a psychological and thus logical (not cosmological, not natural) difference, can potentially be established within any phenomenon regardless of whether on peaks or in vales.

Geistigkeit is the soul's nature; it is, we might say, the soul of soul. What constitutes the soul aspect of phenomena is nothing but their "*geistig* side", which simply refers to the soul's meaning structure, the "about structure". Jung's

38 This quote follows our first citation from *MDR*, 168. I changed "the chthonic" into "a chthonic" according to the German original. The problem with Jung's expression is of course the mythologizing language which might make credulous people think that he posited different personalized spirits in the plural, when what is meant is only the one *Geist* that can also manifest itself in the more natural, sensuous (here by Jung called "chthonic") sphere.

"'psychology with soul,'" is "based on the hypothesis of an autonomous *Geist*"[39]: it is not *based* on image! Image (because it too has this "about structure" and expresses specific meanings in pictorial form) is itself merely one frequent form in which soul as *Geist* appears. *Geist* has no problem at all with or hostile feelings towards image or the imagination. What it finds fault with is the *abstractness* of the image approach, when image is no longer seen as a form of manifestation of thought, but set up in absolute opposition to thought; when the psychological mind becomes identified, in its own structure, with the image approach and consequently also identifies soul with image. We could also say: when "image" is turned into a belief system and declared to be the fundamental *basis* of the very theory of soul.[40]

Geist in this sense is not a mysterious ("mythological") being or agent behind the scenes, nor a special realm, nor a subsisting substance or substrate. No, it is a specific logical *structure*, a structure not in the static, rigid sense (like a building), but living, dynamic, active: that structure that we earlier provisionally characterized as the "about structure" and that we now want to elucidate a little more closely.

When Jung writes "In myths and fairytales, as in dreams, the soul speaks about itself, and the archetypes reveal themselves in their natural interplay, as 'formation, transformation/the eternal Mind's eternal recreation'",[41] he actually describes the soul's *Geistigkeit* or *Geist*-nature, in the somewhat flowery language of the poet. For *Geist* is that structure or activity/process ("eternal recreation") that has the following moments: it is (1) a speaking or producing or manifesting; it produces meanings in the form of images, dreams, myths, rites, tombs, paintings, poems, philosophical works; but (2) *what* it produces or speaks about is only *itself*, its own truth or reality. In other words, it is a self-production or self-presentation, self-display. And (3) in this speaking about itself, in its revealing itself together with its internal logical complexity (the "interplay" of opposites), and in this giving itself a real and visible presence in the world, it obtains its *self-knowledge*. It comes home to itself.

Wherever this logical structure is at work, we have a *Geist*-phenomenon. The three moments are not three separate phases but in their interrelation make up the internal structure of all those events or phenomena that have *Geist*-character or in which soul in its *Geistigkeit* manifests—in contrast to all phenomena in *nature* with its clear cause-and-effect and temporal-sequence structure.

It is crucial to understand that the "beginning" of this process is not *a spirit who* speaks, not really an "eternal Mind" as an existing subject. No, it "begins" with speaking as such; there is only this activity or performance—without a performing agent. And when I said that *Geist* comes home to itself, I now have to add that only in this home-coming and self-knowing does it *begin* to exist. Self-knowing is precisely not secondary, not a result. It is also what inspires the original speaking;

---

39 Jung, *Gesammelte Werke*, Band 8, § 661, my transl.
40 But unwittingly even imaginal psychology itself admits that image is implicit thought. For it does not merely mutely stare at images and adore them, but it *works* with them, says something about them, interprets them, i.e., it tries to bring out into the open their inherent meaning and this means, *sit venia verbo*, the thought enveloped in them.
41 Jung, *CW* 9i, § 400, transl. modif.

the achieved self-knowledge is in itself productive, creative, a speaking. We could therefore say this movement is uroboric. The only remote analogue in nature to *Geist* is life. Both life and *Geist* are not a substance. Life *is* only where and for as long as something has the power to perform, and in fact performs, the act of living. It is a doing, not an ingredient in an organism. Analogously, *Geist is* only where the process of self-manifestation and self-knowing actually happens. Being a structure it can—as (to some extent) life and like language (which is of course merely an example of *Geist*)—at one and the same time be concretely and powerfully real in a this-worldly sense and yet be fundamentally "over and above" all positivities, all natural, factual existence.

Because soul, due to its *Geistigkeit*, is a doing, it does not have a permanent (thing-like) existence. Dreams, e.g., as written texts or as memories are not *per se* soul. The soul's speaking about itself only takes place when (and for as long as) we are actually performing the act of interpreting and comprehending them. This is why Jung advised us concerning dreams, or rather concerning what dreams say: "say it again, as best you can". It is only in this saying it again that the dream begins to speak in the first place and that soul comes into existence. The same can be said about religious dogmas, mythic tales, poems, and so on. They certainly are expressions of soul, and yet they are not, not until and unless the soul or *Geist* in a human subject actively appreciates them in their depth. A work of art is not simply empirically given as a work of art, but needs to be re-created afresh by the viewer. And it exists only in this act of re-creation and only as long as it lasts and is maintained, kept alive. In other words, the "*geistig* side" has the character of a doing, a performance, and precisely not of an existing entity: a positivity. *Geist*, we can say in general, has fundamentally act character. As essentially performative and as production it is not tangible, but fleeting. Just like a musician re-creates *on the literal, physical level* a piece of music by playing the notes written on the sheets of music in front of him, so the mind that apperceives a sculpture or painting truly as a work of art performs, *on the no longer physical level* and therefore *subliminally*, the act of re-creating it from the visible sculpture or canvas in front of him using them as clues or instructions for how to push off from them.[42]

By the same token it needed the soul or *Geist* in C. G. Jung to bring to life, through his mentioned late works, sexuality's "*geistig* side" as it had expressed itself in alchemical tracts. But he brought it to life only for himself, not for us. For us it remains just as entombed in his writings as it had for him been entombed in those

---

42 What for the viewer of a work of art is the visible sculpture or canvas is for the audience of a concert the physically played music. The musicians' playing is *not* as such the re-creation of the musical piece as a work of art. The work of art only comes about in and through the *re-creative* hearing of what is physically played, the hearing of it both in the playing musician and in the members of the audience. The difference between the playing musician and the audience is primarily that for the literally playing musician the creative hearing must *precede* his playing if he is to be really up to the true art character of the work of music, whereas for the audience the physical hearing of the playing logically comes first, and the re-creative production of the piece of music is entirely dependent on the physically playing.

tracts—until a reader possesses the intellectual power and depth to "say it again, as best he can".

But even if the dream, the work of art, the alchemical tract, or Jung's interpretations of those tracts require an appreciating, comprehending human subject to come alive as soul or *Geist*, this "*geistig* side" is not at all anything merely subjective. Rather, *Geist* is the overarching relation between the objectively given text/work/religious symbol/phenomenon as the hard fact in this world that they are *and* the comprehending subject. It is itself the psychological difference: the opening up of the distinction, and at the same time its overarching the thereby distinguished opposites (e.g., its seeing the "*geistig* side" *in* the concrete empirical phenomenon of sexuality). *Geist* is not hovering above the world. Nothing transcendent, other-worldly. It is a very sober, unemotional and uninflated concept. It does not imply idle fantasizing or "free association". On the contrary, it requires the labor of the concept.

3.3 Beyond the personalistic. The dimension of generality

A while ago I used the phrase: "until and unless the soul or *Geist* in a human subject appreciates them [dreams, myths, dogmas, etc.] in their depth". This phrase entails an important point and corrects my formulations in the last paragraph that focused on the human subject. I now have to emphasize that in contrast to the focus on the human subject the soul in its *Geistigkeit* speaks only to *itself*, and it is only the soul or *Geist* in us (and NOT *we*, nor OUR *Geist*, but THE *Geist* as universal[43]) that knows itself through hearing or seeing and understanding what it itself produced. We humans are only the place in which the soul's self-expression and corresponding self-knowledge occurs, if it occurs.

Soul happens for its own sake, its own needs and own fulfillment. It is its own self-contained logical life that uroborically plays itself out. Negatively put: it is not for our benefit, our understanding, our self-knowledge. This is what late Jung (1945) tries to suggest through the Goethe quote about the Eternal Mind's[44] eternal recreation. But as the place in and through which it can realize itself, *we* are nevertheless needed, even indispensable for it, and if we let *it* find *its* "eternal recreation" and fulfillment, then even *we* may, through our participation in it, also find our deepest satisfaction, because in the deepest sense we exist not as organism, but as soul or *Geist*.[45]

Geist wants to know *itself* and has no other (separate or prior) existence than in the *events* of such actually happening self-knowing. Again, this has the further

43 In the same sense that language is not the private language of each speaker, but conversely, every speaker avails himself of a language that is the property of the generality.
44 "Mind" is again a stopgap. The German is: *des ewigen Sinnes. Sinn* does by no means imply a kind of mythological being or subject. One could interpret it as the meaning level, the logos, the *Geistigkeit* or mindedness dimension of existence.
45 This satisfaction would not be Meaning, but only (only?) the event of meaning, of *Geist*.

ramification that soul in its *Geistigkeit* is a *different dimension* from the world of nature, from all natural (sensuously given) things or processes or experiences: Jung's "over and above" dimension. It is the sphere of generality (the fundamental sharedness-character of meanings) and as such also of logical negativity (*absolute negativity*). Jung's misnomer, "the collective unconscious",[46] can now be comprehended as actually intending to give expression to this sphere of generality "over and above" the positive-factual aspect of things, to the sphere of *Geistigkeit*.

Soul events may at times occur in only one single individual, but they are nevertheless not *his: a priori* they do not belong to him the way merely psychic events belong to him. This is precisely what distinguishes "the *psychic*" from "the *psychological*". Psychic events, our emotions, perceptions, desires, fears, fantasies, dreams, etc., are clearly contained in the individual as human animal and are in this sense his property. But the psychological is *geistig* and thus logically universal (Jung would have said: collective). To the extent that soul events are truly soul events they originate as (and have the logical [not the empirical] character of) sharedness, of generality. They do not belong to anybody. Indeed, although occurring in the natural world, *as themselves* they do not "exist" in the natural world.

When Heraclitus (fr.45 DK) said, "You would not find out the boundaries of soul, even by traveling along every path: so deep a *logos* does it have", we now have to point out that it is not the *boundaries* of soul that cannot be found anywhere on earth, i.e., in positive-factual reality, but much rather soul as such in the first place: the "*geistig* side" of real phenomena, because only like sees like. The "*geistig* side" is only accessible to *Geist*. Now we can say that the reason why Jung's "Freud" was unable to see this "*geistig* side" of sexuality was that he insisted on approaching phenomena exclusively as empirical ego and did not rise to the standpoint of *Geist*. The ego's "terminology and theory" are by definition "too narrow" and "concretistic". Jung's shift to the "*geistig* side" and his coining the concept of the (unfortunately so-called) "collective unconscious" as the sphere of generality are one and the same move.

The phrase "Eternal Mind's eternal recreation" also allows us to point to another feature of the dimension that we call soul, a feature intrinsically connected with the soul's absolute negativity and its status of fundamental generality, namely, its total "uselessness" (from an empirical-practical point of view). Particularly those writings in which Jung said he explored the "*geistig* side" of sexuality, *Mysterium Coniunctionis* and "The Psychology of Transference", but also all his other works devoted to alchemy, to the transformation symbolism of the Mass, the visions of Zosimos, etc. etc., openly display this utter "uselessness". This is precisely part and parcel of their devotion to soul.

And yet: soul as the sphere of generality and absolute negativity does express itself in really existing paintings and sculptures, in the words of language that are

---

46 *Geist* is neither "collective" nor is what Jung means with the collective unconscious "unconscious". The "archetypes of the collective unconscious" played themselves out openly in archaic people's mythological or religious knowledge and cults. Even dreams are always conscious, or else they do not exist.

actually spoken, in texts that are printed, in dreams that occur in an empirical human being. This confirms once more that soul does not hover above the world as transcendent other-worldly reality. It is world-immanent. Now the question arises how these two insights (absolute negativity vs. expression in real phenomena) can be reconciled.

What reconciles them is the psychological difference, that difference that (not literally, empirically, but absolute-negatively) divides one and the same real phenomenon into its two "sides": sexuality into Freud's biological function and into Jung's invisible "*geistig* side"; a statue by Praxiteles into the positivity of a stone object as perhaps seen by a dog and the not simply empirically given and *vorhanden* ("present to hand") presence of a god as seen by the artist himself; a text as the printed letters in a book and the nowhere literally existing or subsisting, and in this sense logically negative, story or theoretical discourse; and, of course, also man himself as the natural animal that he is (remember Jung's "human stable"?) and the empirically unprovable and yet undoubtedly real soul or *Geist* that he is. The whole of human culture here on earth and the fact of language as such are evidence of man's soul nature.

3.4 No transcendence. Only "this valley of the world"

Therefore I fully concur with Hillman when he writes in his essay, "psychological method remains within this valley of the world, through which history passes and leaves its traces, our 'ancestors'".[47] For as we have seen, Jung's "over and above" dimension and his emphasis on *Geistigkeit* really do not refer to the peaks of trans-cendence, but to the sphere of absolute negativity and generality opened up within the Real (wherever it be). And like life, *Geist* is a this-worldly reality and yet not a positivity.

However, for two reasons I don't believe that what Hillman says is really valid for himself. The first is that a psychologist who settles in the vale (image) side of the peak–vale, thought–image dichotomy and who needs to rage against the peaks of spirit has himself really not really arrived in the valley of the world and along with it in modernity. For if he had arrived, the valley would not be anything special, nothing to make a fuss about, and above all: not just one side of two. Rather, he would know that modern existence is characterized by the fact that it inescapably has its place in this valley of the world, more than that, that this valley of the world is the only place there is. There is no "peak" anymore as in earlier times (which is precisely why some people today crave for peak experiences and spirituality: emotions, felt experiences as substitutes for the lost "cosmological" peak or heaven). We today are always in the valley. Even literal mountain peaks, indeed even distant galaxies, are part of this valley of the world, as Jung knew only too well.[48] The whole "cosmological" dichotomy—heaven *above*, earth and underworld *below*—no longer

47 Hillman, *Puer Papers*, 61.
48 Jung, *CW* 9i, § 50.

exists. Today heaven and hell are just as above as below; the whole "cosmological" above–below distinction has become obsolete. Psychology is as a matter of course only concerned with this real world, with the soul of the real. However, in order to be *psychology*, it has to be aware of the soul's essential *Geistigkeit* and the psychologist's task of "saying again".

Above all, are not the (metaphoricized) "Gods" that Hillman's psychology insists on the semanticized and barely concealed form in which the *syntax of otherworldliness* is surreptitiously packaged and slipped into the—today unavoidably prevailing—valley of the world as a kind of fifth column?[49] And is this valley, as the soulless and literal "universe" (in Hillman's view the radical opposite of "cosmos"), for him not ultimately a "fallen world" and as "fallen" viewed from a standpoint *above* this valley of the world?

The second reason for my not believing that Hillman truly means what he says with all its consequences is that a mind that wishes for a reversal of history and a return to or resuscitation[50] of bygone things does not seem to respect history, which is above all characterized by its *irreversibility*. Without this sense of irreversibility history is not history. But Hillman insists on Gods as timeless structures of consciousness and denies that Gods (as well as the power of "image") can become historically obsolete. How then can he say, "I ride this horse of history until it drops, for I submit that history has become the Great Repressed",[51] if he nevertheless denies irreversibility and obsolescence?[52] We see: it is not really the soul's history itself that intrigues him; he merely *uses* selected past events for *blaming* his discontent with today's situation (the "malnutritioned" Western psychological culture) on certain forefathers (namely, those "theological, spiritual men" of more than a thousand years ago),[53] much like neurotic psychology tries to blame the patients' present-day neuroses on what their parents did to them in early childhood. And he uses the past, conversely, for selectively picking out certain figures (such as Plotinus, Ficino) as good ancestors of archetypal psychology to provide this modern school of thought with a noble lineage. But just as, biologically speaking, our genetic heritage is our genetic heritage, so also, in psychological and *geistig* regards, our ancestors (*all* of them, the "good" and the "bad") are our ancestors, whether we like it or not. They are *ours*, ingrained in *our* historically grown psychological constitution. We are *their* results. No choice.

---

49 Here it is important to remember that the notion of *Geistigkeit* does not in a similar way involve a betrayal of "this valley of the world", just as the claim that words have a meaning does not leave *this* world in favor of the "peaks" of otherworldliness (transcendence).

50 Hillman, *Puer Papers*, 56.

51 Hillman, *Puer Papers*, 62.

52 Hillman immunized his ahistorical aestheticizing stance against historical arguments by denouncing them as being guilty of what he calls the "historical fallacy" and literalism.

53 By contrast cf. Jung: "The true cause for a neurosis lies in the Now, for the neurosis exists in the present. It is by no means a hangover from the past, a *caput mortuum* ... Because the neurotic conflict faces us today, any historical deviation is a detour, if not actually a wrong turning" in Jung, *CW* 10, § 363, transl. modif.

If more than a thousand years ago "long battles between spirit and soul" were fought in the Councils of the Early Church and "images were deprived of their inherent authenticity", then the *psychologist* who truly rides the horse of history would have the task of comprehending this as a soul-internal process, one induced by the soul for its own purposes, as the soul's *opus contra naturam*. Otherwise he would himself depotentiate and deprive soul of its all-comprehensiveness, himself exile from it certain of its moves. He would have to comprehend and affirm what exactly the soul's specific necessity and purpose was in depotentiating and depriving image of its authenticity during those long-bygone centuries. What was its telos? What was to be achieved? It will precisely not do to approach this historical shift dogmatically from an external superior standpoint with moral judgments (good-bad, right-wrong) or emotions (hatred). I submit, these long-ago battles can be understood psychologically as part of the pivotal events through which the soul's stance towards its own experience was slowly heaved from its habitual "cosmological" (the *An-sich*) orientation to the emerging fundamentally new "psychological" one.

Jung, by contrast, when saying, "without history there can be no psychology",[54] fully acknowledged the irrevocable historical ruptures and losses. He knew that "our time [is distinguished] from all others"[55] and that "we cannot go back to [what] is gone".[56] This awareness of the irreversible processes of history fits to the soul's *Geistigkeit*. In its deepest layer (covered, of course, by incredibly many serendipitous, meaningless, human-all-too-human occurrences, be they disastrous or happy), human history as a whole is the slow process of the soul's speaking about itself and coming home to itself, from the earliest prehistoric times down to medial modernity and in all likelihood also beyond the latter.

Looking back upon the "peaks–vales" distinction we can say that if one bases psychology on the *corresponding* notion of soul, one would establish a *false* psychological difference. "False" here is not my personal judgment. This difference is *intrinsically* false because it is not different enough.[57] Peaks and vales belong to the same (empirical, "geographical") category. Such a difference is six of one and half a dozen of the other. The real psychological difference, as for example expressed in Jung's statements about sexuality that we started with, brings a breakthrough to a totally other dimension, from the world of positivity ("biological function", "personal significance") to absolute negativity ("its *geistig* side"), from the imagery of

---

54 Jung, *MDR*, 205.
55 Jung, *CW* 10, § 161.
56 That the "quest of meaning" Jung nevertheless entertained the utopian hope that the lost truth would become "true once more" in "a new form" is another story.
57 It would also be possible to describe this situation exactly in the opposite way, namely that this difference is not "same" enough. By imaginally *distributing* the two sides of the difference onto two from the outset empirical-factually different, separate things, the difference stays external and abstract (literal otherness, two alternatives). This being condemned to externalize is the congenital defect of the imaginal approach. The difference does not come home to itself and thus does not become psychological. In fact, it ceases to be a real *difference* and instead turns into a dissociation or split. The psychological difference, by contrast, is opened up within *one and the same* phenomenon.

empirical, sensually given things ("peaks" and "vales") to the thought of *Geistigkeit*, which as thought is not positively given and has no positive existence. This is also why the "rise" to the "over and above" level is not an attempt to leave the valley in favor of some mysterious height after all. This (indeed) spatial metaphor of verticality is here an a priori sublated metaphor and what it refers to is by no means a literal upwards movement in extensional space, but in reality an "*intensional*", strictly *logical* movement of negation, an "alchemical" evaporation, distillation.

The true psychological difference can be interpreted as the absolute-negative interiorization-into-itself of the external ("cosmological" or imaginal) peaks–vales dichotomy. We already heard that the latter has, as a whole, gone under into the "vale" side of itself, into the all-comprising inescapable "valley of the world". For the former dichotomy this process of the psychologization of "the cosmological" amounted to a coagulation, a toughening, hardening, of its "vale of soul-making" side into positive facticity, on the one hand, and to the distillation of its former "peak" side into *Geistigkeit*, on the other hand. The "*geistig* side" of phenomena is the *psychological* successor to imaginal psychology's still "*cosmological*" "peak".

4 No ruling dominants. Only: "when the time is fulfilled"

In closing I briefly point to one (major) aspect of Jung's psychology which is incompatible with his own awareness of the *Geistigkeit* and historicity of the soul. This is his theory of the archetypes. As long as they are conceived as mere *forms* or *types* or *patterns* by which human thoughts, images, and experiences inevitably have to be molded if they are to appear at all, the idea of archetypes causes no problem, nor would one's seeing them as a kind of reservoir of sunken substantial contents ("meanings"), as the sedimentation of cultural-historical developments that may re-emerge occasionally. The problem I see comes only because they are also asserted to be timeless, ever-present "archetypes in themselves" that are "the dominants which rule human existence throughout the millenniums",[58] "factors" in the literal sense of "makers", or even "personal agencies".[59] "The word 'type' is, as we know, derived from τύπος, thus an archetype presupposes an imprinter".[60]

With this concept we get mysterious agents behind the scenes, after all, and we are back to a thinking in substances rather than only in living processes, in terms of the soul's self-unfolding logical or *geistig* life. At the same time, this valley of the world has also been left. We now have clearly transcendent causes that "*rule* human existence" fundamentally *heteronomously*. It is, according to this scheme, not the inner logic of a person's as well as society's real nature and situation with its internal and external determinants and contradictions that moves human existence psychologically. No, that existence is governed from outside, by "higher" external forces. The archetypes in their inalienable otherness, if not other-worldliness, are

---

58 Jung, *Letters* 2, 540.
59 Jung, *CW* 5, § 388.
60 Jung, *CW* 12, § 15.

the true effective causes. The real *power* of images in psychic life (that often is experienced as so-called numinosity) comes from them.

I contrast this conception with another one to be found in Jung. He once wrote, "I have often been asked [by analysands seeking help], 'And what do you *do* about it?' I do nothing; there is nothing I can do except wait, with a certain trust in God, until, out of a conflict borne with patience and fortitude, there emerges the solution destined—although I cannot foresee it—for that particular person".[61] It is clear that "trust in God" and "destined" are used only metaphorically. What Jung wants to indicate is of course not that God directly brings about this solution or that the latter is preordained by fate. On the contrary, the result is effected simply by the self-development of the psychic process itself. No dominant. Nothing ruling from outside. Rather, the internal logic of the conflict, provided that it is borne with patience and fortitude (that is, that it is not subdued, dulled, numbed, but kept alive in its unmitigated acuteness), works itself out in an unforeseeable (productive) way. Emergence. The efficacy and the energy behind the change towards a solution comes from *time* (and thus from this valley of the world). The solution comes when the time has come, or as the Bible says, when *the time is fulfilled*.[62]

This theory, elaborated a little more in Jung's idea of the "transcendent function", of the formation of "uniting symbols" through the tension of opposites, is clearly incompatible with the theory of archetypal dominants that *rule* psychic life. If the latter were the rulers, they could bring symbols and conflict solutions at any time and would not be dependent on opposites.

If the source of energy and effective power ("numinosity") really resided in the *archetypal images* themselves, then all archetypal images would inevitably always have to take hold of the consciousness of people. A psychotherapist who hears numerous dreams from his patients and may meet quite a few archetypal images during one day could not help being swamped by their numinous power, pulling him in all sorts of different directions since people may present to him rather different or even contradictory images in the course of his working day. But this awful effect does by no means occur. As a rule, the therapist can calmly listen to and interpret these dreams and stay personally largely unaffected. This is because the power of images or ideas is not inherent in them *as* images or ideas. *In themselves images and ideas are harmless, neutral.* They do not *come* with numinous power, nor are they loaded with that power by mysterious "imprinters" or ruling dominants. The possible "tyranny of unconscious presuppositions" is also not *caused* by archetypes, not even by the "archetypal", "numinous", i.e., *geistig*, character of those presuppositions. No, the possible power of archetypal images and ideas to fascinate (or sometimes even to tyrannize and possess) consciousness is—very much down to earth—*given* to them by the concrete historical situation of the psyche, the particular locus, be it in the soul history of an individual or in the soul history of a whole people or society. Depending on where one stands in one's psychic development,

61 Jung, *CW* 12, § 37.
62 History! Not the power of timeless images.

be it personally or collectively, images become powerful, or lose their gripping power (or do not move one from the outset). This is why images that may once upon a time or in foreign cultures have given rise to great passions or even to wars may not touch us anymore. For us, they are merely curiosities of historical, scholarly, psychological, or touristic interest. The same reason explains why gods and symbols die.

There is no good reason why this "transcendent function" way of conceiving the emergence of something new in the soul should be restricted to solutions of seemingly insolvable internal conflict situations in individuals and to the birth of uniting symbols out of the clash of opposites. It should much rather be the general way of conceiving the appearance of new contents (dream images, visions out of the blue, so-called numinous experiences, new ideas in intellectual history, even neurotic, psychosomatic and certain psychotic symptoms), namely as the very natural emergence into consciousness, *when the time is fulfilled*, of those new contents from out of the internal logical or *geistig* life of the soul; as the soul's pushing off to a new status of consciousness; as the unforeseeable creative result of its internal tensions, contradictions; as its reaction to the pressures arising from all that it is confronted with in real life. No need for ruling dominants. No need for the mystification of "images" as originators and "powers".

But this renunciation of the "ruling dominants" does not detract from the "*geistig* side" of psychic phenomena, which is what represents the inalienable "main concern" and unique specialty of Jungian psychology.

5 Departedness

Reflecting upon this main concern, there is, however, no denying the fact that it is devoted to a thing of the past, to what belongs to former world conditions in the history of the soul, namely, to the bygone ages of classical metaphysics and religion. Today, in medial modernity, it cannot be a present reality; it can only be a historical presence, a presence in Mnemosyne. In its commitment to soul, psychology in the tradition of C. G. Jung relates to all actual occurrences of soul as being present only *as absent*; it respects their logical status, namely that in themselves and in their presence they are a priori and irrevocably departed. It is precisely their intrinsic departedness (their presence *as* absent) that identifies them as events of soul[63] in contrast to "*psychic*" experiences of the human animal.[64] If and where psychology nevertheless insists on their having to be a present reality or immediate

---

63 In contrast to the belief that "soul is constituted of images". "Image" is an *empirical* criterion (it is set off against other possible empirical criteria, thought, emotion, desire, drive, etc.). "Departedness" is not empirically determinable. It reflects the soul's absolute negativity.

64 From a Jungian point of view (and in contrast to their own self-understanding) we could say that all psychologies that are openly personalistic isolate the moment of "absence" contained in the phrase "present only *as absent*", take it literally, and absolutize it, so that soul is nothing, simply does not figure in their theories and thinking

presence—as, for example, in the form of peak experiences, "high"-feelings, the emotion of numinosity, the veneration of "the imaginal", the presence of "the sacred", "the Gods", "Angels", or the discovery of "one's personal myth"—there it would turn into kitsch, and soul into a consumer good for the gratification of the greedy ego.

(Fr. A. Lange coined the popular phrase "psychology without soul" in 1866). They cannot hold the dialectical contradiction-and-union of presence and absence and therefore have to choose *either* the one *or* the other moment. But since history deprived the decidedly modern world of the possibility of immediate presence, they did not *have* a choice: for an undialectical approach, the second moment is indeed, as Lange correctly realized, the only one left: the stance of positivism.

2

"THE PSYCHOLOGICAL DIFFERENCE" IN JUNG'S *MYSTERIUM CONIUNCTIONIS*

Pamela Power

Introduction

"Jung had been familiar with alchemical texts from around 1910. In 1912, Theodore Flournoy had presented a psychological interpretation of alchemy in his lectures at the University of Geneva and, in 1914, Herbert Silber published an extensive work on the subject."[1] In 1928, Richard Wilhelm gave Jung a manuscript of a Chinese alchemical treatise, *The Secret of the Golden Flower.* "The text gave me an undreamed-of confirmation of my ideas about the mandala and the circumambulation of the center," wrote Jung.[2] But it wasn't until 1930 that Jung began to study alchemy in earnest. He acquired alchemy texts, began copying excerpts, and making lists of alchemical terms. Jung had by this time established his ideas about finding one's myth, individuation, active imagination, and the *self.* He encouraged his colleagues and patients to engage in the activities that he had done in his "confrontation with the unconscious" during the years from 1911 to 1918.[3] He recognized a tradition of "active imagination" that in alchemy was called "meditation," and he thought it was a parallel to his work of coming to terms with the unconscious. Jung wrote:

> But when I began to understand alchemy I realized that it represented the historical link with Gnosticism, and that a continuity therefore existed between past and present. Grounded in the natural philosophy of the Middle Ages, alchemy formed the bridge on the one hand into the past, to Gnosticism, and on the other into the future, to the modern psychology of the unconscious.[4]

1 Sonu Shamdasani, *The Red Book* (New York, NY: W. W. Norton, 2009), 219.
2 Jung, *MDR*, 222.
3 Jung, *MDR*, Chapter VI.
4 Jung, *MDR*, 201.

Jung's thought was that the nature of matter was little understood during the time of the alchemists, and this allowed them to see fantasies in the *vas Hermeticum* that were projected and corresponded to their inner, as yet unrecognized psychological transformation processes.

Jung presented his early ideas about alchemy at the *Eranos* Conference Lectures of 1935 and 1936. These two lectures eventually became *Psychology and Alchemy*, first published in 1944. Here, Jung found a way into the complexity of alchemical material in order to demonstrate that alchemy, which had been discarded and ignored, contained a wealth of treasures when viewed from the perspective of depth psychological processes. The first lecture was a series of dreams that demonstrated the theme of circumambulation of a center. In the second lecture, Jung drew parallels between religious motives and symbols in alchemy that appear spontaneously in the "process of individuation."

Mysterium Coniunctionis, Jung's major work on alchemy, written from 1941 to 1954, was first published in 1955. In *Mysterium Coniunctionis* (hereafter referred to as MC), Jung set out his fully developed ideas about alchemy. This book contains in-depth amplification of the welter of images and ideas that Jung had accumulated from his studies of alchemy. Of major importance is the theme of "joining the opposites" in the "alchemical marriage," a theme that had been a special pre-occupation of the alchemists. MC was subtitled "An Inquiry into the separation and synthesis of psychic opposites in Alchemy." Jung wrote, "In *Mysterium Coniunctionis* my psychology was at last given its place in reality and established upon its historical foundations. Thus my task was finished, my work done, and now it can stand."[5]

Giegerich's view of alchemy and "the psychological difference"

Those who have studied Wolfgang Giegerich's work on alchemy know that in many regards, he has a fundamentally different position about alchemy than did Jung. In *The Soul's Logical Life*, he wrote:

> [With] Jung's evaluation of alchemy as the missing link connecting him (and modern psychology) with the imaginal tradition of antiquity, we can say that alchemy is seriously underdetermined with this characterization. For one thing, alchemy is not merely a passive link guaranteeing the undisturbed con-tinuation of a tradition. It is also an active agent, a dynamic force, a historical motor, a transformer. It has a job to do. And secondly, the particular job it has to do is the historical task of *within* the imaginal tradition undoing the imaginal tradition, and thereby in fact transporting the mind to a radically new status of consciousness.[6]

5   Jung, *MDR*, 221.
6   Wolfgang Giegerich, *The Soul's Logical Life* (Frankfurt am Main; New York: Peter Lang, 2008), 159ff.

Giegerich views alchemy as belonging to a specific period in the historical life of *soul*. The soul's *opus magnum* is a historical process of soul that is reflected over the centuries in cultural expressions of the arts, science, political changes, literature, philosophy and religion. One cannot say that Jung did not recognize that the *opus* of the alchemists was work that belonged to this larger historical process. He did. An example is the ubiquitous theme of renewal and regeneration of the King.[7] Jung saw in the alchemical death and rebirth of the King that the "dominants of consciousness," i.e., the current status of soul, was undergoing radical transformation.

However, *most* important for Jung was his view that the alchemists did not recognize that they were projecting their unconscious psychic processes into the little understood physical/material substances. In MC, Jung moves back and forth from the impersonal (Giegerich's *opus magnum* of soul) to the personal level (Giegerich's *opus parvum*) and does not always make the differentiation clear. This is to be understood because Jung's emphasis on alchemy was primarily to demonstrate and affirm his ideas about the transformation processes that occur in the individuation process of modern individuals.

With this emphasis, Jung obscured the psychological difference, conflating the *opus magnum* of soul with the *opus parvum* (small work) of the individual. In addition, Jung was well aware of alchemy as an *opus contra naturam*, but at times he appeared to use alchemical notions not as operations of negation, but as operations to create positivity. When he did this, Jung stopped short the ongoing work of alchemy. It emphatically stopped, in Giegerich's view, when Jung placed the individual as the centerpiece of the *opus magnum*, and when he equated the production of the quintessence, the lapis, the stone, as creating the ontological, personal Jungian *self*. Reading *Mysterium Coniunctionis* through Giegerich's understanding of alchemy may serve to further distill and refine, separate and synthesize Jungian Psychology, which is Jung's *opus magnum*.

The Conjunction

The first chapters of *Mysterium Coniunctionis* are descriptive details and lengthy amplifications of numerous images of "the opposites" that are to be reconciled and joined together to create the *self*. These are symbolic entities that represent the disparate aspects of the psyche, such as sun and moon, salt and sulphur. The most basic disparate elements, according to Jung, are the conscious and unconscious. To create the whole man, the *homo totus*, these many pairs of opposites must be reconciled, joined or brought together. Chapter VI, "The Conjunction," is the culmination of MC and sets out the notion of the conjunction of the opposites that were described and amplified in detail in the five previous chapters ("The Components of the Coniunctio," "The Paradoxa," "The Personification of the Opposites," "Rex and Regina," "Adam and Eve").

---

7   Jung, *CW* 14, Chapter IV.

For this last chapter, Jung relies heavily upon texts from the 16th-century alchemist, Gerhard Dorn, to elaborate upon the stages of the *coniunctio*. The first stage, according to Dorn, is the establishment of the *unio mentalis,* a union of the "soul" ("soul" for Dorn was specifically the seat of emotions) with the "mind," and according to Jung's reading of Dorn, the *unio mentalis* brings about a separation from the body when the "soul" joins the "mind."[8]

Jung described the achievement of the *unio mentalis* as establishing a spiritual counter-position to the purely natural. As such it is, according to Jung, an achievement of mental control over the realm of affects and instincts, which more naturally incline toward the body. The *unio mentalis* establishes consciousness of itself, over and against itself, and it destroys the natural unity, the *unio naturalis,* of mind-soul-body. The *unio mentalis* is a goal of any religion or philosophy that strives for mental discipline over affects and instinctual urges. In this way, Jung describes the *unio mentalis* as a general collective achievement.

In *personal* development, Jung described the *unio mentalis* as the stage when one has achieved knowledge and insight about one's unconscious, primarily about the shadow. However, this knowledge has reached only a theoretical stage and, according to Jung, requires a further stage, that the knowledge gained from achieving the *unio mentalis* is applied to actual, embodied life. Jung wrote,

> The reuniting of the spiritual position with the body obviously means that the insights gained [in the first stage] should be made real. An insight might just as well remain in abeyance if it is simply not used. The second stage of conjunction therefore consists in making a reality of the man who has acquired some knowledge of his paradoxical wholeness.[9]

The achievement of the *unio mentalis* leaves a dissociation, a split between "mind" (in union with "soul") and body. Individuation, according to Jung, repairs this split, thereby healing the individual and the collective split of our times.

Jung looked to the alchemists to see how *they* handled what he viewed as this problem of dissociation. Dorn described the creation of a uniting substance that would join the *unio mentalis* to the left-behind body. For Jung, this meant to unite the conscious to unconscious standpoints, to join spirit to matter, and to unite *all* the opposites into the *complexio oppositorum* (combination of opposites).

Dorn begins this procedure with a *further operation* to distill the *caelum,* or "sky stuff," from the body that had been left behind. Dorn wrote, "In the human body there is concealed a certain substance of heavenly nature, known to a very few, which needs no medicament, being itself the incorrupt medicament."[10] Beginning with this *caelum,* other ingredients are added to make a robust "arcane substance"

8   Jung, *CW* 14, § 671 and following paragraphs.
9   Jung, *CW* 14, § 679.
10 Jung, *CW* 14, § 144, n. 30.

that will hold body and spirit together in the *coniunctio*. Jung understands the *caelum* as the creation of a third, a substance to hold the dissociated parts together. Using these descriptions from Dorn, Jung finds an analogy between this stage of Dorn's *coniunctio* and the creation of the Jungian *self*. The *self* repairs the dissociation that is both individual and collective.

In reading these texts of Dorn that Jung quotes, one may wonder if this is what Dorn intended. As Giegerich wrote, Dorn and all the alchemists had no means other than imaginal language to describe overcoming the imaginal. Jung reads Dorn in a positivistic manner, *and* he applies it to the individual psyche. Jung surprisingly becomes almost literal about the ingredients to be added to the sky stuff, the *caelum*: honey, chelidonia, mercurialis, rosemary, red lily, and blood. Jung amplifies these images as symbolizing the opposites within each image, some version of poison/panacea or poison/antidote, and these being necessary to create the third thing in which the opposites are conjoined. Jung offers rich amplification of the imagery and symbolism of these ingredients seeing them as symbolic, of course, but *almost* not treating them as such.

One can also read Dorn as describing *negated* substances. Over and over, the ingredient is something that is not what it is, and it is specifically, determinately not. Applying negation after negation, negating highly sensuous ingredients, this is suggestive of homeopathic remedies in which the actual ingredient is diluted (i.e., negated) to make varying strengths; and the strongest, *most potent* concentration of a homeopathic remedy is one in which there has been so much dilution that the remedy no longer contains any molecules of that *specific* ingredient at all!

After elaborate procedures leading to the creation of the *caelum* mixture, Jung quotes Dorn's description of what comes next:

> At length the body is compelled to resign itself to, and obey, the union of the two that are united [i.e., soul and spirit as the already accomplished *unio mentalis*]. That is the wondrous transformation of the Philosophers, of body into spirit, and the latter into body, of which there has been left to use by the sages the saying, "Make the fixed volatile and the volatile fixed, and in this you have our Magistery."[11]

Does this not sound like an invitation to, as Giegerich describes it, "the liquidity of dialectics"?[12] Does it not suggest that Dorn was wildly intuiting, albeit with his imagistic language, a consciousness beyond what he had realized? This sounds more like a transformation, a negation of both, indeed a sublation, in which that which is fixed becomes volatile and that which is volatile becomes fixed; and for Dorn, this is the best image for overcoming the imaginal, using the language of the imaginal, that he could produce.

11   Jung, *CW* 14, § 685.
12   Giegerich, *Soul's Logical Life*, 190.

The problem of the third

For Jung, the *unio mentalis* was only half way to the *coniunctio*, and to Jung's naturalistic thinking, this required a rejoining of these disconnected "opposites." Jung understood Dorn's *caelum* mixture as the creation of a "third" with which to join those opposites, the "body" to the "soul–mind" union of the *unio mentalis*. However, Giegerich criticizes the use of the "third." He writes:

> It is the imagination that imagines the overcoming of the opposites in terms of a Third in between. By stationing itself on the middle ground, it ipso facto stations itself in the stationary or fixed as such, in the ontological. It settles in an externalized mental reservation. It is working with frozen images and holds itself, its own life, in suspension. It avoids the liquidity, or Dionysian frenzy, of dialectics. By taking recourse to a Third, it precisely does not *overcome* the alternatives, inasmuch as it only escapes from the ideational *contents* of the alternatives, but retains and rescues the same *logical status* of consciousness they belong to.[13]

Giegerich has also described the *unio mentalis* as a general achievement that needed further work to be fulfilled.

> [By around 1800] "The soul," by having shown itself to be consciousness rather than a content of consciousness, i.e., an object in the world, had come home *from* externality. But this still does not mean that it had come home *to* itself. What had so far been achieved was only the full realization of the interiorized *general form* of consciousness, of what the alchemists called the *unio mentalis*. As such it was still something like a promise of a future that needed to be fulfilled, a projection that needed to be caught up with.[14]

Both Jung and Giegerich view the *unio mentalis* as incomplete, as an initial stage. The major difference is that Jung saw the *unio mentalis* as a dissociation that required repair whereas Giegerich views the *unio mentalis* as the beginning of the overcoming of imaginal, ontological thought. An accomplished *unio mentalis* for Giegerich would mean a sublation of the positivity of the opposites to that of *thinking* the opposites *dialectically*. It is *not* dissociation but a radical overcoming of the imaginal; an overcoming that leaves nothing behind. An accomplished *unio mentalis* for Giegerich would be a complete "working off" of the imaginal mode of consciousness to that of logical thought. It is the accomplishment of a new status in the soul's life. It is not a separation of mind from anything, but a mind that includes everything in the sense that it uroborically can think everything. This does not mean, however, that the imaginal has no place, as Giegerich has written:

13 Giegerich, *Soul's Logical Life*, 190.
14 Wolfgang Giegerich, *The Soul Always Thinks* (New Orleans, LA: Spring Journal, Inc., 2010), 320, italics added.

The psychological difference, however, is also the difference between the imaginal and the logical. This difference is a genuinely *psychological* difference, which means that psychology exists as the distance and tension between them, encompassing both.[15]

However, as long as the imaginal mode prevails, it prevents *soul* as consciousness from being alive with its own self-movement.

Jung conceived the *unio mentalis* as creating a division, separation of mind–spirit from nature–body. It was dissociation. To Jung's naturalistic thinking, this required a rejoining of these disconnected "opposites." But for Giegerich, the whole point is that soul has moved beyond nature and body. As Giegerich notes, "If the *unio mentalis* had been truly accomplished in the first place, there would be nothing to go back to."[16]

Jungian psychology and the end of alchemy

According to Giegerich:

> To do justice to alchemy you have to include its decline in the definition of what alchemy is about … This decline is both alchemy's destruction *and* its final fulfillment. It had been the job of the alchemical opus to ultimately render itself superfluous.[17]

Alchemy would render itself obsolete once the "work of alchemy" is complete, meaning "*within* the imaginal tradition undoing the imaginal tradition, and thereby in fact transporting the mind to a radically new status of consciousness."[18]

For Psychology as the Discipline of Interiority, alchemy as a vehicle for soul has already happened. From this perspective, *Mysterium Coniunctionis* may be disregarded and discarded as a work of mere historical interest. It does not go far enough; it is no longer relevant to *soul*, and it is no longer where soul lives.

Considering *Mysterium Coniunctionis* as a document of Jungian psychology, we can see from what has been shown that the alchemical opus was stopped by the creation of the Jungian *self* as an ontological entity for the "reconciliation of the opposites," conscious and unconscious. But, if *we* continue to think the problem that Jung was trying to solve when he turned to the alchemists and with *his* reading of Dorn, if we continue to think further negations suggested by Dorn, perhaps *misread* by Jung, Jungian psychology can be alive with its own self-movement.

Perhaps Jung himself had intimations of something beyond his own established ideas. In *Mysterium,* Jung wrote:

15 Giegerich, *Soul's Logical Life*, 124.
16 2013, personal communication.
17 Giegerich, *Soul's Logical Life*, 160.
18 Giegerich, *Soul's Logical Life*, 159–160.

the mystery of the stone, or of the self, will then develop an aspect which, though still unconscious to us today, is nevertheless foreshadowed in our formulations, though in so veiled a form that the investigator of the future will ask himself, just as we do, whether we knew what we meant.[19]

Did Jung get caught on the jagged edge of Dorn's production of the *caelum*, the quintessence? We cannot really know what was on Dorn's mind with his stages of the *coniunctio*, or precisely what he meant by his "mind-soul-body"; it is clear, however, he is describing a series of operations. Separation, synthesis, and transformation: process was the message of alchemy, nothing pinned down, and nothing is what it is said to be. There are a thousand words for the arcane substance—not to keep it arcane, but for it to be a substance that is *not* a substance.

What if Jung had allowed his own intimation of, as he wrote, a future "foreshadowed in our formulations" to be realized by himself? What would it mean if *Mysterium Coniunctionis* were to undergo a further negation of itself, so that "within the Jungian tradition, there is an undoing of the *reified* Jungian tradition" leading to an accomplished *unio mentalis*? We can speculate that for Jungian psychology, the "left behind body"—that which has not submitted to the *unio mentalis*, what has not joined the liquidity of the dialectic, to being thought rather than imagined—is Jung's understanding, his *misunderstanding*, of the role and importance of the individual *and* the ego. This ego "entity" requires further separation, distillation, *and* negation.

Gerhard Dorn made such statements as, "Thou wilt never make from others the One which thou seekest, except first there be made one thing of thyself…"[20] and, "Transform yourselves from dead into living philosophical stones!"[21] These exhortations were highly suggestive to Jung that Dorn was *one* alchemist who seemed to be aware that he was actually working on himself, and they confirmed Jung's idea of placing the human enterprise at the center of the *opus magnum*.

However, is it not true that any serious project requires passion and dedication that might be described by such expressions? One is not doing something as much as allowing something to happen *in* and *through* oneself. This, according to Giegerich, is the dialectical opposite of "working on oneself." Instead, importance is placed on soul such that, to paraphrase Giegerich, "The alchemist allowed himself to be turned into a sublated moment of alchemy."[22]

In MC, Jung wrote, "*An experience of the self is always a defeat for the ego.*"[23] This statement reflects an undialectical relation of ego and *self*; it is generally understood as a simple negation of the ego. But in the logic of the dialectic (as a speculative sentence), one must additionally read this as a defeat for the *self*. When one sees that the *self* is often treated as a Jungian reification done by the ego to sidestep and avoid further negation, that it serves to preserve metaphysics in the form of the

19 Jung, *CW* 14, § 213.
20 Jung, *CW* 14, § 685.
21 Jung, *CW* 12, § 378.
22 Wolfgang Giegerich, *What is Soul?* (New Orleans, LA: Spring Journal, Inc., 2012), 98.
23 Jung, *CW* 14, § 778.

god-image—and in this way is a neurotic compromise formation—we see that any defeat of the ego is in addition, always a defeat for the *self*. This *seeing*, this consciousness is a defeat of the *self* and the ego because it is a negation and sublation of both. The *self* would then not be a reified "thing" but would be experienced as the dialectical tension between the current status of consciousness and the edge of the future consciousness. The dynamic tension between them is the psychological difference.

As for the ego, Giegerich wrote:

> The term "logical" comes as a narcissistic insult to the ego, the ego that naturally clings to the natural and wants to shift the burden of the *separatio* (if it becomes aware of it at all) away from *itself* to the experiential level and to the level of its contents of consciousness (its teachings) in order for the *logical structure* of consciousness to be able to remain in its virginal innocence as "natural" consciousness. But psychological consciousness has to take its own medicine, nay, it *is* only psychological consciousness in the first place if its having taken its own medicine lies behind itself.[24]

The unrefined ego resists the liquidity of the dialectic. It resists reflection and the work of thinking. Positivity of the ego inclines toward certainty, fixity, the natural, emotions, and experiences. For Jungian psychology, the un-distilled, un-negated ego is surely one aspect of the "body left behind," rather than any literal body. Jungian psychology, as given in MC, is in a state where the *unio mentalis* is not complete, only hinted at. Jung struggled with a conundrum but could not see clearly through it. If the ego, as Dorn's "left behind body," consents to join the *unio mentalis*, the liquidity of the dialectic, then surely it will be an ego that is continually negated; indeed it is already a negated ego in the dialectic. I see it as the dialectic and tension between what Giegerich referred to as "me-as-ego" and the "Psychological I."[25] It is the space of the psychological difference *in vivo*. There is a continual "pushing off" to create the space of the psychological difference. This is the living, dynamic force of thinking that has overcome the imaginal style.

Once there is a "Psychological I", there is possible further negation and further *unio mentalis*: there is further thinking all the way through from mind to include body.[26]

Giegerich wrote:

> And a psychology informed by alchemy would have the task of freeing "the spirit Mercurius," i.e., the thought that is imprisoned in "the matter" (in the

24 Giegerich, *Soul Always Thinks*, 332–333.
25 Giegerich, *What is Soul?*, 300ff.
26 The plethora of body-based therapies (as useful as some may be) is *not* the body joining to mind. This is not "thinking the body." Thinking the body is hardly advanced past the stage of the most simplistic dream interpretations.

image, the emotion, the body symptom) imprisoned in the Real. In general, we could establish the following series: body symptom is submerged emotion, emotion is submerged image, image is submerged thought, and conversely, thought is sublated image, image is sublated emotion, emotion is sublated body reaction or behavior.[27]

We can sometimes think our thoughts and sometimes think the image and the emotion, but thinking the body symptom requires first some intuition of what that might even be. The task of "freeing Mercurius" from body "is like a promise of a future that needs to be fulfilled."[28]

Continuing the negation

It is remarkable, and to his credit, that Jung came to value alchemy so highly. In spite of seeing it primarily as a historical link to his own psychology of the unconscious, it appears that alchemy worked on Jung: alchemy put Jung into the alchemical vas and, at times, brought Jung very close to dialectical thinking. Alchemy distilled and refined Jung. For example, in MC, Jung wrote,

> Although the alchemists came very close to realizing that the ego was the mysteriously elusive arcane substance and the longed-for lapis, they were not aware that with their sun symbol they were establishing an intimate connection between God and the ego ... [N]ature herself is expressing an identity of God and ego.[29]

Jung's recognition that ego *as* consciousness, *as* God, *as* the arcane substance, suggests the beginning of Jung's knowing that God *as* soul *as* consciousness would eventually come home to itself, in this case home to Jungian psychology, and would no longer be estranged in externality, in the "other" as the unconscious, the god-image, the *self*.

The mysterious, elusive arcane substance, the longed-for lapis, the philosopher's stone, is no less elusive or nonexistent in Psychology as the Discipline of Interiority; however, in the latter it is *not* enshrouded in mystification, nor is it banished to a realm of unattainable "otherness." Rather, such a further distilled and refined consciousness only *seems* elusive because it is not something to be merely longed-for, or accomplished, once and for all. Such a consciousness, Giegerich writes,

> requires a depth and cultivation of thinking and feeling that enables one to see through to the "psychic background" of the real rather than being taken in by appearances and imaginal likenesses, a mercurial mind which is up to the

27 Giegerich, *Soul Always Thinks*, 334.
28 Giegerich, *Soul Always Thinks*, 320.
29 Jung, *CW* 14, § 131.

uroboric dialectic and absolute negativity of the soul's logical life, and, not to be forgotten, the I's clear distance to itself, i.e., *my* distance to myself (the ability to *abstract from* one's personal needs, wishes, preferences, and prejudices).[30]

Conclusion

Jung's perplexing conundrum around the *unio mentalis* remains, as Giegerich wrote, a "projection that needs to be fulfilled, a projection that needs to be caught up with." Uroboric, mercurial, dialectical thinking, today, is hardly an accomplished fact. In *this* respect, *Mysterium Coniunctionis* can point to furthering the work of Jungian psychology.

It may be thought that Jungian Psychology has already fulfilled itself with its methodology of creating a relationship between the ego and the unconscious, with creating the *self* as the reconciliation of "psychic opposites" along with its concurrent belief that the individual is a cosmic centerpiece and the "sole carrier of mind and life."[31] However, this ontological system, with its conflation of the individual with *soul*, denies Jungian Psychology its own further internal self-movement. Recognizing "the psychological difference" between that of the individual *opus parvum* from that of the *opus magnum* of soul would amount to a Copernican revolution within Jungian Psychology as ontologically understood. No longer the individual *with* soul, but individual *within* soul. Not consciousness discovering and "realizing" the *self*, but seeing through that goal to the current status of soul as *that which must be made in and through us*. As Giegerich wrote:

> We must not dissociate ourselves from what is happening, whatever it may be. On the contrary, much as Jung said about God that He needs us for His becoming conscious, this process needs us, needs our heart, our feeling, our imaginative attention and rigorous thinking effort so as to have a chance to become instilled with mind, with feeling, with soul. It must not be left as something that happens totally outside of us and apart from our consciousness. It must, as it were, be reborn through the soul and in the soul: in our *real* comprehension, i.e., in us as the "existing Concept" (Hegel).[32]

Nowadays, it would be unfashionable to claim that Jungian Psychology as a prime matter "has everything it needs within itself."[33] Indeed, the daily clinical practice of Jungian psychology has benefited much from the addition of psychoanalytic, trauma-based, and developmental theories. However, if Jungian psychology is to

---

30 Giegerich, *What is Soul?*, 292.
31 Jung, *CW* 10, § 457.
32 Wolfgang Giegerich, *Flight Into the Unconscious: An Analysis of C. G. Jung's Psychology Project (Collected English Papers, Vol. V)* (New Orleans, LA: Spring Journal, Inc., 2013), 348.
33 Jung, *CW* 14, § 749.

grow from the *inside*, rather than through accrescence, it must remember the far reaching significance of what originally gripped Jung, the notion of *soul*.[34]

Giegerich wrote that *both* alchemy and the Enlightenment had the job of overcoming the imaginal. He reminded us that the Enlightenment was one-sidedly destructive toward the imaginal by its wholesale dismissal of it whereas alchemy "worked it off" and thereby included the imaginal at a higher level. He wrote:

> [S]ince in alchemy the prime matter (the imaginal) cannot escape, there is a continual feedback or return of the opus contra naturam to its own results, on account of which the prime matter is preserved, but forced into higher statuses of itself, rather than being *replaced* by rationalistic concepts.[35]

Contemporary Jungians of many schools, even Psychology as the Discipline of Interiority, may follow the pattern of the Enlightenment, moving sideways to a simple negation, and repudiation, of the Jungian ontological position. But with alchemy as a continuing dynamic force within Jungian psychology, it *still* has a job to do. And that job, to paraphrase Giegerich, is "within the Jungian ontological tradition to work off the Jungian ontological tradition," thereby forcing Jungian Psychology *as a prime matter* "into higher statuses of itself."

34 See Giegerich, *Soul's Logical Life*, 40ff.
35 Giegerich, *Soul's Logical Life*, 160, n. 154.

3

JUNG'S SUBSTANTIAL DENIAL OF "THE PSYCHOLOGICAL DIFFERENCE"

Yasuhiro Tanaka

Introduction

In his *Memories, Dreams, Reflections*, Jung reported one of his dreams that he had during his preparations to write about the Book of Job in the Old Testament. The dream started with Jung's paying a visit to his long-deceased father. It runs as follows:

> He was living in the country—I did not know where. I saw a house in the style of the eighteenth century, very roomy, with several rather large out-buildings. It had originally been, I learned, an inn at a spa, and it seemed that many great personages, famous people and princes, had stopped there. Further-more, several had died and their sarcophagi were in a crypt belonging to the house. My father guarded these as custodian.[1]

The dream-father was "not only the custodian but also a distinguished scholar in his own right—which he had never been in his lifetime."[2] In his study, he began interpreting a certain passage in the Pentateuch of the Old Testament. His "argument was so intelligent and so learned" that the dream-Jung, Dr. Y., and his son in their stupidity simply could not follow it, although "it dealt with something extremely important which fascinated him" and "his mind was flooded with profound ideas."[3]

Then the scene changed. The dream-father and dream-Jung were in front of the house and entered it. The dream-Jung saw that it had very thick walls. They climbed a narrow staircase to the second floor. There, they had a strange sight of a large hall, which was "a high, circular room with a gallery running along the wall,

1   Jung, *MDR*, 217.
2   Jung, *MDR*, 217.
3   Jung, *MDR*, 218.

from which four bridges led to a basin-shaped center. The basin rested upon a huge column and formed the sultan's round seat…The whole was a gigantic mandala".[4]

The dream finally reaches its climax as follows:

> I suddenly saw that from the center a steep flight of stairs ascended to a spot high up on the wall—which no longer corresponded to reality. At the top of the stairs was a small door, and my father said, "Now I will lead you into the highest presence." Then he knelt down and touched his forehead to the floor. I imitated him, likewise kneeling, with great emotion. For some reason I could not bring my forehead quite down to the floor—there was perhaps a millimeter to spare. But at least I had made the gesture with him. Suddenly I knew—perhaps my father had told me—that upper door led to a solitary chamber where lived Uriah, King David's general, whom David had shamefully betrayed for the sake of his wife Bathsheba, by commanding his soldiers to abandon Uriah in the face of the enemy.[5]

Concerning this dream, Wolfgang Giegerich has already thoroughly examined it as a proof of "feigned submission" and "clandestine defiance" included in Jung's religious psychology under the title of "Jung's Millimeter".[6]

In this chapter, I will thus attempt to elucidate how this distance between the floor and Jung's forehead has *systematically* existed in his psychology, and then how and why Jung planned to substantially deny the psychological difference in his psychology.

Jung's *double* disunion with himself

As clearly seen above, the dream-Jung *could not* "bring his forehead quite down to the floor—there was perhaps a millimeter to spare." Although the dream-Jung did not know the reason he could not do that, which was well proven by the words "for some reason", this action in the dream *never* took place of his own *will*. Nevertheless, the after-awakening Jung made a surprising remark on it as follows:

> Something in me was saying, "All very well, but not entirely." Something in me was defiant and determined not to be a dumb fish; and if there were not something of the sort in *free man*, no Book of Job would have been written several hundred years before the birth of Christ.[7]

4   Jung, *MDR*, 218.
5   Jung, *MDR*, 219.
6   Wolfgang Giegerich, "Jung's Millimeter Feigned Submission—Clandestine Defiance: Jung's Religious Psychology," in *Dreaming the Myth Onwards: C. G. Jung on Christianity and on Hegel Part 2 of the Flight Into the Unconscious (Collected English Papers, Vol. VI)* (New Orleans, LA: Spring Journal Inc., 2014), 3–46.
7   Jung, *MDR*, 220, my italics.

On the one hand, the dream-Jung *just could not* do that, but on the other hand, the after-awakening Jung interpreted it as his own determination not to be a dumb fish; he *dared not* to do that based on "something of the sort in *free man*." This is really dissociative!

It appears to me that here the after-awakening Jung fell into a kind of "self-deception," that is, "disunion with himself," which he himself critically expressed as a main etiology in his psychology of neurosis. He himself *imitated* the mountain climber who was portrayed as an example of how a person could deceive himself, or get stuck with an internal conflict, in his own paper, "The Theory of Psychoanalysis."[8]

Here, I will summarize Jung's description as follows: The mountain climber who was attempting the ascent of a certain peak happened to meet with insurmountable obstacles, for instance, a precipitous rock-face that was so sheer that it would be impossible to ascend. After vainly seeking another route, he turned back and regretfully abandoned the idea of conquering that peak. In such a case, if he had really met an insurmountable difficulty, his decision would have been adaptive. On the other hand, if the rock-face had not really been unclimbable, he would have deceived himself. Jung said:

> on the one hand he has a correct appreciation of the situation, on the other hand he hides this knowledge from himself, behind *the illusion of his bravery* ... He draws back not because of any real impossibility but because of an artificial barrier invented by himself. He has fallen into *disunion with himself*. From this moment on he suffers from an internal conflict.[9]

As he mentioned, "the illusion of his bravery" herein, Jung himself fell into "the illusion of freedom" in making the above-mentioned remark on his actual incapability of submission. With "the illusion of freedom," I mean that Jung's idea of freedom, or of free man, was not at all based on the reality of the dream; for living in "the illusion of his freedom," the after-awakening Jung intentionally neglected what really happened to him in the dream. This is the after-awakening Jung's disunion with himself, which rather came from his neurotic resistance.

In the dream, we can find another, that is, the dream-Jung's disunion with himself—Jung's *double* disunion with himself. However, this other disunion is quite different from that of the mountain climber. On the one hand, the self-deceiving mountain climber pretended to submit himself to the mountain objectively; by so doing he concealed himself from the fact that he submitted himself to it subjectively, or truly submitted himself to his own cowardice. In that sense, we may say that he pretended not to submit himself to himself internally; it was a matter of his personal and neurotic self-relation. On the other hand, the dream-Jung pretended to submit himself to "the highest presence" in imitation of the dream-father. The

8   In Jung, *CW* 4.
9   Jung, *CW* 4, § 381.

dream-Jung simply made the gesture with the dream-father who was able to completely touch his forehead to the floor. It was not at all a matter of his personal and neurotic self-relation but of his relation to "the highest presence" behind the small door at the top of the stairs.

As Giegerich pointed out, in terms of "freedom" in his relation to "the highest presence," the dream-Jung should have *freely* submitted himself to it in imitation of the dream-father because such "submission is simply inherent in the notion of 'the highest presence,'"[10] but he could not, or did not, do so in actuality. In that sense, we may describe that the dream-Jung rejected "the *reality* of his freedom" while the after-awakening Jung escaped into "the *illusion* of his freedom," as mentioned above. Needless to say, these are also both sides of the same coin. That would be the reason I have selected the word "double" for depicting Jung's disunion with himself in relating to the dream.

From one point of view, it can be said that this double-ness made Jung completely and safely distant from the nature of "the highest presence." He was completely exempt from touching, or being touched by, it; he was perfectly immune from it. In that sense, we can say that "Jung's millimeter" functioned as a flawless shield to keep himself untouched. Moreover, although the dream-father said, "Now I will lead you into the highest presence," he did not take him to the top of the stairs but just "knelt down and touched his forehead to the floor" on the spot, that is, where he was standing. This would mean that where the dream-father wanted to lead the dream-Jung was not *over there* but *here*. As, in another paper, Giegerich discussed Jung's rejection of the *hic* ("here" in Latin) in his first participation in the Communion ceremony,[11] I am of the opinion that the same kind of rejection of the *hic* also took place in the dream. In this context, we can see that the above-mentioned Jung's double disunion with himself surely contributed to this rejection of the *hic* by dissociating himself from where he was standing and what really happened to him in the dream; this "distance between the floor and Jung's forehead" was fabricated with his rejection of the *hic* as its foundation, although he himself stated in *Memories*, "My watchword was: *Hic Rhodus, hic salta!*"[12]

10 Giegerich, "Jung's Millimeter," 8.
11 Here Giegerich described Jung's rejection of the *hic* as follows; "because the Communion turned out a terrible disappointment, Jung flatly rejected it as his *hic*, going to alibi ('somewhere else') instead" (Wolfgang Giegerich, "The Rejection of the *Hic*: Reflections on C. G. Jung's Communion Fiasco," in *The Flight Into the Unconscious: An Analysis of C. G. Jung's Psychology Project (Collected English Papers, Vol. V)* (New Orleans, LA: Spring Journal Inc., 2013), 115). As discussed below, Jung himself, or Jung's psychology, had a difficulty of staying *here*, developing a certain tendency to escape from *here* to *somewhere else*, that is, the mythological world; within his *discipline of psychology*, he carefully made preparation to *safely* look upward to divine images already lost in modern times. This upward-looking tendency was clearly shown when he stated, "Since the stars have fallen from heaven and our highest symbols have paled, a secret life holds sway in the unconscious. That is why we have a psychology today, and why we speak of the unconscious" (Jung, *CW* 9i, § 50). This is the rejection of the *hic*, or the flight into the unconscious, in Jung's psychology, as Giegerich pointed out.
12 *MDR*, 214.

It appears to me that this tendency to reject the *hic* can consistently be observed in Jung's psychology. In order to make it clearer, I will first present an example of a dream from one of his patients and his interpretation of it. Then, I will examine its validity.

"Crossing the river" and "reaching over" as a therapeutic destination

Jung referred to the following dream, which was reported by a female patient, in "On the Psychology of the Unconscious":

> She [the dreamer] is about to cross a wide river. There is no bridge, but she finds a ford where she can cross. She is on the point of doing so, when a large crab that lay hidden in the water seizes her by the foot and will not let her go. She wakes up in terror.[13]

In interpreting this dream, Jung presents two different approaches, i.e., an analytical (causal-reductive) interpretation and a synthetic (constructive) interpretation, in which the meanings of the crab are different from each other. In the former, the crab is interpreted by devotedly reducing it to the dreamer's actual interpersonal relationship, but in the latter, the symbolic meanings included in the crab-image are highly valued; the crab is viewed as a representation of unconscious contents.

On one hand, we can say that these two approaches are quite identical with each other in the sense that they both see that the obstacle which the crab symbolizes is hindering the dream-I from crossing the river. As similar to the dreamer's association to the river, "I ought to reach *the other side*",[14] Jung interpreted that *what the dream was demanding of the dream-I was to reach the other side by overcoming the obstacle*, which could be regarded as riding "the same hobby horse"[15] with the dreamer. However, this "other-side oriented" tendency may be viewed as extremely *natural* when we pay attention to the historical background of depth-psychology, including Jung's psychology as summarized below.

The polytheistic mythological world had spread out between Heaven and Earth before Christianity arrived.[16] People living in this world were completely surrounded by Gods and Goddesses, or Nature; the sun, the moon, the stars, weather phenomena (such as rain, lightning, and thunder), animals, plants, trees, and stones. All of these were experienced as "divine," invoking in people so-called feelings of awe which deeply penetrated their life as a whole. However, the Christian-monotheistic God had deprived nature of its threatening power, that is, its holiness, and thereby

---

13   Jung, *CW* 7, § 123.
14   Jung, *CW* 7, § 124, my italics.
15   Jung, *CW* 10, § 362.
16   Wolfgang Giegerich, "The Burial of the Soul in Technological Civilization" in *Technology and the Soul (Collected English Papers, Vol. II)* (New Orleans, LA: Spring Journal, Inc., 1983/2007), 155–211.

succeeded in establishing a new *Weltanschauung* for many centuries to come. In addition, the Enlightenment decisively cut away the connection with the "City of God" through "the Church." That is, the concept of "deism" or "rational religion," which was created by the spirit of Enlightenment from the 17th to 18th century, inevitably included the thesis that it is now important for us human beings not to "believe in God" naively but to "know it" with our reason. Of course, we cannot find therein a direct intention to negate the existence of the "City of God" as such, but just thereby, we have lost connection with it, and have been ultimately destined to leave the mythological world; it would be impossible for those who really lived in the mythological world to *know* it with their reason. This is because it was surely a "cosmos" by which they were surrounded or in which they were embedded, and not an object "opposed" to them. In that sense, we can say that by positing ourselves in opposition to God and comprehending God as an "object," the spirit of modern rationalism was established.

This spirit has endowed us with many good *fortunes*, such as the remarkable development of the natural sciences and the Industrial Revolution by which we have come to enjoy unprecedented material prosperity. On the other hand, it has also brought many ills upon our psyche. As Jung said, "it is one of the curses of modern man that many people suffer from this divided personality."[17] He believed that we have suffered from opposing tendencies that have abided within us since the birth of modern consciousness, for example, spirit and body, civilization and nature, reason and instinct. That is, we have completely lost the images of Gods and Goddesses, or the mythological world, in exchange for the development of material civilization.

Hence, in the depth psychology movement which started between the end of the 19th century and the beginning of the 20th century, and especially in the Analytical Psychology founded by Jung, restoring lost divine images within our psyche has always been *believed* as an important task. This seems to be confirmed by the high value that Jung placed on the *research* of myths or fairytales in his psychology. From one viewpoint, we might contend that Jung attempted to vividly reconstruct the pre-modern mythological world which had been excluded by the spirit of modern rationalism, and he was thereby very successful in establishing a new theoretical horizon for depth-psychology. I am of the opinion that the above-mentioned historical background of depth psychology has largely affected its practice as well.

The following serves as an example. As shown in many case studies, the communication between "this side" and "the other side" has been attached great importance in so-called image-centered psychotherapy mainly dealing with dreams, sand-plays, drawings, and so on. Although, in some cases, this is described as vivid, or creative, communication with the other world and in other cases as regarding this world, in both of them we can extract the common attitude which aims at *reaching another side from one side*. This attitude is well expressed in the fact that

17   C. G. Jung, "Approaching the Unconscious," in *Man and His Symbols* (New York, NY: Laurel, 1961/1986), 5–6.

Jung's psychology thinks much of "conscious assimilation of unconscious *contents*"[18] or that psychotherapy based on depth psychology broadly aims at patients becoming conscious of *something* unconscious within themselves. Of course, there we can suppose this side as consciousness and the other side as the unconscious.

Such difference between this side and the other side should be seen as really substantial, not psychological at all. Jung's psychology as depth-psychology, having literally *two* different layers, or sides, of consciousness and the unconscious, has cherished longing, or admiration, for the other side as elsewhere (*alibi*) in order to evacuate from this side as here (*hic*), which was well reflected in Jung's interpretation of the dream quoted above; he one-sidedly regarded the dream-I's crossing the river and then reaching the other side as a psychotherapeutic destination. However, it appears to me that the *hic* in this dream was the dream-I's incapability of crossing due to the crab's seizing her by the foot. In this context, we may see that Jung rejected this *hic* in the *same old* depth-psychological trick (*modus operandi*).

Jung's substantial denial of the psychological difference

Based on the above-mentioned "other-side oriented" tendency included within depth-psychology, Jung *believed* that the dream-I *ought* to overcome the crab as an obstacle and then cross the wide river from this side to the other side. However, when staying in, or diving into, the *hic* of her incapability of crossing, we may see through the crab's nature not a mere obstacle hindering her from moving *horizontally* from this side to the other side but an initiator *vertically* moving the dream-I from *a ford where she can cross* to *a depth where she cannot move*. What the dream-I had to realize was not her *horizontal* movement as an objective goal to be completed in the future but her *vertical* movement as a subjective predicament to be involved *in the present*.

As well shown in the title of one of Giegerich's early papers, "The Present as Dimension of the Soul: 'Actual Conflict' and Archetypal Psychology",[19] we psychotherapists should concentrate on *this* phenomenon, symptom, problem, dream, or drawing at hand, and only by attempting to stay *here now* in psychotherapy are we at our best. Concerning this point, Giegerich stated, "With this emphasis on the present we see that the 'eachness'...needs to be complemented by 'nowness' and, I might add here, by 'my-ness,' as the three characters of psychological truth."[20] The "eachness" means the dedication to the soul's movement that "now continues in the form of an unreserved commitment to the psychological phenomenon (the projected content) so as to exclude anything from outside that does

18 Jung, *CW* 16, § 326, my italics.
19 Wolfgang Giegerich, "The Present as Dimension of the Soul: 'Actual Conflict' and Archetypal Psychology," in *The Neurosis of Psychology (Collected English Papers, Vol. I)* (New Orleans, LA: Spring Journal, Inc., 1977/2005), 103–117.
20 Wolfgang Giegerich, *The Neurosis of Psychology (Collected English Papers, Vol. I)* (New Orleans, LA: Spring Journal, Inc., 1977/2005), 11.

not belong".[21] This "emphasis on the present" may be closely related to the conception of "the psychological difference," which he first introduced in that paper.

In this context, we have to see that Jung's interpretation of the crab dream lacked this dedication to the soul's movement, or intention, of the here and now; he missed the moment of the dream-I's being initiated, or stepping into, her own actual conflict here now by staring past the *hic* at the other side *in the distance*. Herein, the three characters of psychological truth, "eachness," "nowness" and "my-ness," were altogether missing, and therefore, the psychological difference also could not be respected. Here, Jung could not *distinguish* the finality of the dream *from* that of the dreamer.[22]

The *similar* "other-side oriented" tendency and thereby neglect of psychological truth may be observed in *another* form in the dream-Jung's incapability of bringing his forehead quite down to the floor as mentioned above. As Giegerich properly described, "If it had not been Uriah but a majestic God who was the highest presence, then, I presume, Jung *could* have willingly touched his forehead to the ground without hesitation,"[23] but the dream-Jung still desired to be "an upward-looking child of God"[24] and thus was unable to ultimately submit to "the human loss of faith or loss of God ('My God, my God, why hast thou forsaken me?' referred to by Jung in connection with Uriah)"[25] at his feet; he "really refused to go along with the soul's move into modernity,...with the Christian religion's self-movement to its own deepest point, its own absolute negativity."[26] This was Jung's rejection of the *hic* as a modern man, which probably forced him to *nostalgically* say in his closing years, "Man feels himself isolated in the cosmos, because he is no longer involved in nature and has lost his emotional 'unconscious identity' with natural phenomena."[27] As a modern psychologist, Jung was not *here now* but *elsewhere elsewhen* in lamenting for the human loss of "emotional 'unconscious identity' with natural phenomena" by renouncing the three characters of psychological truth.

By the same token, the dream-Jung's consciousness was persistently oriented *over there*, toward a small door at the top of the stairs behind which, he suddenly knew, there was a chamber where Uriah lived. He only imitated the dream-father's *posture* and did not really touch the ground at his feet by himself; he could not accept modern human suffering, "the human loss of faith or loss of God," which was prefigured by Uriah whom his lord "had shamefully betrayed for the sake of his wife Bathsheba."[28]

In the former section of this chapter, I said in contradistinction to the mountain climber's disunion with himself, "It was not at all a matter of his personal and

21 Giegerich, *Neurosis of Psychology*, 10.
22 Giegerich, "The Present as Dimension of the Soul," 111.
23 Giegerich, "Jung's Millimeter," 13.
24 Giegerich, "Jung's Millimeter," 16.
25 Giegerich, "Jung's Millimeter," 17.
26 Giegerich, "Jung's Millimeter," 22.
27 Jung, "Approaching the Unconscious," 85.
28 Jung, *MDR*, 219.

neurotic self-relation but of his relation to 'the highest presence' behind the small door at the top of the stairs." Here, I will have to correct it in our context as follows: what was expressed in his relation between the dream-Jung and the highest presence also should have been a self-relation, but it was not at all his personal one but the human historical and cultural one in modern times.

Jung refused to enter this modern situation that the soul created. By keeping the difference between this side and the other side substantial, that is, always orienting himself toward the other side as an objective goal to be reached, or searched, he could immunize his psychology from the soul's ongoing movement in modern times. In addition, although "for psychology there is no Other. Or, the other that there is is 'the soul's' own other, its internal other, that is to say, itself *as* other,"[29] his psychology often attempted to *conceptually* create the literal, or substantiated, *others* (for instance, "the collective unconscious," many kinds of "archetypes," "Self" etc.). This is the substantial denial of the psychological difference; the word "denial" means that Jung was only half-conscious of the soul's ongoing movement and refused to receive it entirely.

The burial of the mythological world

Jung's halfway-consciousness is well expressed in the following dialogue with himself, with which, we may assume, he commenced his "Confrontation with the Unconscious":

> But in what myth does man live nowadays? In the Christian myth, the answer might be. "Do you live in it?" For me, it is not what I live by. "Then do we no longer have any myth?" "No, evidently we no longer have any myth." "But then what is your myth—the myth in which you do live?" At this point the dialogue with myself became uncomfortable, and I stopped thinking. I had reached a dead end.[30]

Through the process of establishing his own psychology after this dialogue with himself, Jung dedicated himself to studies of mythology, Gnosticism, and alchemy, as many well know. However, it appears to me that what he actually accomplished by so doing, whether or not it was against his wishes, was not the "reconstruction" but the "burial" of the mythological world.

This is well proven in "the dream of the house" that Jung had in a lecture tour of the United States with Freud in 1909. Although he himself regarded this dream as "a guiding image"[31] and his "first inkling of a collective a priori beneath the personal psyche,"[32] what the dream-Jung discovered on the lowest floor were the

29 Wolfgang Giegerich, David L. Miller and Greg Mogenson, *Dialectics and Analytical Psychology: The El Capitan Canyon Seminar* (New Orleans, LA.: Spring Journal, Inc., 2005), 26.
30 Jung, *MDR*, 171.
31 Jung, *MDR*, 161.
32 Jung, *MDR*, 161.

"(scattering bones and broken pottery, like) remains of a primitive culture" and the "two human skulls, obviously very old and half disintegrated".[33] In the context of the present argument, however, we may clearly see that discovering these things did not necessarily mean their revival but rather, confirmation of them as already lost and past.

This phenomenon is also present in the dream that he had during his preparations to write about the Book of Job in his later years. In this, the dream-father was not only a custodian to guard the sarcophagi of the great personages, famous people, and princes but also a distinguished scholar to study the Old Testament. As Giegerich pointed out, "What the custodian is guarding and as private scholar studies is not 'the great personages' (the archetypes') present reality, but 'their sarcophagi,' i.e., their *historical* presence in Mnemosyne, their memory, *Erinnerung*."[34] The dream-Jung could not *follow* the dream-father as such all the way through this dream even about 40 years after he had "the dream of the house."

As shown in *Memories*, Jung began to *study* myths and fairytales very extensively after the lecture tour of the United States of America with Freud. But, by earnestly *studying* them as an object, just as the above-mentioned "deism" or "rational religion" did, Jung inadvertently proved that he himself, or we modern human beings, no longer *lived* in any myth. In our context, we can also say that his longtime intensive studies of the human historical and cultural inheritance *produced* "the sarcophagi"— in this case an appropriate vessel to interiorize the "scattering bones and broken pottery like remains of a primitive culture."

It appears to me that the burial of the mythological world could have been psychologically completed only by the dream-Jung's sincerely imitating, or following, his father as a custodian and scholar, and then succeeding to his father's work and knowledge. However, he did not do that; he renounced his father's *intangible* inheritance. That is the reason, it seems to me, Jung could not bring his forehead to the floor in imitation of his father and at the same time, not admit the real value of his *own* work and knowledge in modern times. Herein, the dream-Jung and the psychologist-Jung were perfectly identical with each other, in the sense that both were really *dissociative*.

Conclusion: moving Jungian psychology forward *here now*

As seen above, Jung certainly refused to go along with the soul's move into modernity with his substantial denial of the psychological difference in his psychology.

He was aware of his task as a psychologist, when he stated, "By becoming conscious, the individual is threatened more and more with isolation, which is nevertheless the *sine qua non* of conscious differentiation,"[35] or "in the cold light of

---

33 Jung, *MDR*, 159.
34 Giegerich, "Jung's Millimeter," 38.
35 Jung, *CW* 13, § 395.

consciousness, the blank barrenness of the world reaches to the very stars";[36] he noticed that modern men dwell only with themselves. On the other hand, as seen above, he attempted to make his psychology immune, or exempt, from this psychological task, or predicament, for modern human beings. Throughout his life, Jung had only half-way realized that entering the pre-modern mythological world could not bring about its resurrection; it could merely serve as a *methodology* for his psychology in modern times.

This personal limitation of Jung's was commonly shared by the collective in the time in which he lived. This is because, as Bruno Latour, a French sociologist, has pointed out, "We have never been modern";[37] even for those of us living in the time called "post-modern," it would be the most difficult task to psychologically go through, or realize, modernity as such. While Jung was *literally* a modern man, he was unable to *be* modern by all means.

In that sense, we may say that moving to a post-modern mentality should be tantamount to truly seeing modernity and thereby *having become* modern. As far as we have no way to go back into the past and thus can, or *have* to, only go forward, psychologists living after Jung must fully analyze and criticize Jung's unwillingness to follow the soul's move into modernity. Only by so doing can we make Jungian psychology move forward *here now*.

A truly modern psychologist, in place of Jung, must respect the psychological difference. As Giegerich describes, "in order to do psychology, a change of consciousness is needed...It is first necessary to struggle to get ourselves to the point where we can begin to think psychologically."[38] *Doing psychology* needs a quite different mode of consciousness from the ordinary one—an *opus contra naturam* which could be completed only through our real struggle, or actual conflict; the modern psychologist must allow his or her forehead to touch the floor.

I believe that this can be said in our *doing psychology*, or moving Jungian psychology forward *here now* as well.

36 Jung, *CW* 9i, § 29.
37 Bruno Latour, *We Have Never Been Modern*, trans. C. Porter (Cambridge: Harvard University Press, 1993).
38 Wolfgang Giegerich, *Neurosis: The Logic of a Metaphysical Illness* (New Orleans, LA: Spring Journal, Inc., 2013), 3.

4

INTERIORIZING AN UNDERLINED SENTENCE INTO ITSELF

Some reflections on being *"only* that!"

Greg Mogenson

Introduction

A friend of mine, like me a prairie boy, spared himself the price of a trip to India, or for that matter, of one of the many meditation courses that were available to him locally, by thinking up a mantra of his own to chant. Hearing of this, I wondered what mine might be. Never mind that I am not a meditator and have no plans to become one, at least not in the usual sense. That my friend had come up with his own mantra set me to wondering what I would come up with. Or perhaps it is more accurate to say, it served to make me aware that I already knew what my mantra would be, indeed, that I already had one in mind!

> "I am *only* that!"
> "I am *only* that!"
> "Ultimately limited."
> "I am *only* that!"

Adapted from a statement of Jung's that appears toward end of the "On Life after Death" chapter of his autobiography,[1] these are the words that came into my mind when I asked myself what *my* mantra would be. Chancing upon them some thirty and more years ago, I even now recall how my spirit was so quickened with intimations of their import that I immediately took up my reader's pen and lay claim to them as my own. Though Jung was their author, they were at the same time mine inasmuch as they had struck such a chord within me. And so it was that I put my line beneath Jung's words. But here, now, as I recall that moment, another memory comes. With equal urgency I am prompted to recall that when

---

1   Jung, *MDR*, 325.

Joseph Campbell was asked what yoga he practiced the answer he gave was "Underlining sentences!"[2]

This, surely, was a splendid reply. Campbell was a scholar of myth. With pen in hand, a great part of his life was spent reading. His spiritual practice—his yoga—was not something separate and alongside this, the main thrust of his life. It was not, in the manner of what Hegel diagnosed as the bad infinite, something external to, separate from, and bordering upon his finite, workaday scholarly pursuits. It was rather the meditative inwardness of these.

Speculative underlining

In keeping with Campbell's characterization of underlining sentences as a kind of yoga, I shall be dwelling in what follows with that line from Jung that my reader's pen laid claim to as my mantra—dwelling with it, delving into it, reading and re-reading it. It may also be said that I shall be meditating upon it. In contrast to my friend, however, whose meditation practice consists of interiorizing the sound and sentiment of his mantra into himself by chanting it silently, my meditative practice will be one of reflectively interiorizing the sentence that with a pen-stroke I claimed as my mantra, not into my inner, not into me, but contemplatively into *itself*.

Now the first thing to be grasped as we set out upon this venture is the "unity of the unity and difference" of a reader's underlining and the text that is underlined. Many years ago on a panel discussion with James Hillman, I declared my underlining of his texts to be as inspired as those texts themselves, earning from him a "high five" for my comment.[3] What I was getting at with this comment was the mutually determining and mutually constituting interdependence of reading and writing. Reading and writing imply one another. Indeed, each, it could be said, is as the unfolding of the other even as they readily turn into one another. Though empirically, of course, the author's text comes before the reader who later comes upon it, it may sometimes work out that a reader's underlining, if it be a soulful underlining, is logically prior to and conceptually deeper than the author's original text.

Limiting myself to a single example, I am reminded of the Jungian analyst, Wolfgang Giegerich's underlining of those passages in Jung's texts in which Jung speaks of psychology's lack of an Archimedean point of perspective outside of the psyche.[4] Giegerich, as it has turned out, has been a deeper, more serious-minded and thoroughgoing reader of these lines than was Jung, their author.[5] Why, it

2   In an interview conducted by Jeffrey Mishlove, "Understanding Mythology with Joseph Campbell," Campbell recalls his having given this answer to Allan Watts. http://archive.is/tPTd, downloaded September 14, 2016.

3   Panel discussion on the theme of "The Immortals" at the Festival of Archetypal Psychology, University of Notre Dame, South Bend, Indiana, July 12, 1992.

4   Jung, *CW* 8, § 421, 429; Jung, *CW* 9i, § 384; Jung, *CW* 16, § 254; Jung, *CW* 17, § 161, 162, 163.

5   With respect to this claim see Wolfgang Giegerich, "Introduction," in *The Neurosis of Psychology (Collected English Papers, Vol. I)* (New Orleans, LA: Spring Journal, Inc., 2005), 1–17.

could even be argued that his own extensive authorship is nothing other than one long extensive underlining in which Jung's seminal insight is applied to itself and released thereby into what as a *concept* it universally implies. And in this connection, I am reminded of an answer that Giegerich once gave in an interview when he was asked a question about his having written such difficult and challenging texts. Performing what I would claim to be a dialectical reversal, he answered by speaking of himself not as writer but as reader. When it is a matter of his own voluntary reading, avers Giegerich, he only reads books that he does not yet understand. As difficult as such texts may be, if they happen at the same time to be captivating of the interest that has been taken in them, this shows, as Giegerich states further, that "underneath *my* not understanding, *the soul in me* already caught fire by what I read, but do not understand."[6] This, surely, is a familiar experience. As readers of Jung, Hillman, and now also of Giegerich (to name only those key writers of our tradition), we probably all read in this manner, taking up our pens to underline those passages which, even though we may not understand them, have set our souls aflame.

Now what Giegerich refers to as "*the soul in me* [having] already caught fire by what I read," and what I, with a nod to Campbell, have referred to as the meditative practice of underlining sentences, corresponds to what in the Psychology as the Discipline of Interiority is called speculative self-relation,[7] on the one hand, and the implicitness/explicitness dialectic,[8] on the other. Born of the aforementioned insight that for psychology there is no external vantage point, no Archimedean position outside, Psychology as the Discipline of Interiority concerns itself wholly and exclusively with unfolding the soulful depths of whatever the phenomenon may be that has drawn its attention and that it has claimed as its own. I say "claimed as its own" because in the relation that is involved here subject and object, self and other (this, that, and the other thing) do not stand apart from each other, external to one another. It is a matter, rather, of their speculative identity, which is also to say, of a difference-trumping or difference-sublating self-relation in which like knows like and difference is regarded as unfolding nuances of the same. As the discipline of Archimedeanlessness, psychology meets itself in its topics and subject matters even as, according to another passage of Jung's that I am sure I am not alone in having underlined, "we meet ourselves time and again in a thousand disguises on the path of life."[9]

---

6   Wolfgang Giegerich, "Love the Questions Themselves," in R. & J. Henderson, editors, *"Enterviews" with Jungian Analysts*, Vol. 3 (New Orleans, LA: Spring Journal, Inc., 2010), 279.

7   My paper, "Entering the Speculative Mind," presented at the Summer workshop of The International Society for Psychology as the Discipline of Interiority, Chestnut Conference Centre, Toronto, Canada, July 20, 2013.

8   Cf. Wolfgang Giegerich, *The Soul's Logical Life: Towards a Rigorous Notion of Psychology* (Frankfurt am Main; New York: Peter Lang, 1998), 45–50.

9   Jung, *CW* 16, § 534.

Meditative reading

My remarks thus far are sufficient to show the speculative character of underlining sentences. With this in mind, we may now turn to the topic of the meditative unfolding of the speculative meaning of such sentences, or as this might also be called, the dialectics of soulful reading.

Coming pen in hand upon a sentence in a text that moves us to underline it, or upon a life situation that could be expressed in sentence form, psychological methodology endeavours to fathom its immanent meaning and intrinsic sense as a statement of the soul about itself. This, as I mentioned, is a matter of our taking Jung's insight into psychology's lack of an Archimedean point to heart, just as, for example, Giegerich has done with his companion insight that "for psychology there is no Other. Or [rather] the other that there is 'the soul's' own other, its internal other, that is to say, itself *as* other."[10]

Taken up in this spirit, the statement to be read is not construed as an object or thing set off and apart from an observing subject in the manner of empirical observation. Nor is the difference of consciousness which is usually drawn between a subject, on the one hand, and its object, on the other, distributed between the reader and the text, or even for that matter (and this is the more salient point) between the sentence subject and its predicate. It is a matter, rather, of their speculative identity. But what, more precisely, does this mean? Legend has it that Luther threw his inkwell at the devil and thereafter wrote with the devil in his ink. Throwing the ink of our underlining at a particular text we may find, similarly, that both we as reading subjects and the topic we had thought to be the subject of a sentence or paragraph are speculatively changed up, speculatively redefined.

Now, I say "speculatively" here because a passage from Hegel I once underlined imparted itself in this very manner to my own thinking as a psychologist. In his *Phenomenology of Spirit*, Hegel discusses what has variously come to be called the philosophical proposition, the speculative proposition, or more simply put, the speculative sentence. Interestingly, given what we have already had to say about reading challenging texts, the context within which this topic is discussed has to do with guidance Hegel offers with respect to the complaint that is often levelled against philosophy books that they are so dense and abstract that by the time the reader comes to the end of a sentence or paragraph he or she is unsure of what these had seemed to be about only a moment ago and has to go back over them again, even many times perhaps.[11] As Hegel puts it, "We learn by experience that we [as earnest readers] meant something other than we meant to mean; this correction of our meaning compels our knowing to go back to the proposition and understand it in some other way."[12] What Hegel is driving at with this description

10 Wolfgang Giegerich, David L. Miller and Greg Mogenson, *Dialectics and Analytical Psychology: The El Capitan Canyon Seminar* (New Orleans, LA: Spring Journal, Inc., 2005), 26.

11 G.W.F. Hegel, *Phenomenology of Spirit*, A.V. Miller, trans. (Oxford: Oxford University Press, 1977), § 63.

12 Hegel, *Phenomenology of Spirit*, § 63, p. 39.

of what I am sure is a familiar reading experience is that philosophical sentences are self-defining, or rather, self-redefining sentences. It is not because they are poorly written that we have to go over them again. On the contrary, it is because our first grasp upon the subject is oftentimes completely challenged by the end of the sentence or paragraph, our sense of its meaning perhaps entirely changed.

Ordinarily, of course, when we are reading a text or experiencing life events, a firm distinction between subject *here* and object or attribute *there* holds sway. Taken straightforwardly, the subject is regarded as a substance that has various properties and attributes, on the one hand, and which borders upon and interacts with things that are external to it, on the other. Expressing this in grammatical terms we could say that the subject is characterized by or discussed in terms of *quality*-specifying predicates. Of a particular topic or subject matter, this, that, or the other thing may be asserted or described. The speculative proposition, by contrast, sublates this ordinary manner of cognition by reading the predicate as an *essential* predicate. Far from indicating a mere quality of the subject, the predicate is regarded as being the subject all over again, itself a second time.

Our sentence and its context

"I am *only* that! I am *only* that! Ultimately limited. I am *only* that!" Before we examine what Jung had meant to mean with these words, let it be noted that their main sentence—"I am *only* that!"—has the form of a speculative sentence. Like Hegel's examples of such sentences, "God is Being" and "the *actual* is the *universal*,"[13] the sentence subject of this mantra-worthy line meets itself once again in its predicate. Its "I" we learn is not "I" in the straightforward, presumptively self-identical I = I sense of formal logic and subject-attribute grammar. Nor is it, as we may have assumed at first glance, a positively existing entity that *has* this, that, or the other positive quality. Rather, reading and re-reading, its meaning discloses itself via the logical movement of the thought that it is within its self-relation as subject and essential predicate. It is a matter of mediation. Reflected in a predicate which despite apparent differences is expressly identified as being the same as itself, the subject "I" is re-definitionally mirrored more rigorously and concretely into its concept. It is not an I that first exists and then, humbling itself, avows that it is "*only* that." On the contrary, it only exists in the first place as the result of its own divestiture, that is, by virtue of its only-that-ness.

But what *had* Jung meant to mean with these words? In their own context, within their own time, before readers such as you and I have claimed them as our own with our underlining, what had he meant to mean when he spoke of one's being "*only* that"? In keeping with the tenor of his life's work as a whole, Jung's statement is taken from a time and spoken into a time when the religious formation of the soul had largely gone under into its successor form, psychology. Whereas in an earlier age its topic would have been the Christian concern for the

---

13 Hegel, *Phenomenology of Spirit*, § 62.

salvation of one's immortal soul, in its own, now psychological times, it had to do with helping the individual of modern times *who is bereft of such a conception* to discern what is essential in his or her life and to live in devotion to it. As Jung put it in the paragraph immediately above the one that contains his statement about being "*only* that":

> The decisive question for man is: Is he related to something infinite or not? That is the telling question of his life. Only if we know that the thing which truly matters is the infinite can we avoid fixing our interest upon futilities, and upon all kinds of goals that are not of real importance. .... In the final analysis, we count for something only because of the essential we embody, and if we do not embody that, life is wasted.[14]

Jung, of course, is referring exclusively to modern man, not to our forbearers. Only in modern times do men and women find themselves faced with what Jung calls "the decisive question." For previous ages it was entirely otherwise. As Giegerich has put it, having not yet been born out of the soul, religious man had simply lived with the answers to begin with.[15] Fully provided for in metaphysical regards, he was not faced with essential questions on his own, let alone with the so-called "decisive question" that subsequently came to confront modern man as to whether "he is related to something infinite or not?" He did not have to, and indeed could not have, confessed himself as being "*only* that." Vocation, gender, family roles, civic office, and the stages of life quite simply had the character of infinitude built into them even as they were conferred upon him by a still vital and longstanding tradition.[16] As someone who would have to make up his or her own mind about these matters, the individual did not yet exist. And here it could be argued, in true Jungian spirit, that psychology and its touchstone, man as individual, were constituted by the very divesture that the words, "I am *only* that!," confess, own up to, acknowledge to be true. For indeed, it is against and in contrast to the earlier situation of religious man's self-evident knowing of himself as being in the soul, a child of God, and the possessor of an immortal essence, that one now finds oneself to be "*only* that."

Now the chapter of Jung's memoirs from which our underlined passage is drawn, "On Life after Death," is a case in point. Jung's mantra-worthy declaration—"I am *only* that!"—follows upon a lengthy discussion of a collection of dreams and experiences from which he had built up his own personal views on the afterlife.

14 Jung, *MDR*, 325.
15 Wolfgang Giegerich, "The End of Meaning and the Birth of Man: An essay about the state reached in the history of consciousness and an analysis of C. G. Jung's psychology project," in *The Soul Always Thinks (Collected English Papers, Vol. IV)* (New Orleans, LA: Spring Journal, Inc., 2010), 216–217.
16 Wolfgang Giegerich, *What Is Soul?* (New Orleans, LA: Spring Journal, Inc., 2012), 299; also his *Neurosis: The Logic of a Metaphysical Illness* (New Orleans, LA: Spring Journal, Inc., 2013), 83–101.

The point to be grasped, however, is that the tribute that Jung seems to pay to this traditional concern of the soul is actually a departure from it. For never before in the Christian past had the afterlife or hereafter needed evidence to be amassed in support of the inference that it might be so. It was simply an existing concept, a vital communal fantasy, a soul truth believed by everyone everywhere. Imparted through the sacrament of baptism, eternal life and the salvation of one's immortal soul had meaning as this-worldly truths throughout the whole of one's life and prior to death. Proof had nothing to do with it. It was only after the birth of man—after, that is to say, our being born out of religion and metaphysics into enlightened modernity—that doubts concerning the veracity of the afterlife spurred empirical efforts such as Jung's to shore it up against its evident demise.

The truth of Jung's times, it follows, was by no means what he as erstwhile exemplar of modern man in search of a soul was anachronistically drawing forth from his inner and decorously setting down in his *Red Book* and memoirs. It was rather, as Nietzsche had announced, that God, and along with him the hopes of the faithful for salvation in the eternity of an afterlife, was dead. And this, the death of God idea, was no more in need of proof than the living God had been in all those previous epochs in which deity-symbols were a vital expression of the communal soul and the logic of actually lived life. It was enough that the idea could be formulated, enough that it could be announced so openly and publicly, without bringing down any firestorm about heresy upon its speaker's head.[17]

The empiricism/speculation difference

I said that the tribute that Jung seems to pay to the afterlife in his "On Life after Death" chapter is actually a departure from that traditional truth of the soul. Indeed, one only needs to compare the spurious experiences and dream material from which he cobbled together his personal views on life after death to the weighty reality this concept held as a communal truth within the doctrines and sacraments of the Church to find little wonder in the fact that, breaking off from his discussion of life after death, Jung goes on in the last pages of his chapter to declare "I am *only* that!" The shortfall here stems from Jung's taking an empirical approach to what traditionally had been a speculative truth. Though he readily acknowledges that the topic of life after death is beyond the reach of the empirical sciences, he nevertheless makes a passionate plea for the life-enhancing benefit of each individual establishing for him or herself an empirically based conception of

---

17   Concurring with this view Jung writes: "When Nietzsche said 'God is dead,' he uttered a truth which is valid for the greater part of Europe. People are influenced by it not because he said so, but because it is a widespread psychological fact … [His statement] has, for some ears, the same eerie sound as the ancient cry which came echoing over the sea to mark the end of the nature gods: 'Great Pan is dead.'" C. G. Jung, *Psychology and Religion: West and East (The Collected Works, Vol. 11)*, ed. Sir Herbert Read and Gerhard Adler, trans. R.F.C. Hull, 2nd edn (Princeton, NJ: Princeton University Press, 1975), § 145.

life in the hereafter based upon "hints sent to us from the unconscious."[18] Individuals who are able to formulate such views, states Jung, tend to find comfort thereby. "They live more sensibly, feel better, and are more at peace."[19] But here we must object: what does it profit a man to gain all manner of psychic reassurances and lose the soul of the real? Jung, no doubt, is correct in his opinion that many individuals are more at peace when they anticipate that their lives will continue somehow after death. *Psychologically*, however, it is neither here nor there whether the afterlife, or God for that matter, really exists or not. What is important, rather, is what such figures *as figures* show with respect to consciousness and say with respect to the soul during the various historical epochs.

On being "*only* that!"

With the context of the line from Jung that I underlined in his autobiography having been established, we may now give ourselves over to the more meditative task of reading it speculatively. At first glance, indeed throughout almost the entirety of a first reading, Jung's "On Life after Death" chapter seems completely straightforward. In keeping with his intent of presenting experiences that point to the possibility of a life in the hereafter, his sentences have the form of simple statements. We are never in any doubt about what their subject *is*. It is only near the end of the chapter, only with the paragraphs that culminate in our statement "I am *only* that!", that the realization dawns that we may need to "go back to the proposition" of the whole chapter "and understand it in some other way."[20]

The paragraphs I have in mind appear in the last pages of the chapter. After having shared his views on life after death in the preceding twenty-five pages, Jung ends by reflecting soulfully upon *this life*. Compared to the comfort which one's developing ideas about the afterlife is supposed to foster, these final reflections are more serious-minded and psychologically rigorous. They no longer have to do with the ego and its purchase upon the next world, but with what Jung, confining himself to this world and this life, diminutively calls the only-that-ness of one's being self. Quite a come down, this, from the "paranormally" mysterious topic that life after death in our times has become. It is as if, after telling what he calls his ghost stories by the fire,[21] Jung has had to realize that the *kenôsis* that characterizes the self-experience of modernity can be staved off no longer.

Above, I cited the line with which this speculative turn begins, the one in which Jung states, "The decisive question for man is: Is he related to something infinite or not?" Further down the page, he continues, "In the final analysis, we count for something only because of the essential we embody, and if we do not embody

---

18   Jung, *MDR*, 301.
19   Jung, *MDR*, 301.
20   Hegel, *Phenomenology of Spirit*, § 63.
21   Jung, *MDR*, 300.

that, life is wasted." And then, in the next paragraph, we come to the speculative climax of the whole chapter:

> The feeling for the infinite, however, can be attained only if we are bounded to the utmost. The greatest limitation for man is the "self"; it is manifested in the experience: "I am *only* that!"[22]

Notice what has happened here. In these, the penultimate sentences of Jung's chapter, the infinite and the finite come home to one another as the very essence of this-worldly self-experience. No longer are they distributed between consciousness and the unconscious, this life and the next, in a sequential, external, side by side, or one after the other relation. On the contrary, with Jung's having broken off his erstwhile attempt to prop up traditional religious conceptions of the afterlife with empirical hints drawn from his psychic experiences, the relationship of the infinite and the finite can now be recognized as being a this-worldly dialectical one. We can also say, they can be recognized as being part and parcel of one another even as it is by being "bounded to the utmost" that the I as organ of truth and soul of the real is quickened and produced. I am *only* that, indeed!

Psychology as the afterlife of its topics and subject matters

Jung of course knows, as he put it in another context, that "Heaven and hell are fates meted out to the soul and not to civil man [i.e., the ego], who in his nakedness and dullness would have no idea of what to do with himself in a heavenly Jerusalem."[23] He knows, as the poet Wallace Stevens put it, that "heaven and hell/ Are one, and here, O terra infidel."[24] Perhaps that is why he breaks off from his ego-consoling discussion of life after death in the last pages of his chapter, because even here, in his personal memoir, the true psychologist was at work in him after all. Or perhaps, on second thought, it is not Jung as the author of this text that is to be so credited on this occasion, but *we* as the authors of our own underlining. For having underlined, as many of us have, Jung's sentence, "I am *only* that!", it is we who must prove ourselves worthy of that designation, if only by going back over the chapter from which we have been quoting and understanding it in some other way.

I said that the speculative or soul character of an exposition typically becomes apparent only upon subsequent readings. In keeping with this, it may now be noticed that at the very outset of his "On Life after Death" chapter, in a statement that we are not likely to have taken fully into account until a second or third reading, Jung declares that the entirety of his works in psychology "are fundamentally nothing but attempts, ever renewed, to give an answer to the question of

22 Jung, *MDR*, 325.
23 Jung, *CW* 9ii, § 56, in Giegerich's modified translation.
24 Wallace Stevens, *The Palm at the End of the Mind*, ed. Holly Stevens (New York, NY: Vintage Books, 1972), 253–254.

the interplay between the 'here' and the 'hereafter'."[25] But how can this be? Typology, schizophrenia, Christianity, alchemy, fairy tales, myth, synchronicity, UFOs: the list of Jung's topics and subject matters is varied and diverse. What then are we to make of his assertion that the images and thoughts that have buffeted him with regard to life after death underlie all these works?

Speculatively returning from the last paragraphs of the chapter to consider again what it was about in the first place, suffice it to say that Jung's opening assertion that his works in psychology are nothing but "attempts ... to give an answer to the question of the interplay between the 'here' and the 'hereafter'" has a chance of being true only if what he then goes on to say about life after death is no more about the afterlife in a literal sense than what he had said about alchemy had been about alchemy in the literal sense.[26]

Interiorizing the "here" and "hereafter" difference into itself

Earlier, we heard from Hegel about how time and again in the course of our reading we are compelled to go back over a proposition or text until a very different understanding of what it was about in the first place dawns upon us. Explaining this further in a related passage, he writes that "Thinking ... loses the firm objective basis it had in the subject when, in the predicate, it is thrown back on to the subject, and when, in the predicate, it does not return into itself, but into the subject of the content."[27] It is the same with psychology. Psychology, too, loses the firm objective basis it seemed to have as an empirically determined science of the psyche when, in the spirit of being *"only* that," it is speculatively thrown back upon itself by the already psychological character of the topics and subject matters it had at first unwittingly posited itself as. How else could it be? As Jung, reiterating his insight into psychology's lack of an Archimedean vantage point puts it, "whereas in all other departments of natural science a physical process is observed by a psychic process, in psychology the psyche observes itself, directly in the subject, indirectly in one's neighbour,"[28] that is in other fields.

Now with these reflections, the contradiction in Jung's text is laid bare. Relapsing into a substantiating style of thought, Jung designates life after death and the relation between "here" and "hereafter" to be the opposites with which he is concerned. Adopting a quasi-empirical approach to these subject matters, the bulk of his chapter has to do with the individual's edifying him or herself with soulful beliefs built upon the basis of dreams and other psychic experiences that may be suggestive

---

25 Jung, *MDR*, 299.
26 Further to my thesis concerning "psychology as the afterlife of its topics and subject matters," see the section 1.10 of Giegerich's *What Is Soul?* Here (see especially pp. 76–77) the point is made that while all the various fields of study (e.g., the humanities, intellectual history, linguistics, religious studies, etc.) reflect the soul and to this extent together provide, if only implicitly, a soulful psychology, an actual discipline of psychology is still needed in order to study what these various fields, as themselves phenomenal expressions of the soul, have to show or say about the soul.
27 Hegel, *Phenomenology of Spirit*, § 62.
28 Jung, *CW* 17, 161.

of the continuation of personal existence into an actual afterlife. But while this is what his exposition is about, it is also not about this at all. Right at the start, as was discussed above, "the interplay of the 'here' and the 'hereafter'" is described as being what his many writings were essentially concerned with, regardless of the topic. Taken to heart, the implication of this statement is that *psychology is the afterlife of its topics and subject matters*, even as, "sublated from the outset,"[29] it is only through the soul-quickening/psychology-constituting apperception of these as having departed from the "here" of their positivity as the topics of their own or some other science that they can be comprehended in terms of the "hereafter" or inner infinity of what their being-for-consciousness says about the soul.[30]

Back to my mantra

"I am *only* that! I am *only* that! Ultimately limited. I am *only* that!" My return to these mantra-worthy words follows upon a series of digressions. But such, it may be argued, is a familiar characteristic of meditation generally. In the course of any sitting, the attention of the practitioner tends to wander off. Sounds distract, fantasies take hold, thoughts arise. For seconds and even much longer perhaps, one's chanting may cease. This, however, does not indicate a failure to meditate. On the contrary, it is an inherent moment of its dialectic. For just as meditation involves the working-off of the mind's contents (via just such a giving way to thoughts and fantasies), so also and to the same extent it is comprised by its negatively returning into itself as the content-sublating *form* or *result* of all that it has worked off. And so it is that upon noticing himself thinking about other things, that the meditator simply returns to the discipline of his mantra once more as to the inwardness of what from a more external perspective merely is or has been.

Now, of course, our meditative engagement in these pages is very differently conceived than is the actual practice of chanting a mantra. As I stated at the outset,

---

29 For a discussion of the fundamental sublatedness of psychology, see Giegerich, *Soul's Logical Life*, 124; 191–201.

30 Pertinent to these reflections is a statement Jung made about the death perspective that is mediated by the *Tibetan Book of the Dead*:

> It is highly sensible of the Bardo Thödol to make clear to the dead man the primacy of the psyche, for that is the one thing which life does not make clear to us. We are so hemmed in by things which jostle and oppress that we never get a chance, in the midst of all these 'given' things, to wonder by whom they are 'given.' ... A great reversal of standpoint, calling for much sacrifice, is needed before we can see the world as 'given' by the very nature of the psyche. It is so much more straightforward, more dramatic, impressive, and therefore more convincing, to see all the things that happen to me than to observe how I make them happen.
>
> (*CW* 11, § 841)

For more on psychology and its death perspective see James Hillman, *The Dream and the Underworld* (New York, NY: Harper & Row, 1979). Also, Giegerich, *Soul's Logical Life*, 22–24, 192.

our concern is not with interiorizing the sound and sense of a mantra into our inner, but with interiorizing it speculatively into itself. But this being said, the analogy I have just drawn to the digressions and iterations that make up the dialectic of actual meditation remains pertinent in our context. That we in these reflections have repeatedly had to digress into *talking about* Jung's sentence (even as and just as repeatedly we have been prompted by the speculative turn it contains to return to it once more), this I maintain is indicative of the fact that in Jung's psychology there is much to work off.

What I am getting at here is that Jung's psychology is a psychology largely of contents. Jung, for example, writes of the *content* of neurosis, the *content* of psychosis, and of the relations between the ego and the unconscious as positively conceived, entity-like opposites. Likewise, in his writings, the self does not have self character but is discussed as having the character of a revered (and sometimes reviled) object. It is the same for the speculative truths that he wrote about (the mother archetype, rebirth, etc.). Claiming to take an empirical approach to these (when a speculative approach would have been better suited both to them and to his insight into psychology's lack of an Archimedean point of perspective), he studied them in the manner of a naturalist, i.e., as archetypes in front of consciousness, which is also to say, as the contents of the collective unconscious. And this is to say nothing of the importance he ascribed to our giving ourselves over to that embarrassment of riches, the symbolic life. Irritably reaching after myth and symbol, subsequent Jungians have indulged in every sort of nonsense in pursuit of their personal myth. Hero quests, shaman initiations, and the gods and goddesses in every man and woman: no wonder that already in 1966 Philip Rieff could describe Jungian psychology as a "religion of sorts—for spiritual dilettantes, who collect symbols and meanings as others collect paintings."[31]

The question arises. How can the words "I am *only* that!" be uttered by the Jungian subject? Though Jung, to be sure, on occasion also spoke of the need to "stoutly avow our spiritual poverty,"[32] his psychology of the collective unconscious would seem to have made billionaires of us all. And yet these words *are* uttered. Letting go of his erstwhile effort to contrive an afterlife for modern man (and I shudder to think what a pharaoh's tomb that would be given Jung's concept of the collective unconscious!) he humbly drops into his finitude in this life, confronting himself and his reader with the aforementioned "decisive question" as to whether, in and through his finiteness, he is related to the infinite—not after death, but in this life.

Closing reflections

It has been said that all of the various writings of a true thinker are but the unfolding in depth of one thought. Might this also be said of the reader, pen in

---

31 Philip Rieff, *The Triumph of the Therapeutic: Uses of Faith after Freud* (New York, NY: Harper & Row, 1966), 139.
32 Jung, *CW* 9ii, § 28.

hand, who is moved to underline this or that sentence during the course of a life-time of reading? Our pen-strokes as readers, are they similarly the fathoming of the one thought that we find in those authors whom we have been claimed by as by our own soul-quickening other? Suffice it to say that when such is the case, one's underlining is well-characterized, as I have characterized it here, as a yoga or meditation practice.

But now to the end of my reflections. Digressing somewhat (the better to make a last speculative return to that line that I claimed as my mantra), I want to close with three more passages from out of the *oeuvre* of my underlining, one from Yeats and a final two from Jung.

Late in his career as a poet, Yeats experienced a dry spell inspiration-wise. For six weeks, he cast about in vain for a worthy poetic theme. Finally, however, describing himself as "a broken man," the poet realizes that there is nothing for it but that he must be satisfied with his own heart. And so, with this as his topic he "enumerates old themes," the poetic triumphs of his past. These he characterizes as his "circus animals" even as it is from this image that he gives a title to his poem, "The Circus Animals' Desertion." Now I mention all this for the sake of quoting the lines of the last stanza, for these, I aver, may be marked with a pen stroke that is continuous with the pen stroke that I long ago drew beneath Jung's sentence, "I am *only* that!"

> Those masterful images because complete
> Grew in pure mind, but out of what began?
> A mound of refuse or the sweepings of a street,
> Old kettles, old bottles, and a broken can,
> Old iron, old bones, old rags, that raving slut
> Who keeps the till. Now that my ladder's gone,
> I must lie down where all the ladders start
> In the foul rag and bone shop of the heart.[33]

It is especially those last lines that I want to underline here, the ones that state:

> Now that my ladder's gone,
> I must lie down where all the ladders start
> In the foul rag and bone shop of the heart.

Moving on from the I-am-*only*-that-ness of the final lines of this poem to my vignettes concerning Jung, the first of these is drawn from Jane Pratt's account of a seminar that Jung gave in New York during October of 1937. According to Mrs. Pratt, the last of Jung's presentations, a lecture entitled "The Concept of the Collective Unconscious," was largely a fiasco due to numerous technical difficulties that interfered with Jung's didactic purpose. Though attended by "Jung's most

33 W.B. Yeats, *Selected Poetry* (London, UK: Pan Books, Ltd, 1976), 202.

prominent New York supporters and detractors ... the occasion," as Mrs. Pratt explains, "was not propitious":

> The lecture ... required slides, a lot of them, and an enthusiastic follower had volunteered to project them, but either this man's skills were insufficient, or the slides were possessed. They came on upside down or reversed, and fell on the floor when he attempted to right them. If Jung wanted to see one again, they moved forward, if he said to go on, they went back. So Jung stood, pointer in hand, on a raised platform before his huge audience, either waiting for the right pictures to appear, or hurrying to comment intelligently upon them before they passed on. Meanwhile his adherents suffered. Reacting at first with great consideration to the awkwardness of his assistant, his remarks became sharper by shades—since negative feelings will out—and the suffering of his adherents increased. Yet the misfortunate lecture ended without anything basically human being destroyed—not even Jung's relation to the assistant, who admitted the justice of a certain irritation. Only the muddle and all the interruptions had completely destroyed the continuity of Jung's important argument. Later he was reported to have told someone: *"I was analyzed tonight, if never before."*[34]

Apropos of the stanza I quoted from Yeats, this statement of Jung's also has "I am *only* that!" character. This, I believe, is all the more convincing when we examine the transcript of the impromptu talk that Jung gave at the gala dinner later that evening which marked the end of his visit. Published under the title, "Is Analytical Psychology a Religion?", Jung in this talk discussed how psychology, though not itself a religion, has arisen in the wake of the religion that preceded it. Especially noteworthy in our context are his comments about Jesus at the end of his talk:

> And you remember that strange incident, the triumphal entry into Jerusalem. The utter failure came at the Crucifixion in the tragic words, "My God, my God, why hast thou forsaken me?" If you want to understand the full tragedy of those words you must realize what they meant: Christ saw that his whole life, devoted to the truth according to his best conviction, had been a terrible illusion. He had lived it to the full absolutely sincerely, he had made his honest experiment, but it was nevertheless a compensation. On the Cross his mission deserted him. But because he had lived so fully and devotedly he won through to the Resurrection body.[35]

34 William McGuire, ed., *C. G. Jung Speaking: Interviews and Encounters* (Princeton, NJ: Princeton University Press, 1977), 94–95 (italics mine). I want to thank Tom Kapacinskas for making me aware of this text at the 1998 East Aurora Seminar and for his discussion of it as reflecting Jung's own disillusionment with respect to his hypothesis concerning the collective unconscious.

35 McGuire, ed., *C. G. Jung Speaking: Interviews and Encounters*, 97–98.

Reading these words, a retentive mind will remember the quip Jung had made on the heels of his triumphal entry into New York having gone hay-wire earlier that evening, "*I was analyzed tonight, if never before.*" But let me cite a little more from this talk, so that the "I am *only* that!" character of Jung's next sentences may also be appreciated:

> We must do just what Christ did. We must make our experiment. We must make mistakes. We must live out our vision of life. And there will be error. If you avoid error you do not live; in a sense it may be said that every life is a mistake, for no one has found the truth. God indeed becomes man. This sounds like a terrible blasphemy, but not so. For then only can we understand Christ as he would want to be understood, as a fellow man; then only does God become man in ourselves.[36]

Now, to my final underlining. It is from a comment Jung made after being reminded of a letter he had written to Freud some fifty years previously. In that earlier letter, Jung had written with much enthusiasm about the prospect, as he then saw it, that psychoanalysis would

> revivify among intellectuals a feeling for symbol and myth, ever so gently transform[ing] Christ back into the soothsaying god of the vine, which he was, and in this way absorb those ecstatic instinctual forces of Christianity for the *one* purpose of making the cult and sacred myth what they once were—a drunken feast of joy where man regained the ethos and holiness of an animal.[37]

A remarkable statement. Laying it on even thicker, Jung continued:

> That was the beauty and purpose of classical religion, which from God knows what temporary biological needs has turned into a Misery Institute. Yet what infinite rapture and wantonness lie dormant in our religion, waiting to be led back to their true destination! A genuine and proper ethical development cannot abandon Christianity but must grow up within it, must bring to fruition the hymn of love, the agony and ecstasy over the dying and resurgent god ...—only *this* ethical development can serve the vital forces of religion.[38]

But our interest is less in this statement per se than in the difference a half century can make. Though there is much in Jung's subsequent writings to suggest that he actually followed through on this ecstatic program (I am thinking especially of his

---

36   McGuire, ed., *C. G. Jung Speaking: Interviews and Encounters*, 98.

37   William McGuire, ed., *The Freud/Jung Letters: The Correspondence between Sigmund Freud and C. G. Jung*, trans. R. Manheim and R.F.C. Hull (Princeton, NJ: Princeton University Press, 1974), 294.

38   McGuire, ed., *Freud/Jung Letters*, 294.

having styled himself as a therapist of Christianity), when shown this letter some fifty years later he responded with considerable chagrin.

> Best thanks for the quotation from that accursed correspondence. For me it is an unfortunately inexpungable reminder of the incredible folly that filled the days of my youth. The journey from cloud-cuckoo-land back to reality lasted a long time. In my case Pilgrim's Progress consisted in my having to climb down a thousand ladders until I could reach out my hand to the little clod of earth that I am.[39]

"I am *only* that! I am *only* that! Ultimately limited. I am *only* that!" After reflecting upon Jung's statement about being "analyzed tonight, if never before," his image of reaching out his hand to "the little clod of earth that I am," and Yeats' lines about "the foul rag and bone shop of the heart," let us return to this mantra again as to the redefinition of the Jungian subject itself.

---

39 *C.G. Jung, Letters 1: 1906–1950* (Princeton, NJ: Princeton University Press, 1973), 19 (note 8 near top of page). For an insightful discussion in which Jung's image of bending down to himself as clod of earth is interiorized into itself in light of its inherent contradiction, see Giegerich, "The End of Meaning and the Birth of Man," 235–236. There is also a link made here by Giegerich to Jung's "I am *only* that!"

5

IMAGE AS PICTURE, IMAGE AS DEBRIS

Philip Kime

Introduction

Our notion of "image" in analytical psychology rather too often simply means "picture." "Image" is a concept of which pictorial representation is only a small and often not particularly psychologically useful part. There is also a parallel problem with our common notion of "imagination" which all too often simply means "picturing," or forming a more or less visual image, so to speak, in the mind. These two problems, the predominance of literal pictures as examples of images and the predominance of pictorial thinking in imagination are two aspects of the same issue—our tendency to assert as the *essence* of image and imagination merely their most simple and accessible forms.

Pictures are pictures *of* something. There is built in to pictures the grammar of representation, copying, the thing itself being the *subject* of the picture. It makes no difference if the intention is to represent something abstract or to subvert the logic of representation as with some modern art, since in such cases, the core against which one rebels is still the central principle of being *of* something, being *about* some content. Our usual descriptions of images are "contentful"—they concentrate on content, the *things* in them, however abstract. Our imagination is usually described in terms of its content, its characters, events, places, and things. It is this concentration on content which is the problem, as it is predominantly blind to the question of form—and psychology is essentially about form, *not* content. The psychology is in the form, the relations, the shape of the connections, and with this in mind, images, when they are relevant at all, are so only because they are *structural, formal*, and not because they are contentful.

So, I will discuss first the problem in terms of pictures as objects, as a problem of what pictures themselves force on us by their inherent assumptions, and then I will turn to look at the picturing style of imagination and how this has come to dominate what we think of as imagination. Suggesting that image is better viewed as the debris left behind by a failure to capture psychology in an inadequate container, I will suggest that image remains important, but only as the bookends around a process which is essentially not imaginal. One begins with images and ends with them as the objects of a, so to speak, psychological archaeology.

Image as picture

It is not particularly difficult to find in mainstream Jungian thought examples of the equation of pictures with images; for example, Neumann speaks of "the pictorial world of archetypal images"[1] and the "picture world of archetypes"[2] while Esther Harding, Johnson and Mattoon all describe dream images in fundamentally pictorial terms.[3]

As might be expected, Hillman's discussions of image were considerably more sophisticated than the mainstream and are worth considering further. The classic statement of his views on image is to be found in the two *Spring* articles from 1977 and 1978. Hillman argues that images need to be "particularized...precisely qualified"[4] but when one follows the examples of this, one sees that it effectively means "pictured."[5] We are told, "[The pattern of meaning] portrays. It makes a picture of."[6] Further, the dream reconstruction given as an example of his technique uses the trick of turning adjectives into nouns, making for more subtle and nuanced pictures.[7] I will have more to say about the role of nouns in Hillman's view below.

As against this tendency, I believe that the sense in which "image" should be taken has nothing essentially to do with pictorial representation, or indeed *any* particular mode of representation at all. We can represent in words, in music, in dance, or perhaps by mathematics, and these are all equally possible approaches to making an "image," but there is something quite immediately alluring about the pictorial. In the definitions given in "Psychological Types," Jung defines image in a rather abstract way in which no mention is made of the pictorial mode of representation: "The image is a *condensed expression of the psychic situation*."[8] However,

1   Erich Neumann, *The Origins and History of Consciousness* (Bollingen Series XCIX), (Princeton, NJ: Princeton University Press, 1954), 321.
2   Neumann, *Origins and History of Consciousness*, 325.
3   Esther M. Harding, *Psychic Energy: Its Source and its Transformation* (Bollingen Series X) (Princeton, NJ: Princeton University Press, 1948), 166; Robert A. Johnson, *Inner Work : Using Dreams and Creative Imagination for Personal Growth* (San Francisco, CA: Harper & Row Pub., 1986); Mary Ann Mattoon, *Understanding Dreams* (Woodstock, CT: Spring Publications, 1978).
4   James Hillman, "An Inquiry into Image," in *Spring* (1977): 62.
5   Follow, for example, the developed image in Hillman, "An Inquiry into Image," 71–73. The development of the example image makes a progressively more vivid and detailed picture.
6   Hillman, "An Inquiry into Image," 75.
7   Hillman, "An Inquiry into Image," 70.
8   Jung, *CW* 6, § 745.

Jung's particular approach to images and representation in general quite regularly shows that by "condensed expression" he often really means "picture."[9] This clearly shows that one cannot take at face value what is said about images. On the contrary, what is important is rather what one does with them (and the concept in general). That is, one must pay attention to the assumptions and structure that accompany the idea of image.

If a landscape inspires a painter to paint it, we would also naturally say that the painting was a representation of the landscape. That is, there is a relationship leading from the landscape to the painting (inspiration), and there is another relationship leading from the painting to the landscape (representation). Further, the painting is an image of the landscape in both the pictorial and conceptual sense. There is also a very important consequence of this bi-directional relationship; the picture can be used to identify the landscape if we have never seen the actual landscape before. The representational relationship facilitates a connection leading from the picture to that which the picture is "of." We know that early man saw certain types of animals because his pictures look like things we know to be animals. We know his hands were of a certain shape and size because he made pictures of his hands (even better, the earliest such pictures are stencils and are about as representational as you can get). The images, seen as pictures, *lead back* to their source, and they do this in the only way a picture can really lead back—they *look* like their source.

The picture has some often fairly simple structural similarity to its object, and we can hold the picture up to reality to determine whether it is *of* something. This is the point of passports, signatures on credit cards, video surveillance, holiday photographs, etc. It doesn't make an essential difference if the identification is not *easy* in a particular case; a poor picture of a criminal on a surveillance camera does not undermine the simple relationship between pictures and their objects, since it is in such a case merely a practical problem for the police, not a conceptual problem for a philosopher.

Mentioning here the police is quite appropriate since a picture in this simple mode is *evidence* for the subject of the picture. If I have a picture of you breaking into a bank, it is *evidence* that you broke into a bank. I can use the picture to attribute actions and qualities to you. The role of pictures and representation in general is fundamental in science—we use pictures on screens, representations in numbers, graphs, and so forth as evidence that we have identified an aspect of the world. The picture and the representation leads us to the real cause of the picture and allows us to say things directly *about* the cause of the picture. So, the role of representational relationship—of pictures in general—is a very powerful tool indeed. It saturates every aspect of our world. It is, however, completely inadequate for psychology.

---

9   Wolfgang Giegerich discusses various examples of this in *Dreaming the Myth Onwards: C. G. Jung on Christianity and on Hegel Part 2 of the Flight into the Unconscious* (*Collected English Papers, Vol. VI*) (New Orleans, LA: Spring Journal, Inc., 2014).

Given an image A and a putative psychological element or concept B, how do you tell if A represents B if you have never seen B? Further, how do you do this if it is not *possible* to see B? Yet further, what do you say if the concept of "seeing B" simpliciter is completely meaningless? The use of pictorial representation in psychology essentially renders psychology impossible. If one can form a picture of God in essentially the same way as one can form a picture of a dog, then one either makes banal the notion of God or absurdly inflates the notion of dog, both of which analytical psychology is guilty of on a regular basis. The "God image" and the "dog image" are two quite legitimate subjects in mainstream Jungian thought, and regardless of what one says about them both, the common bond manifest in the fact that one can discuss their images is a bond which structurally neutralizes any distinction based on their content that one might like to make. As De Voogd says in a somewhat different but pertinent context, "The 'image of God' is in truth a 'picture of God' (but in that case God must be spatiotemporally present for us to 'take his picture')."[10] Thinking of images as pictures leads, via the logic of picturing—which requires the presence of the subject of the picture, here, the "spatiotemporal presence" of God—to a conceptual confusion undermining any attempt to be adequate to the subtlety of such an idea.

Hillman claimed to reject this representational aspect of pictorial images[11] and rather advocated a procedure of "analogizing," which simply asks what the image is *like*. This is intended to be a fundamentally pluralist view, not "losing" any other analogies one might also draw. This pluralism does not change the underlying thought that images are pictures, but rather says that an image can be seen as multiple pictures. Further, the burden of the pictorial is carried in Hillman's examples by changing the emphasis on the nouns used to describe the dream, and, as every logician knows, nouns carry your ontology. It is therefore difficult to see how Hillman's view is different from one which holds the pictorial and representational structure of images as fundamental. The structural ontological commitment carried by the nouns doesn't particularly care if you add a clause to which you aren't ontologically committed. This of course echoes Giegerich's comment about the ontological commitment inherent in even mythological attitudes towards images.[12]

Between 1977 and 1978, Hillman's ideas about images had sophisticated to address the ontological commitment imported by nouns. We learn now that "it is not that the image *is* a picture, but that the image is *like* a picture"[13] and that "If we can effectively let go of our reliance on nouns, we will have taken an important step away from the symbolic perspective."[14] This loosening of the ontological

10 S. De Voogd, "Fantasy versus Fiction: Jung's Kantianism Appraised," in G.S. Saayman and K. Renos Papadopoulos, eds. *Jung in Modern Perspective* (Hounslow, Middlesex: Wildwood House Ltd, 1984), 221.
11 Hillman, "An Inquiry into Image," 86–87.
12 Wolfgang Giegerich, *Neurosis: The Logic of a Metaphysical Illness* (New Orleans, LA: Spring Journal, Inc., 2013), 265, footnote.
13 James Hillman, "Further Notes on Images," in *Spring* (1978): 160.
14 Hillman, "Further Notes on Images," 166.

import of nouns is demonstrated, for example, in terms of the trick of "reversing" an image content, for example, speaking of a "black snake" as a "snakey black." This however, does nothing to loosen the ontological grip of nouns; it merely shows how central they are, since you can confidently turn anything into one and generally need to in order to form a pictorial image. A "snakey black" is just another thing like a "black snake"—it's nouns, things, all the way down. The desire to be "freed from ... narrational obligations"[15] and the belief that "the chief words in an image do not depend on their grammar"[16] are the indicators here of a wish, unfortunately futile, to believe away the linguistic structures in which we swim, the very structures that make pretending to suspend them seem possible. Becoming "freed from the chains of grammatical usage"[17] has to be seen as a fantasy of a psychology which does not fully understand the structural aspects of syntax and grammar. As Wittgenstein so casually mentions in passing in his "private language" argument, "A great deal of stage-setting in the language is presupposed if the mere act of naming is to make sense."[18] Not only naming, but every aspect of language and mere "grammar." One cannot suspend, wish away, or change the fundamental structures of language which indeed define what concepts like "noun" mean. The problem with Hillman here is essentially that he sees the obligations of language as merely "narrational," but they run much deeper than that. He attempts to demonstrate with: "An arrow may arrow, be arrowly, arrowize. This de-substantiation aids de-literalizing."[19] I do not believe it does. There is no de-substantiation since there is a missing noun in all cases, and a missing noun carries ontology just as must a present one. *What* "arrows," *what* is "arrowly," *what* is "arrowizing"? Simply refusing to respect the question being asked *by the language, by the structure of the medium of the discussion itself,* is merely a game. One can see that it is a game in that when one comes to see how one is supposed to *do* this de-substantiation, one is often disappointed.

Take, for example, the trick of "contrasting"[20] where one asks questions which evoke reasons why a specific dream image was chosen rather than a possible other. I call it a "trick" as it merely tries to disguise the fact that one is utterly embedded in the referential pictorial model by referring to objects *not* in the dream. This is supposed to somehow avoid the ontologically suspect referential model, which it does if one concentrates only on the content of the dream; I claim that I am not ontologizing because I am not referring to things behind the dream images but instead just referring to things closely connected to the images (which somehow doesn't count). Of course in fact it does count since it makes no substantial difference whether one thinks of images as pictures because of an implicit or explicit referent.

15 Hillman, "Further Notes on Images," 165.
16 Hillman, "Further Notes on Images," 165.
17 Hillman, "Further Notes on Images," 165.
18 Ludwig Wittgenstein, *Philosophical Investigations*, trans. G.E.M. Anscombe (Oxford: Blackwell, 1953), § 257.
19 Hillman, "Further Notes on Images," 166.
20 Hillman, "Further Notes on Images," 177–178.

Another example of this tendency in Hillman to not take seriously enough the water in which he swims is the following: "When we look at dreams as images, then we have to look at the dream's words doubly carefully, because there is nowhere else to look to find their significance."[21] There may be nowhere else to look to find their significance in terms of their *content*, but language has already pre-dated any dream which can be discussed, so the *structure* of language is part of the fundamental structure of the world into which any dream is born. Dreams have no power to step out of such a defining context unless perhaps one is merely silent in their presence, but even then, pace Wittgenstein, such silence is utterly bound up with language. Even our silence is not the absence of language.

We might think that the practice of "image amplification" represents a sophistication in the Jungian approach to images. One might argue that here we leave a simple picturing mode and enter a more dynamic or interactive relation which leaves behind a simple representational relation. Again, there are structural elements which render such sophistications irrelevant. For example, the ineradicable tendency to highly value temporally prior images is endemic and strongly encouraged by Jung in both his published works and in the *Red Book*. One legitimizes one's own fantasies by relating them to older mythological images often by a simple process of quickly imagining that a figure, place, or situation "looks like" the imagination one has of some mythological character or place. The temporal aspect of connecting current images with temporally prior images is no accident. A picture painted of a person at the time they were alive is in some way more important, more potentially informative than one painted from memory. A picture painted from a memory separated from the subject by a few days is more valuable as information than one painted from memory after several years. This structural component of the logic of pictorial representation infects our attitude towards images—we are often improperly fascinated by "older" symbols, and the general valuation of myths, images, and fairy tales has an inescapable component which has to do with them simply being "old." That is, there is an implicit and illicit structural component being acted out in the attitude towards them because we imagine that in some sense they are "closer" to their ostensible subject. Of course we can make no sense of this "subject" which an old myth is supposed to be closer to, but this attitude comes along with the idea of images as pictures since pictures as simple representations do have such an element of temporal priority. We like to *refer back* to myths and symbols, that is, refer *back in time*, and this backwards temporal ingredient is essentially part of the language of pictures. It inevitably devalues the present, and this explains somewhat why Jungians are often interested in "older" cultures but are rarely able to coherently explain why this is an interest relevant to psychology. It is usually taken for granted that older cultures and older symbols are more authentic or "closer" in some way to the real concerns of Jungian psychology. This is indefensible, a by-product of an attitude that prioritizes a simple representational pictorial model.

---

21 Hillman, "Further Notes on Images," 170.

So, how might we sophisticate our notion of "image" beyond that of "picture"? Firstly, we must understand that pictorial representation is often not *chosen*; often it is a contingent, perhaps historical fact that it is simply the accepted mode of expression of a people at a particular time. Early man had no spoken or written language, no language at all, and so the cave paintings we find were not a choice of one type of imaginative expression over another. At that time, to imagine was to paint, and there was no other, as we would say now, "mode of expression." One does not *choose* when there are no alternatives to choose from. This was largely the case with the alchemists. There was very little choice but to decorate their texts with pictures because these were likely the *only* way to exhibit and to imagine certain aspects of their work. It is one of the reasons why their texts are so inscrutable, precisely because the texts cannot contain the material. This is *not* because alchemy is intrinsically more expressive than words or that it transcends language. It is largely a historical and not very psychologically interesting fact that at the time, the conceptual structures were not adequate to the task, and so the inclusion of pictures is, in a limited sense, regressive. Jung was motivated to revive alchemy precisely because he thought that he now had a more adequate framework with which to make sense of it, hence Jung's *use* of alchemical images is not at all the use to which the alchemists put them. He *did* have an alternative mode of expression with his new analytical concepts, and the pictorial nature of the images of alchemy are *not* essential or unavoidable for him. He does not let them stand as explanations which need no commentary, but rather he uses them and takes them away from their embeddedness, their original context, and talks about them extensively. I think that Jung devoted so much time to alchemical imagery because such imagery does exhibit a particular structure that is more sophisticated than many pictorial representations. The alchemical images were structurally a sort of emergency flood plain to contain the overspill from the overburdened thought of the time. The subtlety and complexity of the ideas required to do justice to the material which alchemists were concerned with was simply not historically present, and their images are a repository of thoughts and ideas frozen in pictures. They are the place where the undigestible parts of the alchemical material were left. These images are generally very special sorts of pictorial symbols in which the representational aspect is not at all primary. Alchemical "pictures" are not really pictures; they are moving towards something which we can really call "image" because of their overburdened structural inheritance from the ideas which they had to try to contain. They are inherently structural entities, images of structure, of form, of relationships, of the geometry of these relationships. They are an image of structure cast into a (necessarily because of the time) pictorial language with the vocabulary of "above and below," "merging and separation," and the like, compressed into a small physical and conceptual space. They are thus Jung's "condensed expressions." This is, it seems to me, why Jung was interested in alchemical images—because they were an early and burgeoning development of a move towards a real notion of "image." This rather *in spite of* and not because of their pictorial aspect.

It is this condensation of conceptual structure into a frozen form that constitutes the status of "image," and not the pictorial content. An "image" is a "condensed expression," a structural snapshot of something with a literally unimaginable structure. Image is a pattern, it *is* structure—it does not *have* structure like a picture has a structure. It *is* form and does not, like a picture, *have* form. Alchemical images are, in a sense, a picture of a relationship between objects. They are a picture of something which is in motion, though not a picture of the *thing* in motion but, rather, a picture of the motion. By being pictures of the motion rather than the things which are in motion, alchemical images, by being *about* structure, attempt to escape the limitations of pictures. They are *about* the process of the art, and they show the relations between things at various stages. However, they are still pictures, and they still, as pictures, fail to be adequate as psychological material.

Image as picturing

If there are problems with pictures, there is a related problem with the practice of "picturing." That is, the style of imagining which can only conceive of imagination as pictures, usually as something resembling an internal film.

A tourist or reporter may write an engaging account of a city or country, but this is made possible because the relationship is one of picturing, of looking at, and it is not an inhabiting. An inhabitant, a real inhabitant of a city or country, cannot produce such an account, cannot really imagine *how* to produce such an account because they are *defined* by the place. The extent to which a person can have, as we say, "some distance" from something, from somewhere in order to look at it, is precisely the extent to which they have ceased to be defined by it, and therefore the extent to which they cease to really be able to imagine it. We have a rather strange inverted notion of imagination in that we tend to think that imagining something is what you do or what you need to do when the thing is not actually present. That is, it is a substitute action to be performed in the absence of the imagined. We say something is "only imagination" or "all in the imagination," that is, it is a poor substitute to be resorted to in the absence of the real thing. This fits exactly with the notion of imagination as picturing, since we form to ourselves a picture when the thing we form a picture of is not here; imagination as a compensation for the recalcitrance of the world. This is however the wrong way round as Jung intuited in the notion of "active imagination." This practice does not simply augment the "imagination as substitute for the real thing" idea of imagination; rather, it completely replaces it with a different idea that imagination is not a substitute for anything and *is* the real thing.

One must follow this idea through; imagination is only really possible to the extent to which the thing you are imagining is *actually* present—so present that it is the structure in which you exist and which defines you. The dream ego or the imaginative ego does not observe—that is the inadequate pictorial relation. It rather inhabits and, in turn, is defined by this inhabiting. This definitional element has very particular consequences. Imagination may present you with people, places, events, and the like, but these are not relevant. The "bringing back" of these elements—their reporting, their description, their representation—is really to miss the point of imagination completely. The point of imagination is the structural inhabitance, and this cannot be "brought back." For as soon as you are able to uninhabit the imagination enough to describe, report, and represent, there is by the same movement no imagination any more. This is a blow to a psychology addicted to reports of dreams and fantasies, since the reporting itself means that the model collapses into a pictorial model and therefore is not psychological. As an example, Jung's *Red Book* as a catalogue of interesting figures, places, and situations is a mere amusement. Jung was at least careful enough to be adequate to the inhabiting sense of image when he warns quite explicitly that the images in the *Red Book* were of no relevance to anyone but himself.[22] To be generous to Jung, we might say that this is because an inhabitant of those images simply cannot say anything to someone else who does not also inhabit them. Then again, Jung also says that he was the "witness" to the "mystery plays" in the *Red Book*, that is, pulling himself out of them into the role of observer. This is why he could report on them and consider publishing them and ultimately produce the ultimate Jungian picture book, which we must with consistency treat as a book not relevant to psychology. Why? Since we have to consider it as a catalogue of pictorial by-products, the image debris left behind by an assumed psychological process. The *Red Book* is a travel guide to an unimaginable psychological land, which, on being made imaginable in pictures, is no longer psychological.

Imagination proper is an attempt to inhabit a structure—albeit a frozen, condensed, and structural expression of something unimaginable—in order to get some sense of the structure. It is an attempt to inhabit a snapshot of an unimaginable (and therefore currently uninhabitable) structure in order to get a sense of aspects of the unimaginable structure. This is not so different from looking at a two dimensional representation of, say, a four dimensional hypercube which is literally unimaginable because it "exists" in a literally uninhabitable world with four spatial dimensions. Trying to inhabit, to be there in a world where the condensed two dimensional representation manifests, is to try (and to necessarily, perhaps fruitfully fail) to get a sense of the "object itself." This is where feeling has a place in psychology as the "sense" one can get of a structure, in the way the sense one gets as an inhabitant is essentially to do with feeling. To live in Rome, in Paris, in Berlin, or in London as a real inhabitant is a matter of feeling. One feels like a Parisian, a Londoner. Merely being able to describe Paris or London by way of pictures is irrelevant to this feeling of being an inhabitant, or of having roots, which is exactly the feeling of being defined by a structure, of inhabiting a structure. To inhabit a structure is to be defined by it, and to be defined is to be defined in a particular manner. One cannot be defined in the abstract, for not being defined in a particular manner is to not be defined. One cannot be an "inhabitant" in the abstract but only in a concrete manner, as an inhabitant of a particular place for which one then has a

22 C. G. Jung, *The Red Book*, ed. by S. Shamdasani (New York, NY: Norton, 2009), 246.

feeling. Our particular place is psychology, and to imagine is to try to get a sense of what it is like to inhabit psychology. Imagination proper is about nothing more specific and nothing more abstract than this. It is to attempt to sense the shape and the structure of the psyche.

Picturing is crippling to the imagination required for psychology because the ability to imagine structure itself, to feel a way into a subtle, complex structure is atrophied, or more accurately, not developed at all. We fall into St Augustine's "shameful error" where the mind can "no longer distinguish the images of sensible things from itself, so as to see itself alone."[23]

Here again, a distorted attitude towards time interferes. The contents of imagination have a contingent relation to time; they appear, disappear, change, or do not change, and all of this we discuss as events which may or may not have occurred. So, we ask why this or that happened in a dream, and in doing so, tacitly accept that duration is a quality which carries meaning. However, imagination as an *inhabiting* means that duration is not merely contingent for imagination, it is essential. Imagination is defined by duration since an inhabiting is defined by its duration. Imagination exists as long as it endures, and as soon as it no longer endures—perhaps by its subsequent representation *as* image—it is finished. When duration is essential, representation in any medium where duration is inessential means a loss. Kierkegaard, whose work is in part a tremendous treatment of this aspect of time, puts this with typical grace:

> When in a written examination young people are given four hours to write the paper, it makes no difference whether the individual finishes ahead of time or uses the whole time. Here, then, the task is one thing and time something else. But when time itself is the task, it is a defect to finish ahead of time.[24]

With imagination, time itself is also the task because duration is essential. To collapse imagination into image is to finish ahead of time and is therefore a failure of the task, the task here being psychology. This means that imagination which has "results," which reports, brings back, paints, describes or otherwise represents the contents of the imagination, is not really imagination since for the contents, duration is inessential. If psychology is imagination, then when imagination is finished with the retrieval or production of an image, psychology is also finished. The concentration on the contents of imagination is to imaginally act out a structure just as falling objects act out the structure of gravity.

One must, so to speak, live in, endure, and inhabit the abandoned dwellings of the psyche and its images in order to get a sense or a smell of what used to live there. One gets no sense of this if one remains outside of the dwellings, looks at

23 Augustine, *On the Trinity: Books 8–15*, ed. by G.B. Matthews (Cambridge: Cambridge University Press, 2002), Book 10, Chapter 8.
24 Søren Kierkegaard, *Concluding Unscientific Postscript to Philosophical Fragments, Volume 1*, trans. Howard V. Hong and Edna H. Hong, revised edn (Princeton, NJ: Princeton University Press, 1992).

them, interprets them, and compares them with other structures which the psyche has also abandoned. The psychological component is the inhabiting, and the scent of the psyche still lingers only inside; it is a structural scent which one tries to grasp. One might observe and examine, analyze even, something which *has* structure, but if something *is* essentially structural, *is* only structure, then it can only be inhabited.

The idea of inhabiting an image is *also* inadequate in the sense that it does not give you the structure you are looking for. As mentioned earlier, it gives you frozen, abandoned, condensed expressions of the structure, and you have to use some sort of analytical instinct to sniff out the traces of the structure. There is nothing you can do as an analyst that will give you the structure you want directly. There is no tool or method that will do this. However, there are some things you can do which will certainly make it in principle impossible, and one of these has been our topic—the confusion of image with picture. Such a confusion is *in principle* inadequate, since its understanding of the psychological structure required is too simple. This simple structure can be had quite easily; it is what we get when we match dream figures to the names of Greek gods or pair fantasies with the names of known fairy tales.

It is a characteristically sophisticated modern development in education that we have moved beyond the old apprenticeship model where the teaching of a task was simultaneously the doing of a task. It was the case historically that every case of teaching how to build a boat was a demonstration of boat building, for example. Today, we have the quite astounding development of the instruction manual. This phenomenon represents several important developments in education. Firstly, it divorces the teaching of a task from its performance—an instruction manual is not a performance of the task it teaches you to do. Secondly, it removes the unbroken duration character of education—a manual skips much of the time required to actually perform the task with phrases such as "continue as before until complete" or "build the left hand side in the same way." Instruction manuals are also highly condensed. They summarize a great deal of effort into sometimes just a few pictures. Of course, nobody could seriously deny that instruction manuals are useful and that they work. As mentioned, however, they are not the performance of the task they instruct the reader to perform, and this is how images and imagination relate to psychology. They are not the doing, the performance, or the essence of psychology but rather can be used as a truncated, condensed description—part of an education in how to begin to construct psychology. They are not psychology itself, as psychology is not imaginal or imagination. Rather, one may use images and imagination to educate in the construction of psychology. As everyone knows, there is a particular art involved in interpreting an instruction manual as one must convert its description of doing into real doing. One must convert its pictures and descriptions, which are in themselves not part of the process of doing into a doing, thereby moving from content to structure. You must move from an examination of the manual to an inhabiting of the process which the manual requires of you. Images and imagination are not what you want, but they may help you to do what you want.

The contents of imagination are helpers. They are real psychopomps in the service of inhabiting the structure as opposed to guides in the pictorial sense which can lead you somewhere. It is not that they demonstrate *to you* the inhabiting; they are the frozen, condensed expressions (recall Jung's term) of the inhabiting, and are psychopomps to the extent to which they exemplify the inhabiting. However, they do not exemplify *how* to inhabit or how *you* should inhabit a structure—they do not "lead the way" in the sense of a pictorial figure walking in front of you, leading you somewhere. The figures are not people in any sense, not even the sense in which you can relate to them as individual figures. They are the frozen, condensed, and phenomenal representations of a literally unimaginable structure.

Image as debris

The mirror of the idea of images as instructive is the idea of image as the debris of a *de*struction. This shows the relation of image to psychology from another side. Images are the residue of the inevitable failure of an attempt to capture psychology in a structure too simple to hold it. However, this should not sound like a resigned statement of futility as the residue is critically important for psychology as it tries to understand the structural requirements for the production of images. The analysis of the waste matter of a process is most valuable and can tell you a great deal about the sorts of things involved. Images are a waste product, a by-product of a process of instantiating an unimaginable structure, of trying to make relations into things. We should recognize the value in this waste product, particularly in analytical psychology, since this is what the alchemical "gold in the dross" theme is precisely about. The gold is the special gold that turns out not to be gold as object, as normal gold, but as the pointer to the structural element, the rarefied trace element in the dross which points to its "origin." The formation of images is in fact the *reverse* of psychology. It is the turning of a structural, logical, and geometrical relation of literally unimaginable sophistication into something imaginable—and thereby essentially unpsychological.

Images are the waste matter of the process of de-psychologizing or un-psychologizing. This process is something like an explosion when one tries to force too much energy into a physical container. What happens is an un-structuring, a concretization, a literalization, a phenomenalization of the structural. The debris of this explosion is images. Just as with nuclear fallout the waste product of the explosion is full of energy, images have what we sometimes call a "numinous" quality. Images, we say, "radiate numinosity," and this analogy with radiation is useful as it highlights the dangerous aspect of the image. The energy, like radiation, is no longer contained in the structure: the images themselves "radiate" and therefore appear to be the source of energy, making it very easy for us to reify and posit a "relation" between images and archetypes, to perhaps say that you can "feel" the archetype through the image. All of this is misleading, as it is attempting to base a psychology on the rubble left over from an explosion caused precisely by the inability to maintain a psychological standpoint. Images in psychology are the ruins of psychology which could not maintain itself and which has therefore collapsed in on itself.

Images are of course not superfluous, such a claim would be absurd. Images are where the instantiation of newly manifesting psychological patterns begin and where the echoes of fading psychological patterns still ring. Like the carrier medium of water in which one can see the wave, the un-imageable energy of the wave is made first visible in the water and fades away in the water as it reaches the shore. Since we are talking about concrete, manifest psychology—human psychology—and not psychology in the abstract, there must be a medium for the wave. However, the wave is not the water. There must be images, but they are not psychology.

We have Hegel to thank for the tremendous distinction between temporal and logical order,[25] which helps us to understand why images seem to be so essential to the empirical understanding. Temporally, images are indeed first. They arise as the first manifestation of a process and provide raw material to interpretation and analysis. However, logically, that is, psychologically, images are the last stage of a process; they are a finished, concrete instantiation of the geometrical process preceding them, summarizing, so to speak, in inadequate form, the unfolding of this process. What is psychologically first is the abstract structure, and what follows is the image, even though the image is the first to be experienced in time. This is why images seem pregnant with the temporal future; they naturally feel to be so since they are the child of a structural, logical past. They logically contain in them the remnants of a structure which, temporally, they seem to imply or lead towards. Put in a rather inadequate but more graphic way, images are the first temporally visible sign of the psychological structure, and anything which is the first visible sign of something is naturally taken to be its first manifestation. This is the natural, empirical attitude and not at all the *contra naturam* required for psychology.

Taken in this way, images can be useful in psychological education. Just as in nuclear physics, where one investigates the structure of the universe by splitting apart, by making structure visible in some way, the image-making process is a (one-way) destruction of a structure which can be examined in order to investigate the way in which it deconstructs. Aspects of the structure are still apparent in the destruction, in the waste matter of the explosions, in the images. Investigating this structure and observing this structure is an essentially scientific, unpsychological further step which is useful in physics since the structure is *of* something, a putative something which *has* structure. However, in psychology, which is *essentially* structure, the structure *is* psychology, so *observing* the structure simply means that you are no longer doing psychology any more. You are observing psychology, doing meta-psychology, a sociological study of psychology, comparative mythology, or whatever, all of which endeavors may of course be interesting and valuable in their own right.

25   Georg Wilhelm Friedrich Hegel, *Hegel: Elements of the Philosophy of Right*, ed. Allen W. Wood, trans. H.B. Nisbet, revised edn (Cambridge University Press, 1991), 32.

The waste product of the de-psychologizing process—the images—have to be inhabited in order to extract the gold, that is, to proceed to the structural point of view. Observing is not enough, and therefore a picturing relation, a "looking at" is not enough. This "getting dirty" is a geometrical getting dirty, not a thinking about or representing contents which one might consider "dirty," i.e. death, dismemberment, incest etc. It is, so to speak, a systemic infection, a radiation poisoning, not a localized wound that can be looked at by a non-infected observer. It is not a further development of images, using imagination, associating to other images, as this is merely a quantitative accretion of yet more of the same inadequate relation. Inhabiting does not mean an imagined inhabiting, an active imagination where one literally in imagination inhabits and augments the pictorial with more pictures. No matter how many rungs you add to a ladder, you will never reach the moon, as a ladder is, given the structure of the universe, a fundamentally, in principle inadequate tool for such a purpose. What we call image is what structure itself "looks like" when it is no longer inhabited and has, like a disused dwelling, collapsed. Discussing the psychological "fog" which Jung says he emerged from suddenly one day in his youth, an event which he held to be a psychological turning point in his development, Giegerich says, "What is this fog? It is the image into which Jung's entire childhood was logically collapsed."[26] "Collapsed" here is very much appropriate, as the fog is the image left after a collapse of an old, personal psychological theory which had run its course and could no longer sustain itself. The "fog" is the debris left over after the collapse of something which is not image and which cannot be pictured. We often say that pictures bring a subject alive, but I think rather that pictures are psychologically already dead, are deceased psychology by them being pictures. This is not to say that a postmortem might not sharpen our idea of life, but in the end, approaching psychology through pictures reminds me of Hegel's favorite criticism of Kant—it is like refusing to go into the water until one has learned to swim.

Since images are the remains of psychology after it has burst or collapsed, one cannot infer anything directly from how matters empirically appear in images. This is another way of saying that images cannot be taken simply as pictures. In order to see this concretely, consider the following dream fragments taken from the same patient over the course of an analysis:

> I find a secret compartment in a cupboard in the house, it is magical and exciting.
>
> I find a secret room under the stairs in the house. There is just a carpet in there, no furniture and again, it is magical and exciting. It is particularly exciting because this room isn't really part of the house—it is something "extra."

26 Wolfgang Giegerich, "Soul and World" (2012). Available on the International Society for Psychology as the Discipline of Interiority (ISPDI) website (http://www.ispdi.org). Society membership is required for access to this paper, located at http://www.ispdi.org/en/2012-berlin-conference-papers/72-soul-and-world.html.

I am in my childhood bedroom. The toy cupboard opens onto a large hidden room with a carpet and some furniture. Larry King (a famous American television host) wants to film his show there. I am happy that I can put my things into this large room.

If we consider these image fragments as pictures, we would be tempted to conclude that the increasing space of the "inner room" in the picture was representative of an increasing inner psychological space or, perhaps, a progressing individuation process. The image of the hidden room which progressively increases in size could, in a simple pictorial way, be seen as mirroring, representing, or showing a process of the subject of the pictures also increasing in size, albeit in a somewhat metaphorical manner. Something in the images "gets larger" which we might take as indicating that something "in the psyche" is getting larger. This implies that we have some simple idea that the notion of physical growth is somehow strongly analogous to psychological growth of some sort. We think we can, as discussed earlier, *identify* the psychological growth by the growth in the pictures. The growth in the pictures is *evidence* for psychological growth. Of course it might be a suspect growth, like the growth of a tumor, but nevertheless there is a simple analogical relationship from the picture to the psychology. The patient might even be helped a great deal by pointing this out, this supposed growth. However, this sketch of a preliminary analysis of the dream fragment series is not psychological in the sense we need. It does not help us understand psychology or develop a psychological understanding because there are disciplines which deal with the matter of "something growing and getting larger" far better than psychology—biology for example. There is nothing psychological about the structure of something which merely gets larger over time, and thus psychology is not needed to account for it. So, here one must give up the information seemingly given by the pictorial representation (the growth). It might be useful to the patient, it might be interesting to amplify, or it might make sense of the analysis. However, it must be forgotten, ignored, or de-emphasized when trying to understand psychology. This is the sacrifice the analyst makes to psychology, the sacrifice of the temptation to think in pictures and thereby avoid psychology.

We must, then, say something about what happens in this series of fragments if we choose (and it *must* be a choice against the pictorial temptation) to ignore the growth in these pictures. By ignoring the pictorial temptation, we then lose the idea of time and the idea of development. We then have to try to inhabit a structure which *looks like growth if you freeze it into pictorial moments and present it in a series*. Without growth, the emphasis falls on what is left, the magic, the "extraness." Then we might see the entire series as one timeless structure which shows different aspects of the concept of "magical." It is a place to "put your things," that is, a place to *be*, but not a real place, as it is a television set, that is, not a real place. Magicalness is not authentic—it is not a real ruling principle but a television host with merely, ironically the surname "King." It is simultaneously (because we removed the element of time by ignoring the temporal implication of growth) small, bare and make-believe. Earlier I mentioned that numinosity in images is related to the excess force left over after psychology has exploded. Here, in these fragments we have an image of that numinosity, ruling inauthentically after the explosion of this patient's whole psychology after the suicide of his father. The images here are the debris of the real event, showing the collapsed structure left behind by the spilling over of psychological materials too powerful to contain. The images are not a picture of the psyche as it is now, but rather a "condensed expression" of what was left when psychology burst its banks and moved on. Refusing to see these images as pictures helps us to get a sense of the structure of the psychology involved. In the actual case involved, simply emphasizing the growth was naturally more helpful to the patient. However, we have two responsibilities, one to the patient and the other to our understanding of psychology, and it is this latter which, as Giegerich so often points out, goes largely unconsidered.

6

A NOTE ON "SOUL", "MAN", ANTHROPOLOGY AND PSYCHOLOGY

Marco Heleno Barreto

Psychology as the discipline of interiority is grounded, as we know, on the notion of psychological difference, which may be expressed as the notional difference between the concepts of "man" (understood as "empirical ego") and "soul" (understood as the logical interiority of a phenomenon). From this notional difference there follows a methodological difference: psychology with soul is constituted by the inwardization of given phenomena into themselves, according to the basic rule established by Jung: "Above all, don't let anything from outside, that does not belong, get into it, for the fantasy-image has 'everything it needs'".[1] Let me insist here on the methodological nature of this rule, for it has a most important consequence in our understanding of our discipline: psychology as the discipline of interiority is just a particular way of approaching some phenomena present in reality, and not a general theory concerning the whole of reality. In other words: psychology is not metaphysics—and, accordingly, it should not be confused with German idealism, despite the many acknowledged debts it has with Hegel's thought.

We are accustomed to thinking another difference that stems from the notion of psychological difference, namely, the distinction between psychology, which is methodologically constituted by the "soul" side of the psychological difference, and anthropology, which is rooted in the concept of "man". However, I would like to examine more closely this distinction, in order to better differentiate psychology from anthropology. As I see it, the specifically psychological distinction should mainly be thought of in terms of the difference between two types of *psychological* approach: the *soul* standpoint (psychology as the discipline of interiority) and the *personalistic* standpoint (ego psychology), so that the borderline between the psychological approach and the broadly anthropological standpoint could be more

1   Jung, *CW* 14, § 749.

clearly traced. That is the main purpose of this brief chapter. My strategy here will consist in examining the two concepts constitutive of the psychological difference: "soul" and "man".

To begin with, let us remark that "soul" has (1) a generic sense and (2) a specific one. In its (1) generic sense, "soul" means the realm of shared meanings and logical negativity: "the generation and entertaining of meanings, of the words of language, of values, ideas, fantasies, laws, institutions, works of poetry, music, art, and so on", comprising "consciousness as such as well as the world as a whole".[2] "Soul" is here coextensive with "communal cultural mind", with existence as mindedness. Hence, the generic sense of "soul" is correlative of the "human mode of being-in-the-world", and as such it has high *anthropological relevance*—if we bear in mind that *philosophical anthropology* is defined as an *ontology of the human mode of being*, of "Man" (*Anthropos*) signifying the whole human circumscription within the realm of being, and not just "man as empirical ego". (N.B.: "Soul" here does not mean a subsisting "part" that human being has, but the *contra naturam* essence of human being's entire world-relation. It is in this sense that "soul" is correlative to the fundamental philosophic-anthropologic object: the human mode of being.)

This does not mean that we are blurring the distinction between psychology and anthropology: first, because psychology refers not to the generic sense of "soul", but to the specific one; second, because philosophic anthropology is precisely an *ontology*, and thus takes "soul" *ontologically*. This means that for anthropology "soul" *refers* explicitly to the human "region" of the real, whereas psychology, despite the obvious fact that it presupposes the human mode of being, is constituted by what may be called a methodological nominalism. "Methodological nominalism" means that all images and concepts in psychology are from the outset taken as self-referential, without taking into account any reference to a reality outside themselves, even if this reality is necessarily presupposed as a condition of possibility of the very existence of psychology. Briefly: psychology *is not* an ontology. Psychological *reality* is the interiorization of the realism presupposed in any *reference* to things in empirical (or metaphysical) reality outside soul itself. This takes us to the next point.

The (2) specific sense of "soul", proper to psychology, is *absolute negativity*, which means that it is constituted through the negation of every determinate referential content of "soul" in the first generic sense: "The negativity of the soul has therewith become interiorized into the concept of soul itself, and through this interiorization the general concept of soul (...) has turned into the truly psychological one".[3] "Soul", in the truly and specifically psychological sense, is "the negation of what the soul itself [in the generic sense] posited, what itself produced".[4] In other words: we enter the psychological dimension through the logical inwardization of certain generically soul phenomena. This is why not every soul phenomenon is psychologically relevant, but only those which, having psychological quality (inner depth),

2   Wolfgang Giegerich, *What Is Soul?* (New Orleans, LA: Spring Journal, Inc., 2012), 74.
3   Giegerich, *What Is Soul?*, 81.
4   Giegerich, *What Is Soul?*, 81.

are negated in their referential structure and thus interiorized into themselves.[5] This means that "the psychological sense of soul is only a methodological one, a way of looking at things brought to bear on given phenomena or material. It is not in any way an ontological one."[6]

The generic sense of "soul" may guide us into *anthropology* provided we take it from an ontological viewpoint, whereas the specific notion necessarily leads to *psychology* proper. Let me insist on this: on the one hand, psychology presupposes the ontological object of anthropology—since there is no soul phenomenon outside the human realm, in a free-floating state—or, the other way around, anthropology includes (indeterminately) psychology (as a specifically human endeavor—there is no psychology in the natural kingdom); on the other hand, as the specific notion of "soul" constitutive of the whole field of psychology is the result of the dialectical *negation* of the generic sense constitutive of the broader field of anthropology, psychology results from the negation of anthropology. We reach "soul" in its specific sense through the crossing from ontology (anthropology) to logic (psychology).

Now let us state without fear this obvious fact: psychology necessarily presupposes humankind (or: humankind as correlative of "existence as mindedness" is a necessary condition for psychology). Furthermore, psychology needs a psychologist, understood as a function of soul itself, the function produced by soul in order to render possible the activity of *making* psychology, and to be concretely actualized this function—obviously!—needs to be performed by very concrete and empirical human beings (who must even have some special talents, such as a developed feeling function—and, I would add, the peculiarity of having been seduced by soul, made pregnant of soul by soul itself). We certainly agree in thinking of psychology as being soul's *opus*, according to what is required by the psychological difference, but sometimes (as can be verified in some moments of theoretical discussions on the website of ISPDI[7], for instance) we tend to hide from ourselves the *obvious* necessary presence of a *human agent* in order to perform the *making* of psychology, as if bringing *any* sign of human presence into our understanding of psychology-making would *ipso facto* throw us back into the personalistic notion of psychology, ego-psychology. This is a gross misunderstanding. Where does it come from?

I think the answer is to be found, first, in a certain form of understanding the concept of "man"/"ego", which is the dialectical opposite of "soul" in one of the formulations of the psychological difference—"man"/"ego" is what must be negated in order to open up the psychological dimension and render psychology as the discipline of interiority possible. In the psychological use, as constituting *one* pole of the psychological difference, "man" and "ego" are equivalent, synonymous, have exactly the same meaning. Hence, as "ego" means "a *mode* of perceiving, a *style* of thinking",[8] this is the meaning of "man", when this concept is taken psychologically.

5　See Giegerich, *What Is Soul?*, 85–86.
6　Giegerich, *What Is Soul?*, 83.
7　International Society for Psychology as the Discipline of Interiority.
8　Giegerich, *What is Soul?*, 296.

In other words: there is no conceptual differentiation between "man" and "ego". One can express the psychological difference as the difference between "man" and soul, or as the difference between "ego" and soul. Both mean exactly the same, and psychologically "man" or "ego" mean "a *mode* of perceiving, a *style* of thinking", not an ontological entity.

Furthermore, the psychological difference *must* be conceived in a dialectical way. How should we understand this?

> The soul as subject is I. However, the I or subject is within itself the dialectical unity and difference between itself as that function primarily oriented towards "survival" in the most general sense, in other words, the pragmatic, technical I (in the sense of the one side of the subject–object opposition), on the one hand, *and* the internal not-I as the subject of true knowing, the organ of truth and of the syntactical or logical form, on the other. The latter is "not-I" because it is the *objective* subject, *experienced* by the ego-personality as an internal other with an intentionality (and often impelling necessity) of its own. We could also say an autonomous other, however one that despite its otherness is nevertheless also I (me). (…) The I as the internal not-I is thus not self-identical and self-enclosed like an entity, and not enclosed in the human individual. (…)
>
> The soul is the whole relation (the entire psychological difference, *homo totus*) and at the same time the one *relatum* of this relation or the one moment of this difference, namely the not-I part, the organ of truth and true knowing, in contradistinction to the other moment, the pragmatic I, the egoic type of knowing and understanding.[9]

The gross misunderstanding that I have pointed out above comes from an *undialectical* and *unpsychological* understanding of the psychological difference, which takes the constitutive terms of the difference ("man"/"ego" and "soul") as simple opposites, excluding one another, and also substantializes both terms as ontological entities. We then should not forget that "soul" designates both the dialectical unity between "ego" (or "empirical man", the "pragmatic, technical I") *and* the internal not-I that is also I. Soul as subject, encompassing the dialectical identity of identity and difference of "soul" and "ego"—the "entire psychological difference"—is equivalent to *homo totus*. The I (soul) as the internal not-I while particularly realized as the subject who makes psychology is called the psychological I.[10] *And the psychological I should not be confused with the human individual*, equated with the empirical subject as such, as an existing positivity in the world. The psychological I *is* soul. On the other hand, as I have said before, *the psychological I requires necessarily a human individual in order to concretely perform its function*—namely, the function of soul-making.

9   Giegerich, *What Is Soul?*, 81, 298–300.
10   Cf. Giegerich, *What Is Soul?*, 300.

By the same token, the "pragmatic, technical I", usually called "man"/"ego", should also not be confused *simply* and ontologically with the human individual, with an existing positivity in the world, because it is also a *function*, a mode of knowing, understanding and acting. As this function is oriented towards the survival of the human individual, or of the human community, we are led to identify it with the concrete individual, but a function is not an entity. We tend to—at least implicitly, subliminally—substantialize the function, *the* ego. It would be better to distinguish concrete individual from "man"/"ego" in the psychological sense, because it is the very same concrete individual who, while ordinarily performing the predominant function of "pragmatic, technical I" in the everyday life, may shift (or be shifted…) to the other function of "psychological I" and become a psychologist, as long as he/she performs the psychological difference within him/herself and "tunes in to" the soul mode of consciousness, leaving momentarily the prevalent ego mode aside. We do not have two different sources of consciousness, but only one, which can be exerted through two modes: the pragmatic and the psychological. Another way of putting it would be: both the *pragmatic I* (man/*ego*) and the *psychological I* are soul itself, though in different modes.

Now, if we concentrate on the psychological difference as being in itself a *psychological* difference, then we may see in the two terms constitutive of the difference two distinct modes of conceiving and doing *psychology*: ego psychology and psychology as the discipline of interiority. And so, if we refrain from challenging or contesting the status of psychology attributed to ego psychology, we have two definitions of psychology: one that takes the psychic material in its reference to the human individual (aiming at understanding the problems, predicaments, sufferings in the personal sphere), and other that takes the same material without that reference (envisaging it as soul's pure self-manifestation). Survival purposefulness (in the broadest sense) versus sheer self-expression of soul. In the first case, the individual is the ultimate concern; in the second, only soul's processes matter. To sum up: ego-psychology may even start from the notional difference of "soul" and "man"/"ego", but then it subordinates the former to the latter, at bottom reverting to the everyday attitude, and in this way "soul" is reduced to "psychic events", and the dialectical strength of the psychological difference is lost; psychology as the discipline of interiority leaves behind "man"/"ego" and sticks to soul's processes taken strictly in themselves, and thus discloses what we are used to calling the *truly* psychological dimension.

However, there is a riddle here: the first form of psychology—ego-psychology—poses no problem, inasmuch as it follows the same line of interests belonging to "ego"; but what leads one to choose doing psychology in the second sense, given that its *telos* is indifferent to those interests and needs, and can even be contrary to them? What is the secret of one's inclination to it? Speaking mythologically: how does soul seduce one into its service, the service of soul-making? For it is not self-evident why one would momentarily abandon the natural/spontaneous concern with one's own vital needs and interests in order to dedicate oneself to performing the function of the psychological I. Quite on the contrary: it is highly unlikely—not to say impossible—that one would *willingly* sacrifice one's needs in order to follow soul's intimations, unless one is touched in such a manner that somehow doing psychology converts itself into a one-of-a-kind vital personal need. Maybe this is an aspect of the "cunning of soul": it touches "man" (here meaning our empirical-personal being) so that in some point of our personal structure arises a *desire* for soul-making. A desire—we all know—is a *psychic* phenomenon, and it has no *psychological* relevance *except* for its necessary instrumental role in rendering soul-making possible and actual, in our case.

Let us read a testimony of this confluence of the personal and the not-personal, of "man" and "soul", in a statement from Wolfgang Giegerich: "I do not confuse myself as private individual, as 'civil man', with the psychologist that (*I hope*) I am."[11] The *hope* to be a psychologist is precisely a *personal desire* of the private individual. It is the sign of the pregnancy by soul, which makes a psychologist in the first place. It is as if "soul" incarnates in "man" and leaves there the seed of itself, a seed that feeds a desire and makes it possible (and, within limits, *desirable*) for the private individual to shift from "civil man" (practical technical I) to "psychologist" (psychological I). This desire is the dynamic force inside the actual soul-making. The "psychologist" needs "soul nourishment", and this *need*, created by soul, becomes one of the many diverse needs operative on the personal individual level. It is one-of-a-kind because empirically it is indistinguishably personal and soul-made—it belongs to "man" and also to "soul", and is responsible for the momentary abandonment of the whole "man" dimension in favor of "soul-making".

Now, how should we understand this apparent suppression of the psychological difference, or its apparent return to an ego-psychological position?

> It is of course possible that the event of a successful truly psychological inter-pretation creates in the person having performed it a feeling of being deeply moved or an emotion of joy and thus a "spark". But this is precisely not itself psychological. Rather, it is a psychic event *in view of* and *occasioned by* an actual happening of psychology, which *itself*, however, remains averted, averted even from the subject doing psychology.[12]

There is no suppression of the psychological difference inasmuch as soul (as psychology) remains averted "even from the subject doing psychology". And this means that the "subject doing psychology" is not intended by the soul process, being only its instrument. His/her "humanitarian" personal gain is only that emotion of joy and that feeling of being deeply moved. And that is fair and enough—at least to me. And in a truly dialectical way, we can say that "soul" is already inside "man" as that self-contradictory point which makes possible the self-negation of the ego mode of consciousness (the everyday attitude) and the con-sequent shift to the truly psychological mode of consciousness. Uroborically, soul

11 Giegerich, *What Is Soul?*, 316, my italics.
12 Giegerich, *What Is Soul?*, 81, 86, note 53.

creates the desire for itself—it is the desire and its nourishment at once. Adapting some words from Augustine for my purposes: *tu autem ad ipsam quaerendo venisti non locorum spatio sed mentis affectu*—"you came to [soul] searching, not wandering through space, but by the desire of your spirit".[13]

(I would like to express my deep gratitude to John Robertson, for his patient reading, commenting and discussing the ideas presented in this note. He also helped to correct my English shortcomings.)

---

13 Augustine, *De Vera Religione*, trans. J.H.S. Burleigh (Philadelphia, PA: Westminster Press, 1953) XXXIX, 72.

PART II

"The psychological difference" in contemporary life and practice

7

A LITTLE LIGHT

Patricia Berry

Introduction

The title of this chapter refers to a dream of C. G. Jung's as referenced by Wolfgang Giegerich in his essay, "A Little Light, to Be Carried through Night and Storm: Comments on the State of Jungian Psychology Today."[1] I will be commenting on Jung's dream as I turn to dreams in general, clinical practice, and other matters. The method I use is my own,[2] which emerged within the atmosphere of early Archetypal Psychology. Most recently, my awareness has been challenged and sharpened through reading and listening to Giegerich and by discussions in the ISPDI.[3]

The first lines of Jung's dream are the following:

> It was night in some unknown place, and I was making slow and painful headway against a mighty wind. Dense fog was... everywhere. I had my hands cupped around a tiny light which threatened to go out at any moment. Everything depended on my keeping this little light alive.[4]

Dream ego

I find it useful in working with dreams to regard the person of the dreamer in the dream as distinct from the dreamer in daily reality. Calling the dreamer in the

1   Wolfgang Giegerich, *Technology and the Soul: From the Nuclear Bomb to the World Wide Web (Collected English Papers) Vol. II* (New Orleans, LA: Spring Journal, Inc., 2007), 333–336.
2   Patricia Berry, "An Approach to the Dream," *Spring: An Annual of Archetypal Psychology and Jungian Thought* (1974): 58–79; Patricia Berry, "Defense and Telos in Dreams," *Spring: An Annual of Archetypal Psychology and Jungian Thought* (1978): 115–127.
3   International Society for Psychology as the Discipline of Interiority.
4   Jung, *MDR*, 87–88.

dream the *dream ego* helps keep this distinction in mind. The idea is that the dreamer, represented by the *I* or *Me* in the dream, is closest to the dreamer's usual, waking consciousness, which is probably why, one might assume, the dreamer experiences himself in the dream as himself in the first place.

Oddly enough, Jung seldom used the term "dream ego." A search of the General Index reveals that the notion appeared only once in the *Collected Works*.[5] While nowadays "dream ego" is more commonly referred to by Jungians, in earlier years or among first generation analysts, it was rare. During the mid-1960s through the 1970s at the C. G. Jung Institute in Zurich, those of us who were students at the time tended to regard ourselves in our dreams more or less unreflectively as ourselves. It generally did not occur to us to think of ourselves in a way that rendered much distance between the dream we brought to analysis and the way we commonly thought of ourselves. What happened to "me" in the dream happened to me for good or for ill, and part of working with the dream frequently involved judging which was which. We were aware of animus/anima, shadow, child, and other such configurations as involved in forming the dream's conceptual framework and dynamics. However, we tended to identify with our self as we appeared in the dream.

The term "dream ego" tends, on the contrary, to demote the dreamer such that we become little more than a figure ourselves. Simply using the words "dream ego" provides this slight separation. One may think of the *I* as in italics or with a single quote mark on each side; identity then becomes "so-called", so-called *I*, so-called *me*. This slight irony or shift in tone creates a reflective space which affects something of a *psychological difference* right there, simply in how one talks about oneself in the dream.

The ability to regard oneself as a figure in a dream influences how one regards oneself in life too. By taking ourselves less literally, we more easily sense the reciprocity between ego behavior in daily life as well as in dreams. Each reflects and affects the other. This has therapeutic implications. One can reflect, "Oh isn't it interesting. Look at me doing that again." "I am afraid of this guy, and so I hide in the closet" or "I hit him" or "I seduce him." The dream ego adopts coping strategies similar to those it draws upon in life. The ego enacts its habits, style, and its favorite behaviors. How we feel and act in a dream is how we tend to handle situations in life.

Getting a sense of this mirroring without identifying or defending against it is an important step, whether dealing with one's own dreams or those of a patient. Metaphorical levels and similarities echo between dream and life, life and dream, in ways that would seem essential to a depth psychology.

Layard's Rule

John Layard was an English anthropologist and a most notable and radical personality. As he tells the story, he once put a gun in his mouth and pulled the trigger. Miraculously, the bullet went through his head in such a way that it did not kill

5   Jung, *CW* 8, § 580.

him or even damage his brain, so far as anyone could tell. This miracle of survival when he had meant himself dead sent him off to Zurich to work with Jung. After a few years in analysis with Jung, he was knighted to become an analyst himself.

I spent a day in the late 1960s with Jim Hillman and Rafael Lopez-Pedraza visiting Layard at his home in Southern England, but it was not until sometime later as I was writing a second paper on dreams[6] (1978) that I learned of Layard's attitude regarding dreams. I promptly put this idea into the paper and named it "Layard's Rule."

The rule goes like this: "Everything in the dream is right except perhaps the dream ego." (*Right* in this context means in its "right" place, as it should be, or simply "what is.") The dream ego may or may not be "right" in the sense of being aligned with the rest of the dream. Sometimes the ego is of a similar attitude, but more often one experiences some degree of tension between the dream ego and whatever else is going on in the dream. This conflict is part of the dialectic of the situation and necessary for the psyche's movement.

I told you the story about Layard's near-suicide because something is horrifyingly apt about the plunge the psyche takes when something as emotionally shocking as the threat of death appears. Often in a suicide attempt, how the individual attempts to commit the act is metaphorically descriptive of what the psyche on an interior level is trying to accomplish; it seems to reflect the soul's effort to get to where it needs to be *no matter what*. For example, a leap off the ledge of a building may convey the soul's attempt to get finally to *terra firma*. The resoluteness of the soul process can be insistent enough to shatter physical being or life itself in the process. It may even kill the life that it must change. Cutting one's wrists might express the soul's attempt to relieve the soul of a too sanguine force of life pressuring it or, to the contrary, lack of pressure, a spiritless, depressive leadenness that deprives the soul of all purpose. Whatever the case, the attempt is like a last act to carry the process all the way unto death, into its necessary negation or "negative" life. As horrible as it might sound, the person might conceivably shoot himself in the head, as Layard did, to get the head "gone" or maybe splayed into multiple bits to vaporize its obsessive thoughts. Whatever the specific *telos* of the interior necessity, it will have its way—and certainly so, it seems to me, when there are no other ways.

Such desperation absolutized is an attempt to get the psyche's dialectic to its next sublation, dead or alive. To the psyche, it does not seem to matter which way it achieves this goal. I am talking about psychological processes in a way that attempts to view the particularity of the soul's desire from within its own interiority. Logically, it is like a radical negation leading to an even more radical sublation.

Not all suicide is of course neurotic. Certainly it can be a shame—as when, e.g., an absolute metaphysic takes hold of an adolescent's sensibility, which anyway tends to absolutize, having not yet developed the skills requisite for dealing with

6   Patricia Berry, "Defense and Telos in Dreams," in *Echo's Subtle Body: Contributions to an Archetypal Psychology* (New York: Spring Publications, 2008) (2nd revised and expanded edn).

profoundly difficult emotional states. In these cases, we would go to great lengths to avert the metaphysical disaster in order to give the youth time to mature and develop the strengths and strategies to handle the inevitability of life's emotional onslaughts.

To help at the deepest levels, one would need to connect with the underlying process—i.e., to get to the soul's most basic movement on an interior level. Such interiority is what the event is *actually* about. As a therapist, one might encourage the individual to talk in as much detail as possible about the suicide attempt. One often finds, however, that many patients will resist such detailed talk, trying rather to escape through vague generalizations or by telling you about suicide from the outside as though you did not understand how it works. Such patients resist because the more details and particular feelings, thoughts, and emotions they articulate hinder the workings of the Metaphysical Absolute—and The Absolute seems to want absolute obedience.[7] As with any neurosis, it is easier to stay with the Absolute on its own terms than to do anything with or about it. Where suicidality is concerned, The Absolute appears to demand the absoluteness of desperation, inflation—*even annihilation*—over articulation.[8]

Layard's Rule has death in it. The rule is subversive. *Everything is right except perhaps the dream ego.* This *"except the dream ego"* punctures the ego's illusion of itself. It is like the witch in the fairy tale whose subtle pricking, poisoning, or needling wounds the ego's sense of itself. With the Layard Rule, the ego becomes weaker and less sure.

The guidance given by Layard's Rule[9]—i.e., bracketing the dream ego from its usual attitudes and narratives—challenges one to look more deeply into the event on an interior level. In conceiving the situation from within itself, one entertains what is *not* ego in the dream as though it were more primary and necessary, rendering negation the most significant aspect of the situation. However, practically speaking, psychic situations are always within certain circumstances or moments. They are not realities for all time. Otherwise, we end up with another fixed positivity. Negation of the ego, as I am speaking of it, is a tool, not a recipe.

Layard's Rule as applied to Jung's "little light"

In Jung's dream of the little light the ego experiences itself as "making slow and painful headway against a mighty wind." The form here is of a progress narrative. The setup implies a tale of progression from one state to the next better or necessary one—toward a goal. (It brings to mind a work like John Bunyan's 17th-century

7   "The Metaphysical Absolute" is explored in Wolfgang Giegerich, *Neurosis: The Logic of a Metaphysical Illness* (New Orleans, LA: Spring Journal, Inc., 2013).
8   I find phenomenal differentiations particularly—including movement, dance, writing, or painting—interfere with the Absolute – which is their purpose.
9   The Layard Rule is not to be regarded as a positivized rule. It is not appropriate in every situation. However, as a hermeneutic, it can be extremely useful as a way of viewing what is going on.

Christian Allegory, *Pilgrim's Progress*, which is construed in the form of a dream.) Certainly, the image of Jung trudging step by painful step sheltering his little light against the wind resonates with a sense of Christian hope, suffering, and courage.

Let us apply the Layard Rule. Were we to bracket the ego's progressive effort, we would have the force of the wind remaining. In other words, the ego is countering the elemental. From the ego's point of view, its movement is heroic and *contra-naturam*. One cannot be heroic unless there is something against which to prove one's mettle, something to counter—an obstacle or enemy. Here, that obstacle is the natural wind.

Alchemy speaks of its work as an *opus contra naturam* (a work against nature). In Jungian thought, the *contra-naturam* is generally considered to be the direction of consciousness, which is usually set up as counter to the elemental or natural course of things. On the one hand, the alchemists were following nature. They diligently studied what they called "The Book of Nature." They were dedicated to nature, but the nature they studied was not simple or singular. A statement summarizing the complexity of the alchemical attitude about nature has been attributed to several alchemists, among them pseudo-Democritus or sometimes Ostanes. To quote Ostanes: "Nature rejoices in nature; nature subdues nature; nature rules over nature."[10]

This more complicated view of nature implies nature flows both with and yet also against itself. This is like saying the *contra-naturam* is itself natural. It is, in other words, part of nature to be against nature, contra-natural. Armed with this more complicated view of nature as both the natural course and nature as naturally moving against itself—"subduing" or even "overruling" the natural course—we might read Jung's dream the other way around.

Let us say actually Jung's *dream ego* is in, as dream egos generally are, its more comfortable, habitual posture, even in its caring concern for the little light, shielding it so carefully in cupped hands against the elements. Imagine the wind is the *contra-natural* element in the dream—*contra* to the more comfortable, usual ego state. Jung speaks of the unconscious as that which crosses one's path. Here, what crosses his path is the elemental wind.

Let us imagine this as the ego's preferred behavior, similar to the examples of ego habits mentioned earlier—the ego always leaving, meeting threat with aggression, seduction, etc. It is not that the habitual pattern is easy, rather that it is *usual* or familiar, and for that reason the ego prefers it. It can be an uncomfortable state, just as neurosis is both uncomfortable and a suffering along with an attachment to the pleasure neurosis creates. It is both a discomfort and a comfort. This combination of both characterizes neurosis and is a most difficult situation from which to free oneself, no matter how one suffers.[11]

10 Jung, *CW* 9ii, § 244n.
11 There is something of a parallel here with Jung's situation, although, I must say, I do not actually regard Jung's attitude as neurotic. The reason is that with Jung there is always so much more going on. Neurosis involves a narrowing, whereas Jung's attitudes almost always, when you look at them within a large enough context, show multiple, even contrary postures.

In this moment in his dream, Jung's posture is that of a figure who carries light against the wind. In this sense he is a Light-Carrier. In creation stories we find various ways in which light comes into being. Perhaps a monotheistic God announces, "Let there be light!" or perhaps a Prometheus steals it, or a Raven, Crow, or other trickster figure fools it into being. We may also find light as an animistic shine within nature itself or a sparkling scintilla in the depths. In Jung's dream the light carrier is Jung himself, an individual struggling heroically against the wind.

Jung was, of course, quite aware of nature's deep contradictory complexity. He taught us of it. But here with this particular dream, in this particular moment, his telling is less complex. Here Jung allows himself a posture of singular heroic progression opposing what would interfere, and this wind he opposes is of course not a meaningless element. Wind evokes spirit, *Zeitgeist*, climates of change, God's creative breath over the deep, and so on. Wind is both elemental and creative at once—not minor in the least.

Let us compare Jung's situation with Jonah's night/sea journey, which is likewise a *contra-naturam* tale. Jonah is swallowed by a whale. The whale swims from west to east against the sun's natural direction. The whale's progress is not a Pilgrim's progress. It is not a Christian allegory of progressive stages of struggle. Rather, the tale is about a man swallowed and carried by a mammoth and mammalian force of elemental depths, carried in a direction *contra* to the natural path of the sun. This *contra-naturam* purpose appears as an impulse from within nature's oceanic depths. It is *contra*-natural yet within the deepest realms of the psyche itself.

A reflection on the little light

The real (and maybe only?) problem with the "little light" situation is that it is exceedingly attractive. Many aspects of it draw us to identify. Its themes are some of our favorites—an individual taking on the storm of life all by himself, courageously determined to counter an "other." We know these themes. And we know what they feel like—what it feels like when everything seems against you, what it is like to shelter something precious, a little light that is so vulnerable it calls for protection. We know the feeling that it all depends on us. Only we with our action can save the situation.

"This little light of mine, I'm gonna let it shine" are lyrics to a song we sang as children in Sunday School in the 1940s to 1950s. In the late 1950s and 1960s, we belted it in earnest during civil rights protests and marches. The song's inspirational, feel-good spirit has made it a favorite in the USA. It has been performed for over 80 years, and we are still not tired of it. The words seem to have derived from The New Testament where Jesus says, "Ye are the light of the world...Neither do men light a candle and put it under a bushel, but on a candlestick; and it giveth light unto all."[12]

12 *Matthew* 5:14.

This "giveth light unto all" feels good and inspires a certain sense of mission. The feeling that it is up to me takes the "*me*" very seriously. One might say it creates something of an ego/Self conflation. Saving the soul of modern man is central to what Jung considered his task—a task that hung on the backs of individuals chosen for *individuation* and their achievement of it. A struggle with the collective winds of the time, whatever the time, seems essential to this heroic sense.

Interestingly, the Jonah tale also frequently comes with a little light. In this Old Testament story, the light appears variously *as* a candle or sometimes a glowing pearl. In some depictions, the light spills out of the whale's mouth, showing the whale itself to be a light creator as it dumps Jonah onto the shore. This is rich Old Testament wisdom where light is part of the whale and elemental within the journey itself. For Jung, as a man in modernity, the situation is different. The most common sensibility in modernity is that man's light exists contra the elemental. In the Old Testament tale, we find light existing more inherently within animal, material, and myth.

"Everything," Jung says, "depended on *my* keeping this little light alive." Everything is a lot. And *it all depends on me and my own little light.* The dream continues:

> Suddenly I had the feeling that something was coming up behind me. I looked back, and saw a gigantic black figure following me. But at the same moment I was conscious, in spite of my terror, that I must keep my little light going through night and wind, regardless of all dangers. When I awoke I realized at once that the figure was a "specter of the Brocken," my own shadow on the swirling mists, brought into being by the little light I was carrying.[13]

Although Jung views the Specter of the Brocken initially as a perceptual shadow cast by the light of his candle, one might assume since he invented the notion *shadow* in its psychological sense, he realizes it in both its perceptual and metaphorical sense. What he does not seem to realize, however, is how his candle-carrying posture *itself* constellates shadow. He seems psychologically less aware of the extent to which his missionary stance engenders what arises behind him. Jung's stated mission was to bring "meaning to modern man."[14] This intent is laudatory, but might we also find some shadow to it?

Jung continues:

> I knew, too, that this little light was my consciousness, the only light I have. My own understanding is the sole treasure I possess, and the greatest. Though infinitely small and fragile in comparison with the powers of darkness, it is still a light, my only light.[15]

13 Jung, *MDR*, 88.
14 C. G. Jung, *Modern Man in Search of a Soul* (New York, NY: Harvest, 1933); also Jung, *CW* 10, 148–196, 275–332.
15 Jung, *MDR*, 88.

Four times here Jung emphasizes the singularity of his little light: "my *only* light," "*own* understanding," "*sole* treasure," "*only* light." Jung's repetitions of the light as the "one and only, his own" creates it as such and increases the intensity fourfold.

Whether the "powers of darkness" Jung refers to at the end of the dream consist entirely of the hulking shadow as Specter of the Brocken or the fierce wind opposing him all along is unclear. What we do know is that what he calls the "powers of darkness" have become increasingly substantial.

Interiorizing the dream into itself: the ego's sublation

So far we have been regarding one part of the dream against the other. We have been treating the wind (using Layard's Rule as buttress) as the primary "given" of the dream, and we have been seeing Jung, the dream ego sheltering his light, as the mutable part of the dream as though this part were what causes the problems, as though if we could just change Jung's attitude, everything would be fine. However, this is not the case.

Now we come to the idea of the "*simultaneity of the image*."[16] What *simultaneity of the image* means to me is to regard the dream as inter-connected as though each part of the dream image were connected with and constellated by all the other parts of the dream. When you look at the situation this way, you realize the dream ego is also part of the constellation. It, too, belongs. So now instead of Layard's Rule—"everything in the dream is right except perhaps the dream ego"—we might say the dream ego is *also* right. Everything in the dream is "right." The dream is simply as-it-is.

Now, on to a more interior level: let us consider this dark Specter as shadow and the negation of the entire dream complex. Jung's "stance," "light," "against the wind," "Specter of the Brocken" are equally part of the situation. Let us say the soul's negation of all this brings the process to a level sufficient for sublation.

But Jung does not let that happen. Instead, at this point in his recounting, he breaks the narration, pops out of the dream, associates, and interprets. He explains the dream as having to do with his No. 1 and No. 2 personalities: "This dream was a great illumination for me. Now I knew that No. 1 was the bearer of the light, and that No. 2 followed him like a shadow. My task was to shield the light and not look back... I must go forward against the storm."[17] Referring to his No. 1 and No. 2 personalities seems to the reader trivial compared with the level of the dream.

Further, Jung views the dream as confirming a choice he had made as a young student concerning which track to study at university. Jung's choice had to do with whether to study on the science or the history/philosophy track. We know in retrospect that Jung ended up drawing deeply from both these areas of study, to say nothing of his integral concern with spirituality and religion, throughout his life.

16   Berry, *Spring*, 1974.
17   Jung, *MDR*, 88.

How could this choice as a 19-year-old have been so important? It was all already there in the beginning and end. Jung did it all. Did the order matter so much, really? Wasn't the notion of choice and its linear illusion something of an ego fantasy?

Jung goes on to interpret the wind as time. The task, he says, is to make of life what one can before the winds have "sucked" it away. This is a strong image, which becomes more potent still when one realizes Jung himself is to die within a couple years. Did he sense the foundations of his physical and psychological life crumbling? Was he less sure about his assumptions or more adamant and identified as he experienced life's brief candle flickering?

Jung sidesteps death (or the negation of the ego) as integrally present in the dream itself, but he picks up the theme of death later in his remarks. He does so, however, by way of more categorical, typological associations in which he characterizes a personality No. 1 versus No. 2 distinction. Why does he position himself in this roundabout manner, removed from the phenomenon itself?

In the language of psychology as the discipline of interiority, one might say that the dream has not gone through the dialectical negations and ultimate sublation necessary for effective change. The dream and psychological situation has not "come home to itself." This leaves the dream and the psychological situation unresolved. I wonder if something of this incompletion is what we Jungians are now picking up and enacting with compelling energy as we carry our little lights into the contemporary world and its difficulties. We want to help as Jung had tried to help. We want to further his message and spread the word beyond what he was able to do.

The little light in contemporary life

The world certainly needs help. Has there ever been a time it has not? Indeed, it is quite a different world today, psychologically and culturally. "The little light" once sheltered in our Jungian introverted hands is now radically externalized, held aloft, politicized, and enacted as we carry our mission and programs to every corner of the world. Our IAAP mission statement, in fact, explicitly states this intent not once but three times.[18] Economic considerations for individual members as well as matters of the survival of the field in general may play a role of course; it is hard to determine where and how much "shadow" is playing into all this, since awareness of shadow has been largely occluded and numbed by our overwhelming zeal and missionary purpose.

The field has changed indeed. It strives now outward—extroverted and exteriorized in ways far beyond what we have ever known as Jungians. Our methodology includes, sometimes quite centrally, that of the social sciences, e.g., sociology, gender studies, and political science—the underlying assumptions and generalizations of which are distinctly different from depth psychology as Jung understood it.

18 International Association for Analytical Psychology, "Mission Statement," n.d., http://iaap.org/about-the-iaap/mission-statement.html.

In recent years even the notion of *soul* has become popularized, simplified, and idealized. The little light, once a tiny sheltered glow, thrives now as a bonfire of pro-active causes. How seldom it is that we find this glow including the ambiguity, complexity, and interiority of Jung's more complicated work. How is it that a subtle notion such as "soul" has come to be a banner waved aloft with such fervor? Where is the subtlety of the little light?

Of course the subtlety may well be working its way concealed within the cracks of the very externalities I am here eschewing. We will get to that in a moment. For now, let us simply appreciate how this little light has indeed expanded far beyond the moment of Jung's dream and reflections upon which we have been focusing. Time changes appearance; things no longer appear in the same forms and ways they did in earlier periods. When most authentic, light appears rediscovered, as indeed it is recreated within time and circumstances. So we may ask, where might we now, in modern times, catch a flicker of what was once this little light?

We might imagine the little light as a *creative* glimmer from within its own negation, its own non-light. The question then becomes how and where does the authenticity of the light hide within the superficiality of contemporary life? In addressing this question, I will use the work of Donald Judd, the artist, as an example.

Judd was an Abstract Expressionist painter in New York City in the 1950s, the heyday of American Abstract Expressionism. This style of painting has perceptual depth in that it builds on layers of overlapping paint, which creates a kind of sub-stantiality and complexity. Suddenly, Judd decided no more depth, not of this sort anyway. He was going to work with objects and concrete, material, and machine manufactured surfaces.

When you take Judd's situation as though it were a dream, what you get is an abstract world of depth created by layers of paint over paint, which evokes inter-esting textures and invites further exploration. Then suddenly, bam! There is surface—manufactured objects and slick, smooth surfaces. That is the image. Rich, individual abstraction in the first part of Judd's career, then flat, machine created surfaces in the second part. If we put the two periods on top of each other in layers, as though they were a timeless image (which I think images are), what we get is *the invisibility of depth within a surface*. This is not dissimilar to the simultaneity of the little light and appearance of the Specter in Jung's dream three-quarters of a century earlier.

For Judd, the contradictions are depth and surface which, in their negation create what one could regard in Judd's work as "a little light." What I am saying is that the creative process at an authentic level produces a spark. This spark is like God and Adam touching fingers—zap!—life, creation. Such a creative spark is the creative moment itself, which can exist anywhere as a consequence of its under-lying contradiction. Here, it exists as the echo of a potentiality between surface and depth, a metaphorical conundrum one might find almost anywhere and in any-thing. It is up to us to develop the eye and ear for it, the "perception" by which we can apprehend this originating moment in its spark. *The point is to get it* and in such a way that lets the psyche be moved by it from within.

Conclusion

In our contemporary period, the little light exists as a light emerging from surfaces and depths *at once*. One way to characterize this is, as I have above, "depth within surface." But however we characterize it, this conundrum is rich only to the extent that we recognize its dialectical origin. Psychologically, i.e., metaphorically, we must give up light as light of the-single-little candle-variety that we have been carrying in Jung's way since Jung's time so that our light may be *real* light, *now*.

Letting this go is like letting the candle as we have known it, go out. Will letting this kind of light and posture extinguish itself result in an extinguishing of the world? So far in the last 2.5 million years (give or take 1000), it has not. But we do not know. Of course we have to attend to now, for this is when and where we exist. We surely love our world physically and culturally. This beautiful world is our home.

In the post-modern view I have (mostly) been taking here, world is inter-connected with everything. Similarly, Jung's dream and comments are interrelated, just as Judd's abstract paintings and radical surfaces interconnect within themselves; everything inter-relates when you look at it that way. With such a view everything is potentially implicated, connected with, and within every other part. When viewed creatively, "meaning" appears not so much as though it were Meaning with a capital *M* in Jung's more ideal sense, but rather more simply as a sense of "significance." No more, but also *no less* than that.

Is the planet finished? Who knows, but certainly it serves us to wear life as a loose wrap—as we probably always should have and maybe always did up until a couple of centuries ago. There once was a time in which we were aware of how gods and disease snuffed out life in closer proportion to birth and survival. That was how life was. The nature of life was close to non-life.

John Layard played his life close to this sense of death. The awareness of death and the importance Layard granted to it brought into psychology a way of thinking about how dreams ought to be embraced. Psychology as the discipline of interiority does that too. Death is folded into its method as the movement and necessity of negation throughout psychic processes. The only way to live on a soul level is to continually die on it. That is how the soul lives. So, too, is the case in art, any art, including the fine art of living. Dying and moments of little light appear together. Dying creates light. Our job is to see it. For me, that seeing is the *psychological difference*.

8

THE LOGIC OF FORGIVENESS

Jennifer M. Sandoval

> [P]ure and unconditional forgiveness, in order to have its own meaning, must have no 'meaning', no finality, even no intelligibility. It is a madness of the impossible.
>
> *Jacques Derrida,* On Cosmopolitanism and Forgiveness[1]

Introduction

This essay explores the psychological nature of forgiveness that emerges in light of what Psychology as the Discipline of Interiority defines as "the psychological difference"—or that difference between the ordinary, subjective, or apparent side of phenomena and the reflected (or negatively interiorized), objective, or underlying logical or meaning quality of phenomena. The psychological difference will allow us to differentiate two different aspects of forgiveness—one utilized by the ego and one reflected by "the soul"—and offer insight on the "impossibility" of forgiveness.

The idea of forgiveness, defined simply as the absolution from blame or sin, would seem to signify profound *psychological* transformation. Is it not strange then, that the matter of forgiveness has been largely neglected by depth psychology? Freud and Jung did not write about the topic, nor did any other major authorities in the field.[2] Whereas in recent years research and literature in mainstream

---

1   Jacques Derrida, *On Cosmopolitanism and Forgiveness* (Oxford, UK: Taylor & Francis, 2007), 45.
2   As noted by T. M. Grant, *Forgiveness in Psychoanalysis*. Unpublished manuscript (1987) and Melvin R. Lansky, "The Impossibility of Forgiveness: Shame Fantasies as Instigators of Vengefulness in Euripides' Medea," *Journal of the American Psychoanalytic Association* 53, no. 2 (June 1, 2005): 437–464. Hillman has written about forgiveness, albeit sparingly. On the one hand he is suspicious of it, noting that the ancient gods wished their wrath to be remembered, not forgiven, yet on the other he intuited that forgiveness "does not come from the ego." Hillman, however, did not examine forgiveness psychologically,

psychology on the phenomenon of forgiveness has expanded dramatically (in addition to a plethora of self-help books and seminars on the topic), its omission as a serious topic of depth psychological study is curious. Indeed, the underlying structure of forgiveness reveals a complexity and character remarkably suited for depth psychological study. For example, forgiveness would seem a paradox, a "madness of the impossible," (Derrida) because, simply put, it both posits and absolves an offense; sin and innocence are mutually constituted—a logical impossibility. Here we are reminded of Jung's transcendent function, which, in holding the tension of two opposites, bestows a *reconciling* symbol.[3] James Hillman describes the alchemical process of "yellowing", where, from an innocent white, through a grueling and putrefying *nigredo* process, we witness the emergence of a second, purer white—a paradox of *forged innocence*.[4] And I suggest that from psychology as the discipline of interiority emerges the idea that the "paradox" of true forgiveness, through absolute negation, acts as an "impossible" bridge between the semantic, horizontal landscape of the ego and the vertical, syntactical sphere of soul, signifying the union of the unity and difference of the opposites. The notion of forgiveness, if allowed to move beyond a simple negation of the offense and logically unfold into its *absolute* negation, reveals the very movement of consciousness itself; that which is forgiven is released into its freedom, into its own inwardness—its truth.

The relevance of forgiveness to psychology in contemporary life

The omission of the concept of forgiveness as a serious topic of depth psychological study may have its basis in the idea that forgiveness does not *belong* in psychology. Given the moral/ethical character of forgiveness and the emphasis of forgiveness in Christianity and other faiths, it is typically seen as more appropriately addressed by religious communities, pastoral psychology, philosophy, and political theory, than depth psychology. Psychoanalytic literature deems forgiving to be generally suspect due to its tendency to unwittingly serve as a repressive defensive structure against conflict; forgiveness is here reduced to an implied masochistic reaction formation. The clear *interpersonal* and *behavioral* nature of forgiveness also puts it squarely outside the bounds of depth psychological study.[5] These reasons support the claim that the notion of forgiveness is unpsychological, i.e., forgiveness does not belong to psychology.

but took it at face value as a "given" so to speak. See James Hillman, *Senex and Puer: Uniform Edition of the Writings of James Hillman, Vol. 3*, 1st edn (Putnam, CT: Spring Publications, 2005).

3   C. G. Jung, "The Transcendent Function," in *The Collected Works of C. G. Jung, Vol. 8*, translated by R. F. C. Hull. 2nd edn (Princeton, NJ: Princeton University Press, 1981), 67–91. Original work published in 1916.

4   James Hillman, "The Yellowing of the Work," in *Alchemical Psychology: Uniform Edition, Vol. 5*, 1st edn (Putnam, CT: Spring Publications, 2010), 204–230.

5   L. Horwitz, "The Capacity to Forgive: Intrapsychic and Developmental Perspectives," *Journal of the American Psychoanalytic Association* 52, no. 3 (2005), 485–511. http://www.ncbi.nlm.nih.gov/pubmed/16045162.

Indeed, how could forgiveness, which in its very *definition* would require a per-petrating "other" as its object, have a genuine place in psychology proper, at the objective level of consciousness that knows no betraying other, but only itself? For psychology, the soul is uroboric, its logical life existing as *self*-expression, *self*-representation, *self*-portrayal.[6] In psychology, there *is* no external other. As Giegerich observes:

> Anger, fury, the wish for revenge or compensation, etc. are unpsychological, namely (if I may say so) "sociological." These emotions establish and uphold the fantasy of the externality of *interpersonal* transactions between people (or between "life/fate/God" and me). But there is no "between" between me and my pain. It is utterly mine or rather me. *I* hurt. Where the pain or wound came from is psychologically absolutely irrelevant. What was done to me by others I have to psychically make my very own, part of my self ... , and without grudge or resentment at that. [Footnote: "This is also why forgiving is psychologically so important. It is not only morally or religiously important. It also helps me to be freed from the constraints of my complex."] I have to embrace it as my very own pain, injury, or loss and these as my new inalienable reality. No otherness. This is the only way I can become free again. Otherwise I will stay caught in the resentment against what happened to me, that is, caught in a *complex*. The flow of life will then be arrested, get stuck (in this area). I have to learn to live with my wounds and deficiencies, to integrate them into my self-definition.[7]

Giegerich deems retributive emotions as "unpsychological" because they are based in a perspective that insists on the "fantasy of the externality of *interpersonal* trans-actions" in lieu of the *psychological* truth that there really is no *literal* other present in the psyche. Psychologically, the "other" exists as self-generated *self-representation*. The wish for revenge exists as an un-psychological projection of one's *own* pain.

Giegerich's footnote highlights forgiving as helpful not only for moral or religious (unpsychological) reasons, but for the psychological benefit of freedom from the constraints imposed by neurotic complexes. Psychological forgiveness would here mean the *recognition of the fundamental nature of psyche as self-relation*, thus "freeing" oneself from the domination and enslavement by a perpetrating other. When the "flow of life" is arrested or stuck, we find ourselves "caught in a *complex*," trapped in a *neurotic* perspective in which the offense is inflated and granted "special" status above other events, "plucked" so to speak out of the normal flow of life and time.

It is crucial here to read Giegerich's comments as strictly *descriptive* as opposed to *prescriptive*; it is not that one *should* embrace pain and suffering as one's own, or that one *should* forgive. Acceptance and forgiveness are rather a condition of psychological freedom. To read Giegerich prescriptively (whether he intends it or not) has us fall

---

6 Wolfgang Giegerich, *What Is Soul?* (New Orleans, LA: Spring Journal, Inc., 2012), 44.
7 Giegerich, *What is Soul?*, 246–247.

into the trap of the "psychic" or ego realm, where forgiving takes on a "project" nature and reifies the semantic level (i.e. maintains a focus on personal wounds inflicted by an external other, be it another person, life, fate, or God). To prescribe forgiving is ineffective at any rate, as the subjective ego cannot *accomplish* true forgiving.[8] No one doubts the ego can certainly *encounter* forgiving and forgiveness, but the event serves only as an *indicator* of a transformation of consciousness at the objective or logical level. Psychological forgiveness, we could say, is accomplished only at the level of the objective psyche or soul. Giegerich's "version" of forgiving, if read *prescriptively*, is itself "unpsychological" and accurately relegated to the status of a footnote.[9]

We are confronted here with the underlying *logical* problem of forgiveness as a psychological phenomenon. The very notion of forgiveness is characterized by a yawning chasm between two selves, the victim and the offender, I and Thou.[10] Forgiveness' inherent stipulation of an offending other (without whom there would be no-one and nothing to forgive) exposes it as a feature of modernity,[11] an indicator that "the logic of otherness rules."[12] As Giegerich has described,[13] modern consciousness, having emerged from a relatively blissful and innocent sense of embeddedness in and containment by the world in former times, now experiences itself as alienated from the natural world. It strives desperately for meaning and a sense of belonging, encountering people and the world as no longer part of itself but as wholly "other." He writes:

8   From Hillman, "We must be quite clear that forgiveness is no easy matter. If the ego has been wronged, the ego cannot forgive just because it 'should,' notwithstanding the wider context of love and destiny. The ego is kept vital by its *amour-propre*, its pride and honor. Even where one wants to forgive, one finds one simply can't, because forgiveness doesn't come from the ego." James Hillman, *Senex and Puer*, 209.

9   It is interesting to note that for Giegerich, forgiveness as a humanistic concept posits a "not-yet-ness" insofar as one's salvation or freedom exists in the future dependent upon its achievement. Of such forgiveness, he writes, "What is in its sites is correction, development, the substitution of one 'wrong' behavior for another 'mature' one; for example: Where there was resentment, there love and kindness shall be." Wolfgang Giegerich, *The Neurosis of Psychology (Collected English Papers, Vol. I)* (New Orleans, LA: Spring Journal, Inc., 2005), 109. Here Giegerich criticizes the use of forgiveness as a tool for self-improvement or betterment of sorts.

10   Though rarely is the perpetrator imagined as a "Thou" but instead reduced to an object, an "it."

11   The notion of personal forgiveness was not practiced in early Western culture and only introduced with Christianity. In Greek and Roman antiquity, the act of "forgiveness" typically referred to the king's prerogative to pardon captured soldiers for political reasons. In early Judaism, forgiveness was reserved for one's relationship with Yahweh, and forgiveness offered to others was mediated by that relationship. See C. L. Griswold and D. Konstan (eds.), *Ancient Forgiveness: Classical, Judaic, and Christian* (Cambridge: Cambridge University Press, 2012).

12   Giegerich, *What Is Soul?*, 246.

13   Wolfgang Giegerich, "The End of Meaning and the Birth of Man: An Essay about the State Reached in the History of Consciousness and an Analysis of C. G. Jung's Psychology Project," in *The Soul Always Thinks (Collected English Papers, Vol. IV)* (New Orleans, LA: Spring Journal, Inc., 2010), 235–236.

122   Jennifer M. Sandoval

In modernity, especially since Feuerbach, the otherness of the Other has become irreducible. I and Thou (just think of Martin Buber or Emmanuel Levinas) stand vis-à-vis each other in mediation-less opposition. In the human sphere, this opposition shows concretely ... in the unbridgeable difference between guilty perpetrator and innocent victim. "Victimization" and the corresponding notion of "traumatization" is a *logical* problem, an index of the fact that otherness rules, and thus clearly a problem and distinguishing mark of modernity.[14]

Forgiveness, in requiring the condition of otherness for its very existence, is a testament to and a symptom of this problem, *posing* as its solution. Forgiveness would seek to bridge the chasm that it itself posited, but it is itself evidence of mankind's modern condition of *otherness*. In its perpetual attempt to cross the (uncrossable) chasm between victim and perpetrator, the promise of forgiveness only serves to reinforce the divide on the semantic and horizontally spatial level of the *psychic*, utterly unable to approach the vertical dimension of the uroboric, self-referential *psychological*. The hope of forgiveness inadvertently and retroactively instantiates a concretized *psychological difference* in the form of "unbridgeable difference between innocent victim and guilty perpetrator." This unbridgeable perpetrator-victim dynamic is the "concrete" or "acted out" manifestation of the psychological reality of modern consciousness. To grasp this is to comprehend and accept the *logical necessity* of the modern construct of the "unbridgeable difference between guilty perpetrator and innocent victim" in the practical sphere as the mere *acting out* of the soul's logic (otherness of the Other)—and therefore no *human* need (or ability) to resist or obliterate the construct.[15]

Giegerich's characterization of the relation in modernity between perpetrator and victim as "unbridgeable" acknowledges the inherent contradiction of attempted reconciliation between the two. The perspective which gives rise to "otherness" is the *same* perspective which gives rise to the ego; from this side, there *is* no bridge to the other.[16] Neither is there a larger notion of soul, nor thus of the

14 Giegerich, *What Is Soul?*, 282.
15 A campaign to "Make Love, Not War," for example, that fails to recognize the inherent character of modern war as an "acting out" of the prevailing logic of the soul (or more accurately, the *neurotic* soul) would likely be an ineffective campaign. While, as already noted, with Freud, Jung lamented, "'*Homo homini lupus*' [man is to man a wolf] is a sad, yet eternal truism," the recognition of its source as an "acting out" of the modern problem of otherness at the level of soul is Giegerich's. While wars are a feature of humanity throughout history, in pre-modern culture it is safe to assume that instinctive "eye for an eye" retributive justice (or worse) was the rule, in contrast to the neurotic perpetrator/victimization dynamic ubiquitous in modernity.
16 Giegerich also writes,

What in this description sounds totally negative and is also experienced negatively, namely as painful alienation and soul-lessness, from a soul point of view, however, has to be conceived as a step forward in the history of the soul. It means that man has become born man and come of age. He is no longer contained in the womb of Mother Nature as her child. Psychologically, he now has to live all on his own account, and with a metaphor of Jung's, has to sew his garment himself (cf. *CW* 9i,

psychological difference. Here forgiveness is trapped in the psychic realm where its inherent *dialectical* aspect is misrecognized as mere paradox.

The contradiction of forgiveness

In her important essay, "Wiping the Slate Clean: The Heart of Forgiveness," philosopher Lucy Allais points out the most obvious contradiction of forgiveness:

> The first difficulty is simply to *make sense* of what is involved in ceasing to hold an action against someone while continuing to regard it as wrong and as attributed to the perpetrator in the way which is necessary for there to be something to forgive. Forgiving seems to mean ceasing to blame, but if blaming means holding the perpetrator responsible, then forgiveness requires *not* ceasing to blame, or else there will be nothing to forgive.[17]

This contradiction lies at the heart of forgiveness. For in saying, "I forgive you for betraying me," one is at once reifying the offense of betrayal while intending it "wiped clean" through the act of forgiveness.[18] This contradiction renders forgiving devoid of logic, i.e., "impossible" to the rational mind, effectively sawing off the very branch it rests upon.[19] The concept of forgiveness is not *rational* at the ordinary, everyday level of discourse or thought, on which level it is logically impossible—a fact which generally fails to discourage the inflated ego from thinking it *can* forgive (or vice versa, withhold forgiving).

Jacques Derrida further describes the typical notion of forgiveness and contrasts it with what he calls "pure" or "true" forgiveness. He writes:

> § 27) on his own responsibility and risk. The mythic garments that preciously had always already been provided for him with unquestionable authority have dropped from him like a snake's old shed skin. Nature and the world have become obsolete (of course only psychologically, not pragmatically). The soul has overcome the world and thus come home to itself.
>
> (Giegerich, *What Is Soul?*, 285)

17 Lucy Allais, "Wiping the Slate Clean: The Heart of Forgiveness," *Philosophy & Public Affairs* 36, no. 1 (January 2008), 33–68, doi:10.1111/j.1088-4963.2008.00123.x, 32.
18 In addition, the offending act is often inextricably bound to the other such that their identity takes on the status of "offender"—or in our case, "traitor."
19 Allais' way of "making sense" of the contradiction is to separate the doer from the deed (or avoid the tendency to "collapse" the offense with the offender), recognizing the inevitable fallibility of human beings.

> Without changing our beliefs in the culpability and wrongness of another's actions, we can come to have an attitude towards her that sees her as better than her wrong actions indicate her to be, and thus can move forward in a relationship that is not bound by past wrongdoing.
>
> (Allais, "Wiping the Slate Clean," 68)

In my view this tactic avoids the contradiction inherent in forgiveness, thus not acknowledging its *logical impossibility* in the ego realm.

> I shall risk this proposition: each time forgiveness is at the service of a finality, be it noble or spiritual ([such as] atonement or redemption, reconciliation, [or] salvation), each time that it aims to re-establish a normality ... then the "forgiveness" is not pure—nor is its concept.[20]

Derrida criticizes the ego's exploitation of forgiveness for its own purposes, including even the "noble" aim of reconciliation. Derrida is critical of the application of forgiveness to accomplish particular ends, for in the effort to correct, reconcile, repair, normalize—in fact, in the attempt to achieve any aim whatsoever— forgiveness is hijacked by the ego and cannot be considered "pure" or psychological.[21]

Derrida continues, "Forgiveness is not, it *should not be*, normal, normative, normalising. It should remain exceptional and extraordinary, in the face of the impossible: as if it interrupted the ordinary course of temporality."[22] One might imagine that Derrida is here describing forgiveness' logical truth as an interiorized soul movement. In the context of the psychological difference, we could even say the characterization as "exceptional," "extraordinary," "in the face of the impossible," and rupturing "the ordinary course of temporality" is a vivid phenomenal portrayal of the absolutely negative *soul* aspect of virtually *any* phenomenon when held up against its unreflected, semantic instantiation. For Derrida, "pure and unconditional forgiveness, in order to have its own meaning, must have no 'meaning', no finality, even no intelligibility. It is a madness of the impossible."[23] In negating the meaning, usefulness and intelligibility of forgiveness, Derrida thinkingly articulates forgiveness' own internal logic, allowing it to come home to itself as a rupturing, syntactic phenomenon, operative on the vertical level of soul. Such forgiveness is indeed exceptional, a "miracle." After all, Derrida asks, "What would be a forgiveness that forgave only the forgivable?"[24]

Derrida asserts the "impossibility" of forgiveness, noting its emergence only in the face of the unforgivable. If the contradiction inherent in forgiveness is *acknowledged and confronted* (rather than avoided or ignored), we are deposited up against solid rock, so to speak, with no way out—in the same spot Giegerich characterizes as a way *in*, an entrance into the soul's interiority. If we can "hold our place in the absolute contradiction of dead end and continued faithfulness to our

---

20 Derrida, *On Cosmopolitanism and Forgiveness*, 31–32.
21 The ego's appropriation of forgiveness to dominate the other or to display moral superiority has been noted by Kenneth Wapnick in *Love Does Not Condemn: The World, the Flesh, and the Devil according to Platonism, Christianity, Gnosticism, and "A Course in Miracles"* (Roscoe, NY: Foundation for a Course in Miracles, 1989) and *Forgiveness and Jesus* (Roscoe, NY: Foundation for a Course in Miracles, 1998) and others. For Derrida, pure forgiveness would make no use of power. "What I dream of," he writes, "what I try to think as the 'purity' of a forgiveness worthy of its name, would be a forgiveness without power: unconditional but without sovereignty" (*On Cosmopolitanism and Forgiveness*, 59).
22 Derrida, *On Cosmopolitanism and Forgiveness*, 31–32.
23 Derrida, *On Cosmopolitanism and Forgiveness*, 45.
24 Derrida, *On Cosmopolitanism and Forgiveness*, 36.

purpose...the experienced stone wall interiorizes our progressive movement into itself so that it becomes an in itself recursive progression."[25] Here the apparent impasse of forgiveness may become instead a place of passing from the semantic level—where forgiveness posits external, literal wounding, the perpetrator/victim dynamic, and the irreducible otherness of the other—into the sphere of logical negativity, or the exceptional, extraordinary, *impossible* realm of the soul.

Neurotic forgiveness

A standard dictionary definition of "forgive" reads simply, to "absolve or to acquit, pardon, release."[26] In particular, the abstract notions of *absolution* and *release* inherent in this definition of forgiveness are essential properties of *absolute negative-interiorization*, or the dialectical act of negation which opens up the space of logical negativity, or soul.[27] However, it is common for psychologists and others to re-define forgiveness to meet practical and/or social demands. For example, a prominent psychologist in the field of forgiveness studies, Robert Enright, dramatically revises the dictionary definition to the following:

> Forgiveness is the willingness to abandon one's right to resentment, negative judgment, and indifferent behavior toward one who unjustly injured us, while fostering the undeserved qualities of compassion, generosity and even love toward him or her.[28]

Forgiveness re-defined in this way allows the forgiver to avoid the absolution demanded by pure forgiveness, opting instead for a simple (or undialectical) negation: one's "right to resentment" is merely suspended, the love remains "undeserved," and a literal offense is explicitly posited and reified (in contrast to the abstract definition in which any offense remains implicit). This definition stays on the *psychic* side of the psychological difference; the semantics are negated, but the syntax or logic that gives rise to the victim/perpetrator dynamic is not left behind (i.e., it is similar to merely rearranging the deck chairs on the Titanic).

Such a limited definition is also *neurotic*, as it relates to the injury as externally caused and unjustified. Giegerich notes, "A neurotic way of erecting and celebrating...one's absolute invulnerability and unwoundedness is by blaming others for one's wounds."[29] As we recall, psychologically, wounds are exclusively one's

25 Giegerich,*Soul Always Thinks*, 172.
26 Forgive, *Roget's II: The New Thesaurus* (Cleveland, Ohio: Wiley Publishing, 2010).
27 *Absolution* and *release* also correspond to alchemical processes which attempted to free the Mercurial spirit from matter (i.e., *putrefactio, mundificatio, solutio*).
28 Robert Enright & The Human Development Study Group. "The Moral Development of Forgiveness," *Handbook of Moral Behavior and Development*, edited by W. Kurtines and J. Gewirtz (Hillsdale, NJ: Erlbaum, 1991), 123.
29 Wolfgang Giegerich, *Neurosis: The Logic of a Metaphysical Illness* (New Orleans, LA: Spring Journal, Inc., 2013), 387.

own, "they are not caused, there is no cause. Any cause is outside the range of [one's] psychological sphere."[30] In maintaining the offender as its object, forgiveness singles out and traps the offense out of the flow of time like a fly frozen in amber. This is precisely what happens with neurosis. Giegerich writes:

> Neurosis begins when a disruption takes place. The stream of events is stopped, the flow of time is arrested. How does this happen? The one disappointing event or condition is singled out, wrenched from, and protected against, the natural process that ultimately would inevitably end in forgetfulness, and is raised to ultimate importance. The one event is frozen, fixated and thereby made to last. It is held on to beyond its time.[31]

A definition of forgiveness that smuggles in the right "to resentment, negative judgment and indifferent behavior" and characterizes qualities of compassion, generosity, and love as "undeserved" unwittingly protects and prevents the offender (and offense) from undergoing the naturally occurring alchemical (psychological) process of time itself. We could even say the neurotic soul, or that element of consciousness which stubbornly insists upon its own untruth, strategically *utilizes* psychic forgiveness to avoid undergoing the process of *actual* forgiveness. Returning to the original abstract definition of forgiveness, we can see that to truly forgive would require not a mere *simple* negation of the offense in question, but its *absolute* negation; only then would the offending event be *absolved* of its semantic content and *released* back into the flow of time, thereby exposing it to the natural process resulting in "forgetfulness."[32] The limited form of forgiveness described above would seem preferable to the neurotic soul, which by definition stubbornly denies the osmotic character of time and insists upon a positive semantic presence in defiance of the soul's absolutely negative *modern* reality as pure subjectivity, or consciousness.[33] Real forgiveness would be unthinkable to the neurotic soul precisely because it would absolve or emancipate it from its identity with The Absolute.[34] By withholding *true* forgiveness, the neurotic soul stubbornly prevents the offense from allowing it to come home to itself as absolute negativity, as truth. Instead, the offense remains categorically characterized as "that which shall not be!"[35]—"frozen, fixated, and made to last."

30 Giegerich, *Neurosis*, 280.
31 Giegerich, *Neurosis*, 280.
32 "Forgetfulness" here does not mean the event is obliterated. The event occurred (as all historical events do) and is recognized as historically necessary; it is therefore *logically* remembered. However its *semantic reality* no longer invades and violates the present moment and is thus phenomenologically experienced as "forgotten."
33 For Giegerich, a neurosis has no redeeming qualities for the person who suffers it. At the objective level, however, neuroses are seen to be the soul's way of making what had been unconscious *explicitly conscious* through the painful "working off" of earlier fragments or statuses of consciousness. See Chapter 4 in Giegerich, *What is Soul?*
34 Giegerich defines neurosis as a "metaphysical illness" in which the neurotic unconsciously insists on attempting to simulate the lost experience of the Absolute (or God) via the neurotic symptom. See Giegerich, *Neurosis*.
35 Giegerich, *Neurosis*, 280.

Psychological forgiveness

In the New Testament, where forgiving is first referenced historically in earnest,[36] forgiveness has two distinct meanings. The first shows itself when Jesus says, "Forgive, and you will be forgiven."[37] The Greek word used is "ἀπολύετε" (transliteration = *apolyete*) meaning to "release" or "set free,"[38] which is consistent with the dictionary definition. The use of forgiveness here is astonishingly psychological in that it negates the semantic reality not merely of the sin in question, but of *otherness itself*, instead affirming the uroboric nature of relating to another as one's *own* other. "Forgive, and you will be forgiven"—if understood as an *observation* as opposed to a dictate—is consistent with the psychological reality of *comprehensive* subjectivity in which "consciousness has its own otherness no longer out there in some Other, but in itself as its own ontological self-contradictoriness: integrated into its very Being, into its Concept."[39] This form of forgiveness explicitly overcomes the neurotic form of forgiving which posits and directs itself toward an external other. Jesus' forgiveness liberates consciousness from bondage to the irreducible logic of Otherness, acted out in the form of the "unbridgeable difference between guilty perpetrator and innocent victim" on the semantic level.

In Jesus' prayer on the cross, "Father, forgive them, for they know not what they do," forgiveness holds a distinctly *different* meaning than the first ("release" or "set free"). Here the Greek word used is ἄφες (transliteration *aphes*), meaning "to allow," "to permit," "to let be," "to suffer".[40] In Christ's petition, "Father, forgive them," we hear the extraordinary entreaty to God to *allow* the event of the crucifixion—God's own death.[41] Christ's injunction to "forgive" the crucifixion can be seen psychologically as a plea from the soul *to itself* to "suffer" this event, "to permit" its own absolute negative interiorization, allowing it to go under into itself, dissolving into "spirit". Forgiveness can be seen here as supporting the movement of the soul's emancipation from itself as substance and its return to itself in truth as

---

36 In ancient Greek culture, the concept functioned primarily as a political tool of rulers in wartime to demonstrate power by granting clemency (or not) to prisoners of war. In early Judaic culture, the notion of forgiveness greatly expanded and was a primary element conditioning one's spiritual relationship with G-d – and was only relevant within that context. Not until Christianity was forgiveness generally construed as relevant to interpersonal relations.

37 Luke 6:37.

38 http://www.biblos.com/luke/6-37.htm

39 Wolfgang Giegerich, *The Soul's Logical Life*, 4 Revised (Peter Lang GmbH, 2007), 106.

40 http://biblesuite.com/greek/863.htm

41 That the object of forgiveness is "them" may foreshadow the imminent *sublation* of the substantial figure of the transcendent God in Jesus into the transubstantiated form of the Holy Spirit, which exists only *as* the virtual presupposition of the activity of finite individuals, in other words, the actions of men, i.e., "them." See Slavoj Žižek and John Milbank, *The Monstrosity of Christ: Paradox or Dialectic?*, ed. Creston Davis, reprint edn (Cambridge, MA: The MIT Press, 2011), 61.

Spirit.[42] Giegerich writes, "The dying on the Cross IS the absolute *kenosis*, the going under, the resistanceless bowing down under evil, and this IS nothing else but a spelling out of what Love is. And it is *in itself* and *as such* absolute forgiveness."[43]

The combination of "releasing" and "allowing" as seen in the New Testament reflects the important dialectical notion of *sublation*. According to Hegel,

> To sublate [*aufheben*] has a twofold meaning in the language: on the one hand it means to preserve, to maintain, and equally it also means to cause to cease, to put an end to ... Thus, what is sublated is at the same time preserved; it has only lost its immediacy but is not on that account annihilated.[44]

For Hegel, Jesus' death on the cross resulted in God's ultimate "sublation" in the Holy Spirit (this includes sublation of both God's human *and* transcendent form). Sublation, however, is "not directly the sublation of otherness, its return into the same, its recuperation by the One."[45] This is evident in Jesus' observation "Forgive and you shall be forgiven," where forgiving yield's not merely a self-same reflexive act, but rather accomplishes an *advance* in consciousness in which a prior state has been overcome or sublated.[46]

With sublation, the dialectical process provides a crucial alternative manner of "holding" reality that reaches beyond other modes, such as denying, forgetting, recalling, or retaining. Where neurotic forgiveness stops short with an undialectical negation, positing the semantic offense as imminent empirical fact, psychological forgiveness recognizes the new logical status of the offense and the logic that gave rise to it as *sublated*, no longer explicit or immediate. It is "released" from immediacy and also "permitted" its existence insofar as it is "not annihilated." In this way forgiveness maintains the psychological difference, engendering a perspective in which the "sin" is seen in a way that is different truly in itself, "that as one and the same is at the same time posited and negated."[47]

---

42 However, not spirit as pre-existing "substance." According to Žižek, Hegel's Spirit

> is a virtual entity [that] exists only insofar as subjects act as if it exists....it is the sub-
> stance of the individuals *who recognize themselves in it*, the ground of their entire exis-
> tence... [T]he only thing that really exists are these individuals and their activity, so this
> substance is actual only insofar as individuals believe in it and act accordingly.
>   (Slavoj Žižek and Boris Gunjević, *God in Pain: Inversions of Apocalypse*, trans.
>   Ellen Elias-Bursac (New York, NY: Seven Stories Press, 2012), 171)

43 Wolfgang Giegerich, "God Must Not Die!" in *Spring 84 A Journal of Archetype and Culture: God Must Not Die! (Or Must He?): Jung and Christianity* (New Orleans, LA: Spring Journal, Inc., 2010), 49.
44 Georg Wilhelm Friedrich Hegel, *Hegel's Science of Logic*, later printing edn (Amherst, NY: Prometheus Books, 1991), 107.
45 Žižek and Gunjević, *God in Pain*, 172.
46 Otherwise one would merely say, "Forgive, and you will be forgiving."
47 Giegerich, *What Is Soul?*, 81.

Here I am not attempting to re-define forgiveness as dialectical or psychological; Jesus' use of forgiveness already *is* dialectical or psychological and illustrates its non-ego or objective form. The sharply restricted form of forgiveness found in modern ego discourse is a neurotic re-definition that deprives forgiveness of its psychological character. To better understand the underlying *logic* of the unrestricted form of forgiveness discussed above, let us utilize the dialectical methodology afforded by psychology as the discipline of interiority,[48] through which we can methodologically think forgiveness forward, negatively interiorizing and fully releasing forgiveness into its truth as a psychological notion.

Interiorizing forgiveness into itself

As we have seen, forgiveness' primary problems emerge as a contradictory positing of the literal offense and the victim/perpetrator dynamic. Our *prima materia* is just this un-psychological nature of forgiveness: its assertion of semantic reality and otherness. And it is this error *itself* that opens up the space to overcome the error.[49] Consistent with the notion of interiorization, "the dialectic proceeds via the self-application of the notion or category that happens to be at stake in each case,"[50] in this case the notion of forgiveness. For to merely apply the notion, forgiveness, to an object (the sin or sinner), we have seen thus far results in only a simple negation, an "acting out" of the concept insofar as an "attempt" to forgive is undertaken. "But [the concept] must also be *er-innert* [interiorized], come home to itself. Physician, heal thyself, take your own medicine. The concept must not remain aloof, itself exempt from and above the sphere of its jurisdiction."[51]

Applying forgiveness to itself—i.e., "forgiving" the notion of forgiveness—would entail both (1) *releasing* the notion from itself, "letting go" of the very construct of otherness, such that the logic that posited the sin and its perpetrator/victim dynamic is itself released, absolved from its intentionality and semantic meaning *and* (2) permitting, allowing, and suffering the construct of otherness and the event arising from it to *exist* in its true or sublated form. The dialectic reveals forgiveness as a fundamentally psychological process which absolutely negates what the soul itself posited, what it itself produced, opening the way to a psychological perspective by methodologically "forgetting" the semantic content of the "sin", thus making possible a structural or syntactical perspective. In this way, forgiveness *transgresses* the psychological difference not horizontally—through a mere simple

48 The dialectical process explicitly reveals soul as the process of reflection *into itself*, thus continually revealing itself as the infinite "bottomlessness of its own ever-negated base, absolute negativity, 'the soul'," in Wolfgang Giegerich, David Miller, and Greg Mogenson, *Dialectics and Analytical Psychology: The El Capitan Canyon Seminar* (New Orleans, LA: Spring Journal, Inc., 2005), 103.

49 Slavoj Žižek, *Less Than Nothing: Hegel and the Shadow of Dialectical Materialism* (London; Brooklyn, NY: Verso Books, 2012).

50 Giegerich, *Dialectics and Analytical Psychology*, 17.

51 Giegerich, *Dialectics and Analytical Psychology*, 17.

negation of the offense—but *vertically*, by leaving behind the logic giving rise to the very concept of otherness ("innocent victim and guilty perpetrator") and revealing a consciousness that recognizes itself *as* and *in* itself *both* victim *and* sinner *and* their difference at once. "The other becomes psychological only when it ceases to have the form of 'other' and is recognized as having the form of self."[52] The recognition of consciousness existing as this contradiction is equivalent to the state of "forgiveness" in which the logic of otherness has been overcome.

Forgiveness is astonishing because it is an inherently dialectical negating process that both *presupposes the fundamental unpsychological errors of semantic reality and otherness* AND *exists as the process of overcoming them*. The paradox of forgiveness "destroys its own premises within itself…. It implies a sublimation or *sublation* of the logical form or status in which the message first occurred."[53] While true forgiveness lives at the level of thought or logos, at the same time, forgiveness has no meaning on that level because there is literally nothing to forgive, no substantiality or content to be attacked or threatened. At the *objective* level of consciousness, there is no "perpetrating other" nor semantic offense in the sphere of absolute negativity, therefore nothing for "the soul" to forgive, other than itself. Forgiveness is utilized by, yet irrelevant to, soul and renders itself obsolete upon reaching its goal.

The logic of love

"In the negation of the negation," Slavoj Žižek explains, "the subject includes itself in the process, taking into account how the process it is observing affects its own position." He writes, "[The] properly Hegelian 'negation of negation' … resides in the decisive shift from the *distortion of a notion* to *a distortion constitutive of this notion*, that is, to this notion as a distortion-in-itself."[54] Similar to an alchemical death through yellowing, "the vessel itself is drawn into the process…. The vessel, too, is subjected to the corruption."[55] True forgiveness includes not merely the object, the offense, but the subject, the "vessel itself." In other words, where true or absolute forgiveness is concerned, the posited error or "sin" undergoes a radical translocation from the object to the subject—it is not *what* or *who* I am seeing that is the problem, but *my* seeing *per se. And* the problem I see is *necessary to exist* so that I may *see* that I am the problem; "for only what is explicit for consciousness can also be explicitly overcome."[56] The negation of the negation involves a shift in methodological approach from *seeking* to *seeing*. True forgiveness allows the corrupted vessel to be infused with and penetrated by the shadow element or "sin" it had been protecting itself against. A fully integrated consciousness would then

---

52 Wolfgang Giegerich, *Soul Violence (Collected English Papers, Vol. III)* (New Orleans, LA: Spring Journal, Inc., 2008), 106.
53 Giegerich, *The Soul's Logical Life*, 261.
54 Žižek, *Less Than Nothing*, 298.
55 Žižek, *Less Than Nothing*, 194.
56 Giegerich, *Neurosis*, 351.

recognize the self-contradiction it exists *as*—or the unity of its unity and (former) difference.[57]

On a human level, to forgive would mean to "reach the truth in its own conceptual element"[58]—in other words, to cross the "unbridgeable difference" from horizontal to vertical logic, from semantics to syntax. The seeming "impossibility" of forgiveness lies in its ability to span this infinite divide. Žižek writes:

> [T]he transubstantiation of the subject from a "concrete" self immersed in its life world into the subject of pure thought [requires undergoing]…a process of "abstraction" which has to be accomplished in the individual's "concrete" experience, and which as such involves the supreme pain of renunciation.[59]

On a human level, forgiveness can be likened to the alchemical acid bath of "silvering" and "yellowing"[60] as Hillman describes, the excruciating purification process of *mundificatio* as depicted in the *Rosarium Philosophorum* woodcuts, or the Judaic notion of *Teshuvah*, in which one dies to oneself and is reborn a "new person."[61] All such processes entail the releasing of one's archetypal "mythical garments," letting go of being identical with the "God-man in the shape of a servant,"[62] suffering the substantial absence of The Absolute, permitting the reality that "'I am *only* that!', neither servant-shape, nor God-man."[63]

True forgiveness functions as a dialectical logic as it relates to and overcomes injustice, the wrongs of the world, and even evil itself. One does not overcome these antagonisms, Giegerich writes,

> by powerful conquest and subjugation, not by rejection and condemnation, but conversely by, with resistanceless sufferance, allowing them to *be*, indeed, even embracing them, and *ipso facto* unrelentingly exposing oneself to them, letting them permeate oneself … [T]his is first of all a concept, an insight, a

---

57 This process is beautifully laid out in Giegerich's essay, "First Shadow, Then Anima" in *Soul Violence*, 77–109, and faithfully documents, as it were, the soul's journey of forgiveness.

58 Žižek, *Less Than Nothing*, 111.

59 Žižek, *Less Than Nothing*, 111.

60 Giegerich writes,

> A real death through yellowing and a yellowing that "applies to psychology itself" would…refer to that process through which, in alchemical imagery, the vessel itself is drawn into the process; it can no longer preserve its intactness as container vis-à-vis the prima material and the corrupting process that the matter undergoes. The vessel, too, is subjected to the corruption.
>
> (Giegerich, *The Soul's Logical Life*, 194)

61 Sandoval, "Forgiveness and the Soul."

62 Giegerich, *Neurosis*, 344.

63 Giegerich, *Neurosis*, 344.

truth on a very deep and remote soul level. It is a *logic* to be comprehended, not a maxim to be acted out. It is the logic of Love.[64]

The "logic of Love" here shares the dialectical logic of forgiveness; a "going under," a "resistanceless bowing down under evil"—this is "*in itself* and *as such* absolute forgiveness."[65] Reflected on the psychic level, such Love takes on an unconditioned, radical, and even "impossible" form.[66] While Love, as the soul's direct knowing of itself, is not in need of forgiveness, the precondition of Love *is* forgiveness as that very bridge that spans the unbridgeable difference between guilty perpetrator and innocent victim, between semantics and syntax, between I and Thou.[67]

Conclusion

In the consulting room, forgiveness may appear as a worthy project taken on by patients and encouraged by therapists for numerous reasons. As discussed above, however, when forgiveness is *intentionally* undertaken, it becomes an ego scheme. From a phenomenological perspective, while true forgiveness by definition overcomes otherness, it does so on a *logical* level; forgiving does not necessarily "fix," "repair," or reconcile the relationship to its former status on a semantic level. From Žižek we read:

> [When] Hegel introduces the notion of reconciliation as the way to resolve the deadlock of the Beautiful Soul, his term designates the acceptance of the chaos and injustice of the world as immanent to the Beautiful Soul which deplores it, the Beautiful Soul's acceptance of the fact that it participates in the reality it criticizes and judges, not any kind of magical transformation of this reality.[68]

While forgiveness *is* a transformation of *consciousness*, nothing actually *happens*, it is not an "experience"; "The change from one stage or logical status of consciousness is something very real…but it cannot be an experience inasmuch as it is something syntactical and not something semantic, something psychological and not something psychic."[69] We must remember that forgiveness is the recognition of "a concept, an insight, a truth on a very deep and remote soul level." Forgiveness

---

64 Giegerich, "God Must Not Die!," 43–44.
65 Giegerich, *Spring # 84 A Journal of Archetype and Culture*, 49.
66 As reflected in the seemingly monumentally impossible entreaty, "Love your enemies."
67 Insofar as it exercises the dialectical logic of absolute negation and sublation, insofar as it transgresses the psychological difference to "reach the truth in its own conceptual element" or absolute negativity, Psychology as the Discipline of Interiority is fundamentally a psychology of forgiveness.
68 Žižek, *Less Than Nothing*, 478.
69 Giegerich, "God Must Not Die!," 54.

would make way for that which remains when the soul is absolved from empirical semantic reality, released into its truth as absolute negativity, as pure consciousness; forgiveness thereby makes possible the soul's direct knowing of itself as Love.[70] True forgiveness is thus the *recognition of a conceptual truth*, a logical shift in perspective, however profound.

Forgiveness in the way described here applies to psychology at large—it is meant to describe the activity of the soul toward itself—and the human person actively involved would be the psychologist (or anyone thinking psychologically) insofar as the soul achieves its actuality in human consciousness. And, when a person finds herself freed from a neurosis, she may find she has forgiven (and been forgiven). In this, we might say, the soul which produces a neurosis forgives *itself* for the very neurosis it creates.

---

70 The relentless interiorization of the positivity of the semantic level that occurs through the process of absolute negation would reveal this underlying logic, i.e., "the soul" would "probably…become apparent as being Love (with a capital L)… [I]nfinite Love as objectively existing Concept (the self-comprehension of the mind), Love as absolute logical negativity, fluidity, interiority, Love as 'self,' inner infinity…" Giegerich, "The Movement of the Soul," in *Soul Always Thinks*, 323.

9

REFLECTIONS ON A CASE STUDY OF NEUROSIS

Daniel M. Anderson

Introduction

In this essay, I examine a case of a neurosis, originally analyzed by Gerhard Adler in his 1961 book, *The Living Symbol: A Case Study in Individuation*.[1] This essay re-interprets certain neurotic symptoms and fantasy material that Adler presented in light of Wolfgang Giegerich's theory of neurosis set forth in his 2013 book, *Neurosis: The Logic of a Metaphysical Illness*.[2] Adler's *Living Symbol* is one of the few book–length treatments in English of a single case from a traditional Jungian perspective. Adler published the material because it "showed so clearly—indeed so beautifully—the stages of the individuation process which C. G. Jung has described in his writings."[3] He analyzes 190 separate dreams and active imaginations. In this short essay I cannot hope to retrace Adler's steps. Rather, I examine parts of Adler's case in order to demonstrate differences between his traditional Jungian approach to the clinical material and an approach informed by Giegerich's psychology and theory of neurosis. I suggest how clinical material might be seen through the lens of Giegerich's *theory*.[4] I focus on the patient's neurotic symptom, which Adler characterizes as claustrophobia. In order to unpack the character of the neurotic symptom I also will examine an active imagination that proved to be a turning point in the analysis.[5]

---

1   Gerhard Adler, *The Living Symbol: A Case Study in the Process of Individuation* (New York, NY: Pantheon Books/Bollingen, 1961).
2   Wolfgang Giegerich, *Neurosis: The Logic of a Metaphysical Illness* (New Orleans, LA: Spring Journal, Inc., 2013).
3   Adler, *The Living Symbol*, 3.
4   What I cannot say is how a flesh and blood therapist influenced by Giegerich's psychology might have *actually worked* with this clinical material.
5   This chapter is a highly condensed version of a re-analysis of Adler's case that I detail in my dissertation. See Daniel Anderson, "Giegerich's Psychology of Soul: Psychotherapeutic Implications" (PhD diss., Pacifica Graduate Institute, 2014).

Adler's view of neurosis

Before turning to the case material itself, let us first compare Adler's traditional Jungian view of neurosis with Giegerich's view. Adler, in laying out his understanding of neurosis, contextualizes it within Jung's thought with multiple citations.[6] A principle purpose of his book is to "make clear" that "any neurosis ... can be defined as a loss of the 'symbolic attitude,' i.e., as a break in the spontaneous relationship between the conscious mind and its matrix, the unconscious."[7] Adler's position is that neurosis arises from disconnection to the unconscious, and its cure lies in a return to the unconscious "world of images" and the archetypes, particularly the archetype of the Self ("the transpersonal archetypal factor of inner order and significance").[8] Adler seeks to, and in fact does, cure his patient's neurosis through extensive work with dreams, paintings, and active imaginations. In other words, he cultivates his patient's connection to her imagination and unconscious images. Reconnection with the unconscious and the Self is simultaneously the realization of meaning and the cure of neurosis. Adler presents this case to demonstrate the clinical effectiveness of the Jungian treatment of neurosis.

Giegerich's view of neurosis

Giegerich's understanding of neurosis is quite different. One difference concerns the purpose of neurosis. For Jung and Adler, neurosis is an ineffective attempt by the psyche to establish equilibrium and heal itself.[9] Healing neurosis, in Adler's and Jung's view, is inseparable from archetypal, or numinous, experience.[10] Analysis, then, aims at facilitating this experience, which often comes in the form of "big" dreams or active imaginations. Giegerich does not see that a neurosis serves a person in any way. It is simply sick and harmful. It is in the patient's interest to be simply freed of it. The *way* to free the person of the neurosis (provided the neurotic soul permits) is through seeing through the neurotic phenomenon to its structure, its mechanism.

Giegerich's stance is that neurosis is a massive project of the objective soul—that is, of Western consciousness. It serves no purpose from the viewpoint of the suffering neurotic, but it does serve a purpose for the objective soul, as shall be seen. Giegerich sees the objective soul as "fundamentally historical, historical process. ... The soul *is* historicity."[11] Giegerich's soul is a *cultural soul*. Cultural institutions, practices, beliefs, art, technology can be seen as "thoughts" of the objective soul.

6   Adler, *Living Symbol*, 9–15.
7   Adler, *Living Symbol*, 9.
8   Adler, *Living Symbol*, 10.
9   "A neurosis always has that particular constructive side to it: it is an attempt at self-cure," in Adler, *Living Symbol*, 61.
10 Jung maintained that "inasmuch as you attain to the numinous experience you are released from the curse of pathology" (*Letters 1*, p. 377, to Martin, 20 August 1945)," cited in Giegerich, *Neurosis*, 63.
11 Wolfgang Giegerich, *What is Soul?* (New Orleans, LA: Spring Journal, Inc., 2012), 73.

Because culture and general consciousness change, this means that, *soul, too, changes.* Since culture and the objective soul mirror each other, culture can never be opposed to soul. If modern culture yields the soul illness of neurosis this is due, *not* to the soullessness of modern culture, but to the modern soul's *decision to become sick.* The soul's *choice* to become sick follows from two basic assumptions of Giegerich's concerning the soul: that soul *is* freedom (choice) and that the objective soul is mediated by culture. *We* are neurotic, each and every one of us, because we parti-cipate in Western consciousness-at-large.[12] This consciousness "carries" neurosis like the air we breathe carries pollutants. One could liken consciousness-at-large to a specific climate and terrain. Giegerich's psychology examines the overarching "ecosystem" of modern Western consciousness and maintains that *it* establishes the requisite level of sophistication for the tricky illness of neurosis to flourish. This consciousness-at-large, and not Jung's unconscious, is the source of neurosis in Giegerich's view. Consciousness-at-large is imprinted with all of Western culture as seen, for example, in experimental science, the subject–object relation, democracy, human rights, free-market economics, the financial system, telecommunications, materialism, consumerism, the media, nuclear weapons, and nihilism. All these realities reflect modern consciousness: they are *central* to it. What is no longer central to Western consciousness is religion. While naturally many individuals still practice religion and believe in God, Giegerich's hard-to-dispute point is that religion is a non-factor in Western consciousness as a whole. It does not inform the way life is really lived. Once at the center of Western society, religion now limps along at its margins. God is dead, as Nietzsche observed over a century ago. God, who once *was* the most real of all realities—more real than transient physical existence—this God is past.

The monumental death of God transforms reality, for a God-suffused reality is saturated with manifest meaning. Giegerich observes that prior to the beginning of the modern period in the West (around 1800) humanity lived in such a sea of meaning.[13] Humanity swam in meaning like fish swim in the sea. All that could be seen, felt, imagined, and thought had its source in God. God was *the* Absolute. The collapse of a foundational world-view grounded in the Divine created a cascade of consequences: the decline of church authority; the replacement of monarchy with democracy; the world's dis-enchantment and the rise of the subject–object relation and natural sciences; the notion of individual rights and human dignity; the creation of psychology. This overall development Giegerich imagines as Man's emergence from the waters of meaning and the birth of modern identity, i.e., the modern self and subjectivity. Giegerich observes that the modern person has a "stable identity such that he also *exists* on the basis of an actual continuous awareness of the

---

12   "There is no exit from the soul, the soul in this general sense, and soul here is synonymous with consciousness," in Giegerich, *What is Soul?*, 75.

13   Wolfgang Giegerich, "The End of Meaning and the Birth of Man: An essay about the state reached in the history of consciousness and an analysis of C. G. Jung's psychology project," in *The Soul Always Thinks: Collected English Papers, Vol. IV* (New Orleans, LA: Spring Journal, Inc., 2010), 189–283.

stability of his sense of I and identity (which is the reason why he *is* I, a unitary personality)."[14] The modern self and subjectivity emerges even as the self-evident reality of God fades. The one is the inverse of the other.[15] Giegerich views this modern, subjective sense of self as the product of an epochal historical process. It is by no means an anthropological constant.

The soul's creation of modern subjectivity comes at the cost of the world's dis-enchantment, the "death of God" and neurosis. Neurosis, in Giegerich's view, is inseparable from the loss of God and the rise of subjectivity. It is a project of the modern soul, whose *ultimate purpose* is to *establish* on a firm foundation modern subjectivity and the self but whose *immediate effect* is to create widespread personal suffering. How does neurosis consolidate modern subjective consciousness? Giegerich argues that, paradoxically, modern consciousness is established by for-cibly installing in individuals absurd vestiges of the Absolute—vestiges of that which once was experienced as God. In other words, it establishes vestiges of the *old pre-modern form of religious consciousness.*

> What is left is only the empty form of the historical relics of the metaphysical tradition, but relics without any living, animating spirit and without any authentication by a living tradition and an objective rootedness in real life and real feeling... .
>
> The very goal and purpose of neurosis is, however, to give The Absolute, in spite of the experienced and understood end of metaphysics and the impossi-bility of a revival, a present reality and an immediate existence. The Absolute is the fundamentally empty form or vacant placeholder of metaphysics, merely its abstracted principle. This Absolute has to become factually real. Materialized, incarnated.[16]

The Absolute, for Giegerich, manifests in neurotic symptoms.[17] So, a plaza is *absolutely* threatening (agoraphobia); one is *absolutely* "fat" and "disgusting" (anorexia); writing a dissertation is *absolutely* impossible (procrastination).[18] Neurotic symptoms are "characterized by the quality of *unconditionality*: something is experienced as *absolutely* intolerable, *absolutely* unthinkable, *totally* menacing, *at all cost* to be avoided, *by all means* to be controlled."[19] Here is Giegerich's radical thesis: phobic terror of a mouse represents a neurotic incarnation of the Absolute, the modern-day, sick

---

14   Giegerich, *What is Soul?*, 261.
15   Giegerich argues that the emergence of subjectivity (and God's submergence) is precisely the *work* of Christianity. It is an (implicit) message of the Incarnation: God gives way to Man. See Giegerich, "God Must Not Die! C. G. Jung's Thesis of the One-Sidedness of Christianity," in *Soul Always Thinks*, 165–242.
16   Giegerich, *Neurosis*, 364.
17   An approximate structural counterpart to Giegerich's "the Absolute" in object relations theories of neurosis would be "omnipotence." However, object relations theory is not grounded in a concept of soul.
18   Giegerich, *Neurosis*, 32–33, 272–273.
19   Giegerich, *Neurosis*, 34.

successor to that which once was worshipped as God, or experienced as a soulful cosmic Order. Neurosis genuinely is a metaphysical illness.

It might seem that this metaphysical illness is merely a (pathological) *clinging* to an old worldview—unconscious nostalgia. But Giegerich argues that neurosis is more than regressive longing; it also (progressively) serves to establish the modern self and consciousness. How? Giegerich maintains that the modern soul already has surpassed the metaphysical/religious consciousness of pre-modern (pre-1800) Western consciousness. This is not an issue, nor is there any going back. The problem is that this new status of Western consciousness is not yet fully consolidated. Neurosis serves to *consolidate* the position of the *already established* modern consciousness. An analogy may illustrate how. One could compare soul's modern status to the status of the American colonies after winning the Revolutionary War with England in 1783. By winning the war, the newly christened United States of America really had become a sovereign nation. It had a Constitution and a governmental structure. But to really *be* a sovereign nation it still had to establish *on the ground and in reality* (i.e., consolidate) an effective and functional Constitution and governmental structure. Democracy had to be made to actually function. This enormous task was in reality more difficult than achieving initial independence and sovereignty. This task parallels the modern soul's task of firmly establishing itself in its own subjectivity, without the support of religion or metaphysics.

Now let us imagine that in the United States of 1783, amidst the arduous task of establishing a genuine Constitutional democracy, a nostalgia for monarchy erupts. While no longer a present reality, there nevertheless remains a powerful monarchical impulse. This shows itself, let us say, in the areas of fashion, manners, and architecture. This initially emerges as a serious cultural trend, which subsequently is seen through and ridiculed. Thus, through the explicit *expression* of monarchy's vestiges—nostalgia in fashion, manners, and architecture—and its subsequent repudiation as pretentious and preposterous, monarchy is finally overcome and consciousness settles into the new democratic reality. It becomes *explicit* for consciousness that a threshold has been irreversibly crossed—in our analogy, the crossing over from monarchy to democracy—and there is no going back. To think otherwise would be absurd.

Neurosis serves a similar function in the logical life of the soul. While the individual neurotic, at times, cannot see the absurdity of her neurosis—just as the man wearing a powdered wig in 1800 America cannot see his ridiculous pretension—the neurotic display performs the indispensable task of demonstrating for consciousness-at-large the absurdity of clinging to the Absolute. For example, narcissism (a form of the neurotic Absolute installed as the individual's demand for perfection) is increasingly *seen through* as ridiculous. The *narcissist* might not see it, but the wider culture does. Humor and satire serve a critical role here. In neurotic symptoms, soul stages a performance of its own obsolescence. Giegerich writes,

> And so, I submit, the soul invented neurosis for itself both as *incentive* and *springboard* to push off from. For the soul it is obviously not enough to simply

(easily, "just like that") *outgrow* metaphysics in a natural developmental process. ... It has to actively, systematically, in detail and full awareness *work off* its own fascination and infatuation with the metaphysical, the mythic, the numinous, and the suggestive power of the imaginal—*through* pulling itself out of its neurosis, *really* stepping out of it and leaving it behind as the nothing that it is.[20]

From the standpoint of culture and of consciousness-at-large, neurosis has a purpose. But from the standpoint of the individual it does not. It is like a computer virus that downloads to one's PC and does nothing but harm. No benefit. From the standpoint of the person, neurosis is simply senseless and sick.

Now, we turn to our case study.

The patient

Adler's patient was born in 1892, and began treatment with him in 1941. Adler does not refer to his patient by name, but I will refer to her as "Elizabeth." Elizabeth was an accomplished woman. Adler notes that she "came from a scholarly family, not of great wealth but with an excellent cultural background."[21] Both parents were educators. Because the family did not possess great wealth, Elizabeth had to "make her way very early in life by winning scholarships." She "did brilliantly at school and later at her university."[22] Though Adler does not provide dates, one might deduce that Elizabeth began her university studies around 1910. She obviously was an enterprising and talented woman to make it as she did through a male-dominated university system on the sheer strength of her academic performance. Later, Elizabeth "joined one of the great international institutions connected with the League of Nations, in Geneva, where she soon attained a responsible position, which she held with marked success."[23]

The presenting symptom

Adler provides the following history of Elizabeth's symptoms:

> The presenting symptom that made the patient come for analytical treatment was severe claustrophobia. She had had very occasional attacks in her middle thirties, and they had always occurred when she was staying at some mountain inn or hotel. ... Gradually, however, these attacks became more frequent and severe—they used to occur every few months—until at the age of 44 she had a particularly severe attack which she could no longer "overlook." This occurred when she was staying at a mountain inn. ...

20 Giegerich, *What is Soul?*, 332.
21 Adler, *Living Symbol*, 19.
22 Adler, *Living Symbol*, 21.
23 Adler, *Living Symbol*, 21.

After this particular attack things went fairly well for some time until, at the age of 47, the outbreak of the war forced her to leave her work in Switzerland and return to England. ...

On the strength of her previous training and experience she quickly found a fairly congenial job in England. Soon, however, her attacks came on much more frequently and violently. At the same time there seemed to be a change in their nature and intensity. Claustrophobia seemed "no longer an adequate description" for them, as they did not occur only inside enclosed spaces but also in the open air, and she felt them to be more like attacks of acute anxiety. In her own words, "the attacks gradually took on a less physical and more mental form," and seemed to be connected with "an acutely distressing and incomprehensible intuition of the nature of the world, of which all that can be said is that there was darkness and emptiness, and no possibility of establishing any relation with it."[24]

The turning point of the treatment

Seven months into her work with Adler, Elizabeth had a critical dream.[25] As the dream's resolution was somewhat equivocal from both Adler's and Elizabeth's standpoint, Adler recommended that Elizabeth revisit the dream by means of active imagination. Elizabeth then undertook a series of active imaginations. The fantasy culminates with a group of four people (which includes Elizabeth) discovering a large underground cavern. In the center of this cavern is a luminescent pool, and many underground rivers enter the cavern and empty into the pool. The pool, as the place into which the converging underground rivers empty their waters, suggests a mandala and the Jungian Self, the central ordering principle of the psyche. Elizabeth's description of the luminescent pool is crucial for understanding the character of her neurosis:

> The water was clear and very deep. Far down in the middle there was something shining; it looks like a crystal, or perhaps a star. Could it be a reflection? They say you can see the stars in daylight at the bottom of a well. I asked Webster, and he said: "that is the Pole Star. All the other constellations revolve around it." "But we are not looking at the sky," I said. "Are you sure of that?" he answered. "You can look at the sky from either end, you know." The mists gathered round closer, until nothing was visible but the blue pool; and it looked as if it might indeed be, not a round pool, but a translucent sapphire blue sphere, with a glittering star at its center. Vaguely shining things moved

---

24   Adler, *Living Symbol*, 21–23.
25   In previous research, I pointed out how this dream tends to *defeat* any thought by Elizabeth to utilize any space underground as a container for cosmic meaning. This, I submit, prompted Adler to suggest active imagination as a sort of corrective to the dream. See Anderson, "Giegerich's Psychology of Soul," 202–212.

round about in it, as gold and silver fishes might in a pool, or constellations, planets and comets in a night sky.

Mr. Webster said: "I understand you used to suffer from claustrophobia. Well, there you have the answer to it."[26]

Note that the character in the active imagination, "Mr. Webster," states that this central pool is the "answer" to Elizabeth's neurosis. In fact, after this active imagination, Adler states that "from this point onwards the claustrophobia disappeared, without any trace, for good."[27] In the sense of curing the neurosis, this image did "answer" the neurosis. But the answer to the neurosis must also represent the fundamental truth of the neurosis. It must offer the key for breaking the neurotic code. We shall examine in detail the character of this code. For now, I will only point out its basic nature. The luminescent pool contains the Pole Star, the sky, the cosmos.

Adler's analysis of the neurotic symptom

Surprisingly, Adler does not explore in detail the fact that Elizabeth's neurosis is (or at least begins as) claustrophobia. He does observe, generically, that the neurosis is connected with Elizabeth's mid-life crisis, and her purportedly insufficient "adjustment to *inner* factors, to the world of *inner* images, access to which goes through the medium of the unconscious."[28] But this only explains why Elizabeth developed *a* neurosis, not why the neurosis she developed was claustrophobia. Adler's only answer to the question, "Why *claustrophobia?*" is offered in a footnote, and is wholly developmental. He suggests that claustrophobia arises when an infant develops an ego that "has been overpowered—[or is] too strongly enclosed—by the mother imago."[29] This conceptualization is informed by a spatial fantasy. That is, the ego is imagined as something like an inflating balloon and the mother imago as an inflexible covering surrounding it—the "fabric" of the mother imago cannot stretch and expand as the ego balloon inflates. The mother image constrains the growing ego, resulting in ego constriction and claustrophobia. For Adler, the mid-life crisis joins forces with this infantile issue to produce a claustrophobia—at least this is how I reconstruct his reasoning. But the character of Elizabeth's neurotic symptom does not really concern Adler. He is entirely focused on *imaginal* contents: Elizabeth's written fantasy elaborations of her symptoms, her dreams, her active imaginations.

Analyzing Elizabeth's symptoms from the standpoint of interiority

I believe that there is considerable meaning in the character of Elizabeth's neurotic symptoms that Adler overlooks. The first step in understanding Elizabeth's initial

26 Adler, *Living Symbol*, 312–313.
27 Adler, *Living Symbol*, 317.
28 Adler, *Living Symbol*, 35.
29 Adler, *Living Symbol*, 40.

claustrophobic attacks is to note a highly unusual aspect of her claustrophobia: it *only* strikes while Elizabeth is vacationing in the mountains. Think about that. When she was working in the city, routinely entering enclosed spaces such as rooms, elevators, subways, buses, and trains, she had no claustrophobia. Her claustrophobia struck *only* when she was vacationing in the mountains.

We therefore must understand this mountain setting and what it might have meant for the soul. Adler reports that Elizabeth "loved climbing mountains and was an expert at it."[30] That Elizabeth enjoyed climbing mountains is one thing, but that she was an expert at it attests to her passion for mountain climbing, her desire to cultivate an expertise at it. Of course, there can be many reasons for mountain climbing: challenge, exercise, the beauty of the setting, perhaps conquest. In Elizabeth's case there is little direct evidence as to what motivated her. But there is a very suggestive comment that she makes in connection with her pivotal active imagination fantasy. In the fantasy Mr. Webster declares that the arrival at the luminescent pool provides the "answer" to Elizabeth's claustrophobia. Adler asks her what the statement about the "answer to claustrophobia" means to her. Elizabeth's answer is telling.

> "There is the sky without and the sky within, that is part of it, but not all. Also, you get to the sky from the cave, not only by going back, but by going on and right through." Then she added: "In claustrophobia you think you are walled in every way, but now you find you're not walled in any way."[31]

Elizabeth clearly connects "getting to the sky," or the inability to do so, with her claustrophobia. To be free of claustrophobia she must reach the sky. Indeed, claustrophobia is synonymous with being "cut off from the psychic sky which is the order of created—as opposed to chaotic—things."[32]

What precisely is that "psychic sky" that Elizabeth sought? Since neurosis is a sickness of the *soul* we must understand what the sky means to *it*. Giegerich provides a beautifully apt description of what the sky meant to the pre-modern soul in his analysis of a poem by the 17th-century poet Andreas Gryphius:

> In 1643 ... Andreas Gryphius published his sonnet, "To the Stars," in which he addresses the stars directly, calling them torches, sparkling diamonds, flowers that adorn wide heaven's leas, saying that in looking at them he simply cannot get his fill here on earth. They are the guarantors of his delight, and many a beautiful night he spent awake watching them. ... It is they whose love ignites his heart and his spirits.[33]

30   Adler, *Living Symbol*, 66.
31   Adler, *Living Symbol*, 316.
32   Adler, *Living Symbol*, 316.
33   Giegerich, *Neurosis*, 114.

Giegerich notes that Gryphius's reaching to a soul-filled Heaven is not "a utopian, idle, deluded reaching out beyond itself! It is not deluded because the soul is nothing else but this reaching out beyond itself."[34] Gryphius "is here still completely enveloped in the soul, much like the earth is enveloped in an atmosphere."[35] "Nature" in this status of the soul "is here still a caring nature, not the absolutely indifferent nature (as pure facticity) of modernity."[36] It is reality still seen through the lens of the Divine.

This provides enough information to surmise why Elizabeth's claustrophobia struck in the mountains. Elizabeth's mountain climbing symbolized an upward-striving in her soul, a yearning for verticality, a striving that only could be satisfied by reaching the sky, but not the modern soulless sky. Elizabeth sought a "soul-filled sky," a "psychic sky which is the order of created—as opposed to chaotic—things." Elizabeth sought the created cosmos where the soul could expand in infinity and dwell amongst the stars as the poet Gryphius's soul did. This was the *absolute* demand of her soul. Yet, the *demand* for a cosmos betrays Elizabeth's (unconscious) knowledge that what she seeks does not exist. An *absolute demand* hints at a desperation arising from knowledge of an absence. Elizabeth's soul demand for a cosmos cannot be realized; more precisely, it can only *be* realized negatively and pathologically, not through infinite expansion, but by infinite *constriction,* claustrophobia.

Elizabeth's acute anxiety in England

Interestingly, Elizabeth's neurotic symptoms changed when she moved from Switzerland to England on account of the Second World War. The attacks no longer occurred in enclosed spaces; they were more mental than physical, and they were accompanied by "an acutely distressing and incomprehensible intuition of the nature of the world."[37] We interpreted Elizabeth's previous claustrophobia to be related to an upward-striving, expansionary soul movement toward "cosmos" that found particular support in her passion for mountain climbing. In England, however, I believe that this upward-striving was frustrated in two fundamental ways so that the neurosis appeared in a new form, not as claustrophobia, but as acute anxiety. Her neurosis thus shifted from a physical to a more mental form.

First, while neurosis in Giegerich's view causes *itself* to come into being,[38] it is not divorced from physical reality. A neurosis—at least like claustrophobia—needs a trigger. Here, in Elizabeth's case, an enclosed space in a mountain setting is such a trigger. "The complex is only an instruction, an algorithm, a computer program, and it needs (a) the trigger and (b) the material substance of a real situation so that

34   Giegerich, *Neurosis*, 114.
35   Giegerich, *Neurosis*, 114.
36   Giegerich, *Neurosis*, 115.
37   Adler, *Living Symbol*, 22.
38   "[Neurosis] is caused by *itself*. It has, as I said, its cause within itself: it *is* its cause," in Giegerich, *Neurosis*, 27.

the program has something with which it can begin its work."[39] Elizabeth's claustrophobia evidently needed the setting of mountain climbing, surroundings suggestive of upward-striving, Heaven, and cosmos. The patent flatness and urban density of London provides no such material.

Second, and perhaps more importantly, the London sky was irreparably ruined as a symbol of cosmos and infinity for Elizabeth. In the pristine purity of mountain heights, the sky could function as a sign of infinity and cosmos. But in London in 1940–1941, the possibility of the sky serving such a function was destroyed by the German bombing campaign of England known as the "Blitz." Now, "sky" was the physical medium that transported modern, deadly technology. At the time of Elizabeth's first severe anxiety attack in January 1941, the Blitz was in its fourth month. Londoners had grown accustomed to the cry of the air-raid sirens and ensuing terror in the skies from whence destruction came, as they hurried underground to air-raid shelters that trembled with each explosion. After four months of this hellish experience, how could the imagination continue to conceive of the sky as Heaven and the expansive realm of the soul? The German aerial Blitz of London ruined the sky's symbolic capacity to hold the notion of soul and upward-striving. No upward-striving and no claustrophobia was possible for Elizabeth. So, how can we understand the change in Elizabeth's symptom from classic claustrophobia to acute anxiety coupled with "an acutely distressing and incomprehensible intuition of the nature of the world?"[40]

A helpful insight may be gained in comments Giegerich makes about a patient's phobia in a different context. In referring to an otherwise physically fit man's fear of swimming across a lake because he would be paralyzed by anxiety at the halfway point, Giegerich writes:

> In therapy a psychology with soul could, however, turn this symptom around. … It could utilize this anxiety for therapeutic, truly psychological purposes and assign to it the opposite meaning by interpreting this anxiety as the (now not neurotic) soul's call to this man to go under, to give himself over to the bottomlessness of existence, to expose himself (not to the literal, physical element of water, but) to the fluidity and absolute negativity of the soul's life as his new ground. It could say that this anxiety points to his psychological task. As Jung repeatedly stated, our fears indicate where we have to go.[41]

In Giegerich's vignette the man imagines being halfway through his swim across the lake when, equidistant from both shores, he becomes incapacitated by fear. In a psychological sense, Elizabeth is also "between two shores." Her claustrophobia reveals an unconscious demand: to be in, and contained by, a meaningful, soul-filled cosmos. At the same time, as a modern, highly educated and highly intelligent

39   Giegerich, *Neurosis*, 309.
40   Adler, *Living Symbol*, 22.
41   Giegerich, *Neurosis*, 430.

woman of the world (she was a civil servant), Elizabeth participates within an objective, cultural soul that knows the futility of this demand. But both her demand and her knowing better occur behind her back, so to speak, the blindness of which is reflected in the incomprehensible onslaught of her claustrophobia.

This is no longer the case with Elizabeth's intense anxiety in London. The veil separating her conscious knowledge from the issues at stake for the soul has slipped. The soul issues are no longer completely hidden in the physicality of her symptom. They have slipped out into the open. Metaphorically speaking, Elizabeth can now catch sight of the "other shore," the truths that are at stake in her neurosis. She can see that what is at stake is the "nature of the world," and she already has an "intuition" about this nature that is "acutely distressing."[42] The "nature of the world" at stake, simply stated, is whether it is an orderly, containing, soul-filled cosmos or whether it is an indifferent universe. Elizabeth's acutely distressing intuition is certainly the knowledge that her demand for cosmic containment is untenable. Elizabeth has caught a glimpse of the other "shore": an explicit philosophical issue concerning the world's nature made all the more pressing by the catastrophe of the Second World War in general and the German Blitz of London in particular. But, like the man halfway across the lake in Giegerich's vignette, Elizabeth, too, seizes up in panic as the issue emerges into consciousness.

In this light, the therapist might have sought to bring these questions out into the open. What is your intuition about the nature of the world? What is distressing about it? That is, make increasingly explicit that which has already emerged into consciousness. Follow the anxiety to its ground. Elizabeth reported that her acute anxiety was accompanied by an intuitive knowledge, but then the knowing mind stopped short at a "darkness and emptiness, and no possibility of establishing any relation with it."[43] But one may "establish a relation" with the question of the world's nature by continuing to reflect. The "darkness and emptiness" at which Elizabeth's thought stopped was by no means a real barrier to thought; it was a barrier generated and posited by aborted reflection. The darkness is the personified image of a refusal to continue thinking. The therapist's task would be to invite Elizabeth to think beyond the point where she left off.

The significance of Elizabeth's cure

Adler notes that with Elizabeth's active imagination fantasy of the shining pool containing the night stars, her "claustrophobia disappeared, without any trace, for good."[44] Before examining why this fantasy cured the neurosis, let us examine the significance of the underground setting. We have noted that the bombing of London ruined the sky as a symbol of cosmos and eternity. What happened when the air raid sirens sounded? The residents of London headed underground, and

42   Adler, *Living Symbol*, 22.
43   Adler, *Living Symbol*, 22.
44   Adler, *Living Symbol*, 317.

surely Elizabeth herself participated in this frightening ritual. We can imagine the
symbolic suggestiveness of this ritual: *underground* as a safe haven from the terrors of
modernity represented by the aerial bombing. And indeed Elizabeth's first association
to the dream which featured an underground motif—and from which she pushed off
into the active imaginations that ended with the image of the underground luminescent pool—was to underground air-raid shelters. With the sky symbolically
ruined, Elizabeth's imagination headed underground, safe from the horrors of
modernity.

Giegerich has argued repeatedly that Jung's theoretical construct of "the
unconscious" is nothing other than a hermetically sealed refuge of the former
archetypal riches of the soul. For example, he notes that "a psychology of the
collective unconscious is dealing only with *former* soul truths, with sunken history,
with fundamentally fenced-in or canned contents—'canned' because they are
encapsulated in our inner."[45] Of course, Gryphius's 17th-century ode to the stars
reflects one former soul truth, the way in which the soul's infinity was experienced
in the stars of the night sky. Another way to say this is that formerly the soul
experienced the starry sky as a cosmos, not as a universe.

At this juncture we can see why with her image of the central pool that contained
the starry sky Elizabeth's neurosis was cured: she "independently," but unwittingly,
generated the "Jungian unconscious." She walked right in Jung's footsteps and
replicated his logical moves. She successfully interiorized the former cosmos, quite
concretely, into the underground cavern that contained pocketed within itself the
soul-filled starry cosmos, now swimming in the luminescent pool. Pocketed
underground, *this* cosmos was safe from the assaults of modernity, just as the literal
London underground protected Londoners from aerial bombardment.

How did this fantasy cure the neurosis? Previously, the demand for a soul-filled
cosmos could only be realized negatively by Elizabeth suffering unbearable claustrophobic constriction. The absolute soul demand for infinite expansion crammed into
the sealed subjectivity of modern consciousness yielded Elizabeth's claustrophobia.
But when the neurotic demand for cosmos was *displaced* from Elizabeth's personal
subjectivity to the fantasy of the cosmic pool, the latter assumed the burden of the
neurotic demand, and Elizabeth was relieved of it. The neurosis remained—
indeed, it calcified as Elizabeth's new conviction concerning the continuing reality
of a soul-filled cosmos—now sedimented into the active imagination fantasy validated
by Jungian theory.[46] There was a transference cure—but not in the Freudian sense
of a displacement of the neurosis into the client–therapist relationship. Rather,
Elizabeth's neurotic demand for a soul-filled cosmos was transferred from her personal subjectivity into a fantasy supported by an objective psychological theory.
The neurosis realized itself as numinous experience and as an exemplar of Jung's

45   Giegerich, *What is Soul*, 146.
46   Wolfgang Giegerich, "On the Neurosis of Psychology or the Third of the Two," *The
Neurosis of Psychology* (*Collected English Papers, Vol. I*) (New Orleans, LA: Spring Journal,
Inc., 2005), 41–67.

notion of the living Self. The dubious character of this realization should be apparent. Is an infinite cosmos contained within a finite pool not facially contradictory?

We are presented with a dilemma. Elizabeth was relieved of her symptom—albeit, by displacing the neurosis onto the psychological theory without really resolving it. In Giegerich's terms, the neurosis was preserved "by kicking it upstairs,"[47] now contained by a psychological theory. In Elizabeth's case, her original demand for a soul-filled cosmos was transferred from her subjectivity to the Jungian "unconscious" where this demand was satisfied. Giegerich addresses this maneuver in the following manner:

> If the patient were to succeed in an attempt of his to take shelter in such a belief-system, he might, of course, indeed be subjectively relieved of the neurotic symptoms and his former suffering (which is something whose value I don't want to underestimate), but the neurosis itself, the neurotic structure, would nevertheless not be dissolved. He would have successfully deceived himself.[48]

Giegerich argues that symptoms can be relieved, but the *neurosis* remains, now *encased* in a theory. This displacement can occur with any psychological theory, Jungian, psychoanalytic or otherwise.

Conclusion

This article seeks not to second-guess Adler, but to show how Giegerich's psychological theory alters our view of clinical material. Real therapy is a flesh-and-blood encounter between two people and is inseparable from the singularity of this encounter. Giegerich observes that a therapist who would work soulfully must possess a developed feeling function: essentially, the capacity to see from the soul perspective.[49] The therapist must discern the objective feeling of the matter at hand (dream, symptom, etc.); the individual client's subjective presence, intonation and posture inform this feeling. Each phenomenon presents a singularity that the psychologist must discern. Giegerich notes that soul phenomena either point to their own flowering (the soul's "anima" need) or deconstruction (the soul's "animus" need).[50] The art of therapy lies in divining with refined feeling each phenomenon's character. The *soul's intentionality, not the therapist's theory*, dictates how clinical material is handled, and the patient's presence is part of this.[51] In a

47 Giegerich, *Neurosis*, 261.
48 Giegerich, *Neurosis*, 83.
49 "[We] probably do not go wrong in stating that what Jung calls 'feeling' ultimately is the soul view of events," in Giegerich, *What is Soul?*, 239.
50 Giegerich, *What is Soul?*, 318.
51 "In the consulting room I try to be present with such a psychologically trained consciousness, but otherwise forget theories and approach the patient unprejudiced." Giegerich,

psychological approach to psychotherapy *any* theory runs the risk of diminishing or concealing the soul's perspective (including a theory about soul!). Genuine, spontaneous, *soulful* work with Elizabeth would have unquestionably involved different interpretations or responses than I have written about here. How could it be otherwise? For soul work to *be* soul work, it cannot exist apart from the moment in which it spontaneously occurs and to which it belongs.

quoted in Ann Casement, "The Interiorizing Movement of Logical Life: Reflections on Wolfgang Giegerich," *The Journal of Analytical Psychology*, 56(4) (2011): 539.

10

THE NUCLEAR BOMB RE-VISITED THROUGH THE EYES OF THE SHOAH

John C. Knapp

> Once upon a time it happened to my people, and now it happens to all people. And suddenly I said to myself, maybe, the whole world, strangely, has turned Jewish. Everybody lives now facing the unknown. We are all, in a way, helpless.[1]

Introduction

When Giegerich's nuclear bomb essays appeared,[2] they opened up a conversation about the nuclear bomb that permitted the bomb to be *thought*. The bomb was, for the first time, considered to have *psychological* significance—both something that was "legitimate" and "indispensable" for the sake of psychology.[3] However, the nuclear bomb papers were written in the early days of Giegerich's thinking. They were comprised before the publication of *The Soul's Logical Life*,[4] where he set out his original vision of psychology, and well before one of Giegerich's most recent and seminal works, *Neurosis: The Logic of a Metaphsyical Illness*,[5] in which he details his highly complex psychological theory of neurosis. Had Giegerich's

---

1   Elie Wiesel, Viewpoint (ABC Television news program), 1983. Accessed on March 28, 2016 from https://www.youtube.com/watch?v=PcCLZwU2t34.
2   Giegerich wrote a two-volume work in German on the nuclear bomb, *Psychoanalyse der Atombombe*, Volume 1: *Die Atombombe als seelische Wirklichkeit. Ein Versuch über den Geist des christlichen Abendlandes*, Zürich (Schweizer Spiegel Verlag, Raben-Reihe) 1988. Volume 2: *Drachenkampf oder Initiation ins Nuklearzeitalter*, Zürich (Schweizer Spiegel Verlag, Raben-Reihe) 1989. The present discussion, however, is based on a select number of these essays that were published in English, located in Wolfgang Giegerich, *Technology and the Soul: From the Nuclear Bomb to the World Wide Web (Collected English Papers, Vol. II)* (New Orleans, LA: Spring Journal, Inc., 2007), 25–115.
3   "…we can say that the Bomb is more than legitimate. It is indispensable, inasmuch as it is our true therapist," in Giegerich, *Technology*, 68.
4   Wolfgang Giegerich, *The Soul's Logical Life: Towards a Rigorous Notion of Psychology* (Frankfurt am Main; New York: Peter Lang, 1998).
5   Wolfgang Giegerich, *Neurosis: The Logic of a Metaphysical Illness* (New Orleans, LA: Spring Journal, Inc., 2013).

understanding of psychology remained the same from the time he wrote these bomb essays to the present, there might not exist a discrepancy between his early thoughts on the bomb and the psychological thinking that emerged later in his life. However, this is not the case.[6] What constitutes the psychological nature of the nuclear bomb thus needs to be revisited.

I will begin by briefly summarizing Giegerich's original interpretation of the bomb insofar as it is relevant to this chapter. I will then explore the relationship between the bomb and a topic that has been seriously neglected in the field of Analytical Psychology: the Shoah.[7] While the bomb and the Shoah might seem like entirely separate phenomena, I will explore how each of these phenomena are related, ultimately suggesting that they are both expressions of the *neurotic* soul. Neurosis, as discussed by Giegerich in his book, *Neurosis*, will be explored in both its dissociative nature and "Absolute" quality. Finally, I will return to Giegerich's original writings on the bomb showing how his analysis of the bomb is un-psychological in comparison to his later theory of neurosis.

Giegerich's interpretation of the nuclear bomb

There are three key features of Giegerich's rich and complex thinking about the bomb[8] that I would like to explore, namely, 1) his psychological attitude towards the "symptom" of the bomb, 2) how he sees the bomb as related to God, and 3) what he sees as particularly "neurotic" about the bomb.

Giegerich's psychological attitude towards the bomb is in the spirit of the traditional Jungian and archetypal theoretical orientation which recognizes the inherent value of pathology, wherein "neurosis is legitimate, even necessary, indeed truly productive."[9] As Jung once stated, "Neurosis is really an attempt at self-cure, just as any physical disease is part an attempt at self-cure … It is an attempt of the

6   In Giegerich's "Introduction," to *Technology and the Soul*, he acknowledged that he was still very much influenced by archetypal and mythical thinking when he wrote the bomb essays. He states, "The papers collected in this volume reflect the status of my thinking reached at the time when they were written. I still stand by the basic arguments presented in them, although if I had to write them now they would not come out the same way," 20.

7   I use the Hebrew term "Shoah" instead of "Holocaust" for *psychological*, not moral reasons. The "Shoah," translated as "catastrophe," captures the *neurotic* nature of this tragedy more fully in that the term is limited to its catastrophic dimension. The term "Holocaust," a word which means "fully burnt," is associated with ritual sacrifices to God; it thus contains elements of a Sacred dimension, which the conclusions regarding the Shoah in this chapter would deem problematic.

8   I attempt to draw out main themes in the way in which Giegerich addresses the bomb, as his later thinking diverges quite drastically from his original imaginal approach. However, it is important to acknowledge that there are moments when Giegerich's thinking about the bomb does live up to the "true" psychology he later espouses, e.g., when he acknowledges the bomb as a product of the *historical* Christian West. See Giegerich, *Technology*, 101–102.

9   Giegerich, *Technology*, 57.

self-regulating psychic system to restore balance,"[10] Giegerich extends the same attitude towards the bomb, speculating upon what compensatory function the bomb might serve. In this, he attempts to listen to the symptom of the bomb, hearing its underlying meaning or message as a statement of the soul.

Situated within this attitude, Giegerich offers an alternative way of looking at the bomb. Instead of suggesting that humanity must work towards either peacefully eradicating the bomb or conversely, aggressively building more bombs, he proposes the rather strange and provocative idea that we must "save" it, where

> saving the nuclear bomb has nothing to do with defending it against the peace movement, but it means a third way beyond the entire alternative of pro or con, war or peace. It means listening to its voice, seeing its face, acknowledging its reality, and releasing it into its own essence. It means saving it from our habitual throw-away mentality. The question is not how to dispose of the bomb, but where to pose it, where to find its legitimate place.[11]

In this, Giegerich's attitude towards the bomb reflects the Jungian notion that in one's symptoms there is also the cure, the "alchemical gold" to be found. Rather than merely ridding the symptom, i.e., the bomb, the symptom is recognized as a failed attempt by the soul to establish equilibrium; it thus maintains some kind of compensatory function for humanity at large. Giegerich notes:

> I am here transferring the depth-psychological attitude toward the individual person's symptom to the way of looking at the symptom of the body politic. C. G. Jung once said that in our "neurosis is hidden our best friend or enemy." He did not just say "friend." He said, "friend or enemy." Put this way, friend and enemy cancel each other out like plus and minus, showing that the entire category of friend or enemy, pro or con, the perspective of our human likes and dislikes becomes irrelevant. What remains is "our best (friend or enemy)," our best, that is to say, the dignity of the real phenomenon itself, independent of, and prior to, our subjective valuation, a dignity even if the phenomenon is as painful as a neurotic symptom or as dangerous if not as evil as the nuclear bomb. "Saving" means restoring the dignity of things.[12]

In this light, "saving" the bomb amounts to neither trying "to destroy it nor to waste it in a one-time explosion."[13] "I would suggest that we ground our existence in it, dwell near it, make our home in it."[14] He continues:

---

10 Jung, *CW* 18, § 389.
11 Giegerich, *Technology*, 27.
12 Giegerich, *Technology*, 27.
13 Giegerich, *Technology*, 35.
14 Giegerich, *Technology*, 35.

> Are you suffering from the loss of meaning? Searching for a spiritual dimension? Wanting to reconnect to the imagination? Longing for a God, a fate, an unprogrammed future? Don't go to India, nor back to classical or primitive mythology, nor off into drugs nor into yourself. Go to *our* reality, try the *real* thing: try the nuclear bomb. All the riches of the imaginal that we think we have lost are there, stuffed away and buried and hidden, *but also preserved* in its terror, waiting to be redeemed.[15]

Hidden in the nuclear bomb are thus the riches of the imagination, a "spiritual dimension," a "dignity," and an ensuing "meaning." In this, one might say the God in the disease is present, and it is our job to locate him.

This leads to the second aspect of the bomb that Giegerich discusses, namely, the bomb's being identified as God. Being more than merely a modern phenomenon, Giegerich suggests that the nuclear bomb is the result of a process that began in the early formation of Western mankind—a historical evolution of the nature of God himself. In his essay, "The Nuclear Bomb and the Fate of God,"[16] he discusses this evolution, seeing the parable of the Golden Calf in the Old Testament as one particular and crucial moment in the life of God that will ultimately relate to the development of the nuclear bomb in modernity.

In this parable, Giegerich suggests that the "scene dramatically announces a change within God" in which "God's nature splits."[17] Moses leaves his people to ascend Mt. Sinai where he will ultimately receive the Ten Commandments. While gone, the Israelites take part in worshipping the golden calf, whereupon returning with the tablets Moses is consumed by rage and anger for their worship of false idols. We have, here, Giegerich suggests, the first notion of the true and the real, i.e., there is now a notion of a true God and a false one, one that prior to Moses retrieving the Ten Commandments did not exist. "The God resulting from the split is the 'true' God; what is left of the bull after the split is, to be sure, visible and tangible, in other words: real, but it is only an idol, a false God."[18]

With this split that occurs in God, Giegerich identifies that "nature" also changes in that it is now split off and separate from God. The animal deity, or golden calf, to which the Israelites worshipped is relegated to a lower status compared to the higher, true God who on the mountain peaks in his invisible transcendence reveals the moral code by which individuals must live. With such a split in God's essence, nature and earthly reality (the now *false* idols) also undergo a transformation in which they are no longer imbued with the Divine. "As God became worldless by his obtaining absoluteness, so earthly reality became God-less."[19] Nature is now in opposition to the true God and the higher principles he espouses.

---

15 Giegerich, *Technology*, 36.
16 Giegerich, *Technology*, 69–115.
17 Giegerich, *Technology*, 75.
18 Giegerich, *Technology*, 85.
19 Giegerich, *Technology*, 79.

According to Giegerich, this split in God in which nature is divested of its divinity amounts to the first nuclear fission, that which would ultimately make possible over the course of many thousands of years the development of the nuclear bomb in modernity. Reflecting upon the consequences of this split, he states:

> Just as God's truth cut off from his reality had striven for the highest heights like a released balloon, so conversely reality, separated from the name of God and thus unleashed, could, and had to, strive to advance its earthly realness to unheard of degrees of intensity in order to correspond to the intensification reached by the predicate "God."[20]

With earthly reality left to its own accord and "abandoned" by God, nature might emerge with little to no ethical or moral constraints—as God is now bound up solely in his *word*—the Ten Commandments—*not* in nature, earth, and matter. According to Giegerich, a world in which the divine is no longer manifest in nature is one in which nature is unleashed and unbridled, thus allowing for man to ultimately appropriate full dominion over nature and manipulate nature as he sees fit. This new orientation to the "real," matter, and nature ultimately allows for the development of the natural sciences and the emergence of modern technology.[21]

Finally, Giegerich suggests that with nature "unleased" and unbridled, the nuclear bomb emerges in modernity as the return of God in the form of matter and spirit reunited, where "[n]ature and spirit are no longer ... absolute opposites."[22] He notes:

> What in the shape of the nuclear bomb is knocking at our door and wants to be received into consciousness is nothing else but God's own reality, that reality that he had centuries ago cast away ... What has been split off must be united with its other half ... God's reality must finally be given back its truth, withheld from it for so long.[23]

In this, the nuclear bomb returns "the face of the dark God"[24] to God himself, thus resolving the original dissociative split in God.

In concluding that the nuclear bomb is God, Giegerich suggests that psychology is able to reach the inner nature of the bomb—*its true psychology*—so that the bomb and psychology do not remain juxtaposed against each other. This amounts to overcoming the "inner" and "outer" split that would mistake the bomb and its

20 Giegerich, *Technology*, 93.
21 Giegerich has noted that Christianity and, in particular, the Incarnation, are most directly associated with the developments of technology in modernity. See Giegerich, *Technology*, 155–211.
22 Giegerich, *Technology*, 98.
23 Giegerich, *Technology*, 95.
24 Giegerich, *Technology*, 35.

true nature, thus permitting a new orientation to the bomb that can see it for what it is. Seeing the bomb for what it is means understanding it at its core; it means that we might relate to it appropriately. Otherwise, "we remain fundamentally threatened because all constraints [on the bomb] have to be imposed from outside, by us, by *our* morality and well-meaning. But such imposed constraints will never be able to reach and affect the inner nature of the bomb and the explosive potential itself."[25]

This leads to the third aspect of Giegerich's writings on the bomb that I would like to address, namely, how Giegerich sees *neurosis* and *neurotic dissociation* in relationship to the bomb, where what is neurotic is not the bomb *per se*, but more so, the particular psychological thinking about the bomb that would keep *inner and outer, physical and psychological distinctly apart*. He describes this neurosis as follows:

> This condition of a split of reality into two realities—one physical and technical and irrevocably non-psychological, one psychological and having the physical object irrevocably outside of itself ... then appears as a most critical condition, as a split of consciousness, as a neurotic dissociation.[26]

Such neurosis can be seen, for example, in the manner in which technology such as the nuclear bomb is often viewed. Rather than technology being seen as an aspect of the soul, or perhaps even having its own soul, the soul is decidedly a *human* soul, independent of physical, technological reality altogether. It is this *personalistic* notion of the soul that is problematic and thus neurotic for Giegerich, wherein he suggests that a *psychological* position would overcome this split between the "inner" and "outer" worlds.

With this understanding of neurosis, Giegerich also proposes that it is not the inner nature of the bomb that is neurotic, but the human beings and their particular neurosis which have led to the creation of the bomb in the first place. He states, "It seems to me that the nuclear bomb is by no means itself the actual pathological problem."[27] Rather, it is the fact that "we, that is to say Western mankind, are residing within a neurosis."[28] He continues:

> And perhaps there has only been this extreme technological development toward the nuclear bomb because technology has been split from the soul, and the soul, as the exclusively internal reality, had been split off from external reality so that the external world could undergo a development without any inherent restrictions or constraints.[29]

Similar to Giegerich's interpretation of the parable of the Golden Calf in which God, as split off from nature, permits nature to develop freely and without fetters,

25 Giegerich, *Technology*, 40.
26 Giegerich, *Technology*, 38.
27 Giegerich, *Technology*, 51.
28 Giegerich, *Technology*, 39.
29 Giegerich, *Technology*, 39.

so too does the split that occurs between human beings and nature amount to nature as unleashed and unbridled. While it is worth noting, here, that neurosis and neurotic dissociation as Giegerich defines it mirrors the split that he says occurred within God, Giegerich does not discuss the possibility that God *himself* was neurotic for the split that occurred in his very own nature. Instead, neurosis is reserved for the human beings who "are residing within a neurosis."

While I will return to many of these ideas later in this essay, these three points set the stage for a new interpretation of the bomb. Still, though, there is one more note that I would like to make regarding Giegerich's thoughts on the bomb before proceeding—one that is an underlying thread amongst the entirety of his nuclear bomb essays. Specifically, I would like to note that despite the fact that Giegerich's view of the bomb is transformative, indeed a *radical* idea in the first place, he is still only addressing one particular quality of the bomb, i.e., he is speaking about the bomb *in potentia*—"its explosive potential"—*not* the bomb in its actual explosion. While he mends a split in consciousness by taking the bomb seriously for psychology, his theory of the bomb remains focused on the bomb as *unused*—a bomb in which God's nature is *preserved* and *waiting* to be redeemed. Despite the fact that he alludes to the exploded bomb when he states that we must be "truly affected and transformed by the fundamental explosion of all our traditional views and expectations during modernity"[30] and, "The Bomb explodes psychology's prison of the interior and opens our eyes to what else there is outside of us as the real Other, the real unconscious, the real world,"[31] Giegerich's take on the bomb has not yet confronted what such actual explosiveness entails. Would this not seem like a rather important aspect of the bomb to address, especially in a discussion on its symptomatic character? Not once does he mention Hiroshima or Nagasaki, or any actual occurrence of the bomb's use. Psychologically speaking, then, we might say his take on the bomb does not live up to the task of the true psychology he espouses because it fails to confront the *entirety* of the bomb, that which would ultimately include *its explosion*. The following sections will further lay out what such explosion might mean for the psychological nature of the bomb, so for now, let us turn to the exploded bomb and that "explosion" as it might be seen in the Shoah.

The Shoah and the exploded bomb

According to some estimates at the end of the 20th century, the materials produced regarding the Shoah were expected to exceed or total the number of items that have been produced on any other subject in human history.[32] Literature, philosophy, history, sociology, theology, political science, psychology, anthropology, and many other disciplines have addressed the Shoah, each with its own theoretical

30 Giegerich, *Technology*, 53.
31 Giegerich, *Technology*, 58.
32 George Kren and Leon Rappoport, *The Holocaust and the Crisis of Human Behavior* (New York, NY: Homes and Meier, 1994).

orientation and methodology. Astonishingly (and perhaps embarrassingly), the Shoah is an untouched topic in Jungian and post-Jungian psychology. While much has been written on Jung and his alleged anti-Semitism,[33] Jungian psychology has strayed from a true confrontation with the Shoah. There is not one significant work or text of any considerable length or value that attempts to thoroughly address this event in history. While the nuclear bomb has also been seriously neglected, Giegerich's work on the bomb has at least begun a conversation about it. Not so for the Shoah.

Why turn to the Shoah, though, in the midst of a discussion on the nuclear bomb? Are these two realities not entirely separate phenomena? Why not, say, look to Hiroshima or Nagasaki, where the actual bomb did explode? For certain, hundreds of thousands of people would die from both the blast and radiation exposure. However,

> destroyed, that is, were not only men, women, and thousands of children but also restaurants and inns, laundries, theater groups, sports clubs, sewing clubs, boys' clubs, girls' clubs, love affairs, trees and gardens, grass, gates, gravestones, temples and shrines, family heirlooms, radios, classmates, books, courts of law, clothes, pets, groceries and markets, telephones, personal letters, automobiles, bicycles, horses—120 war-horses—musical instruments, medicines and medical equipment, life savings, eyeglasses, city records, sidewalks, family scrapbooks, monuments, engagements, marriages, employees, clocks and watches, public transportation, street signs, parents, works of art. "The whole of society," concludes the Japanese study, "was laid waste to its very foundations."[34]

Is the exploded bomb itself and its unspeakable aftermath not enough?

Even more, let us imagine a possible nuclear war between nations. Richard Rhodes, for example, summarizes a 2008 study:

> some of the scientists who modeled the original 1983 nuclear winter scenario investigated the likely result of a theoretical regional nuclear war between India and Pakistan, a war they postulated to involve only 100 Hiroshima-scale nuclear weapons, yielding a total of only 1.5 megatons—no more than the yield of some single warheads in the U.S. and Russian arsenals. They were shocked to discover that because such an exchange would inevitably be targeted on cities filled with combustible materials, the resulting firestorms would inject massive volumes of black smoke into the upper atmosphere which would spread around the world, cooling the earth long enough and sufficiently to produce

33 See Aryeh Maidenbaum, ed., *Jung and the Shadow of Anti-Semitism* (Berwirk, ME: Nicolas-Hays Inc., 2003). See also Andrew Samuels, *The Political Psyche* (London, UK: Routledge, 1993).

34 Richard Rhodes, *The Making of the Atomic Bomb* (New York, NY: Simon and Schuster, 2012), 733.

worldwide agricultural collapse. Twenty million prompt deaths from blast, fire, and radiation, Alan Robock and Owen Brian Toon projected, and another billion deaths in the months that followed from mass starvation—from a mere 1.5-megaton regional nuclear war.[35]

Is the threat of nuclear annihilation also not enough?

These are legitimate arguments and objections, and ones that I am not at all opposed to; the exploded bomb contains everything it needs within itself, so to speak, to arrive at the same conclusions that will ultimately be presented in this chapter. Despite this truth, however, there are many differences in the ways the bomb and the Shoah have been internalized into culture and society. The bomb maintains many romantic undertones, particularly in America, and these could be seen almost immediately after it was dropped: cakes that resembled mushroom clouds; "atomic" sales in department stores; General Mills marketing an atomic bomb ring to children;[36] the naming of the bikini after the atomic bomb testing site; images of the atomic bomb hanging on the walls of psychoanalysts' offices.[37] Even more, it is not uncommon to find many individuals who are willing to argue that dropping the bomb on Hiroshima and Nagasaki was legitimate in the context of World War II. Compare this, however, with the consistent and universal opinion of the inherent evil that was the Shoah. My worry, then, in addressing the actual explosion of the bomb in either Hiroshima or Nagasaki is that because of these undertones it could very easily cloud our judgment and prevent us from fully differentiating the inner nature of the bomb, thus stopping a truly psychological discussion.

Most importantly, however, the exploded nuclear bomb carries within it an idea and possibility of *total* annihilation, e.g., in nuclear holocaust, and thus it is on par with the inner logic of the "Final Solution" which sought the *total* annihilation of the Jewish people. This is a quality of the nuclear bomb that is understated (and perhaps only implicit) when one looks to Hiroshima or Nagasaki and the context in which it was used, despite the *complete* annihilation of the city populous which took place. Thus, it is important not to lose this distinction of "unconditionality" and "totality" that the bomb carries within it. Looking at the inherent evil of the Shoah, then, can assist us in seeing this "unconditional" quality of the exploded bomb. It can help us understand more fully its *neurotic* nature, as will be discussed below. For the present discussion, then, I want to first focus specifically on the Shoah because it is a very clear and universally accepted expression of *true sickness*— one that captures the psychological essence of the exploded bomb—and one that speaks to the neurotic soul as Giegerich understands it.

35   Rhodes, *Atomic Bomb*, 7.
36   Robert Jay Lifton and Eric Markusen, *The Genocidal Mentality* (New York, NY: Basic Books Inc., 1990), 65.
37   CBS News, "How Design Colors the Mind," last modified May 19, 2013. http://www.cbsnews.com/news/how-design-colors-the-mind/

The Shoah as an expression of the neurotic soul

I would like to now explore the idea that the Shoah is an expression of the *neurotic* soul before returning to the nuclear bomb, and in so doing, there are a few preliminary thoughts on this matter that I would like to note before proceeding into a more in depth discussion of two particular aspects of neurosis, namely, its dissociative nature and its Absolute quality.[38] First, I must clarify that from this point forward I use the term "neurosis" in the manner in which Giegerich defines it in his seminal text, *Neurosis*. In this text, he expounds upon the inner logic of neurosis—a far different use of this term than how it has been used in various psychological circles and one that is far different from the manner in which he used it when he wrote the nuclear bomb essays. Again, his notion of neurosis is quite complex, and I cannot hope to do justice to the full extent of his theory in this chapter. However, it is important to note, here, some key aspects of how Giegerich defines neurosis as they are relevant to the present discussion.

The first point concerns the manner in which Giegerich defines neurosis as a *true sickness*, in which there is nothing compensatory or inherently valuable about a neurosis at all. The soul is genuinely sick, and the neurosis serves no function for the person. He notes:

> Neurosis (*if* it is truly a neurosis) is simply sick, a terrible aberration, and a dead end. In contrast to certain other phenomena of psychopathology, in the case of which Jung's ideas are very much in place, it certainly does not cure us. It has, as I said, no redeeming value.[39]

In this, it is radically different from the traditional Jungian orientation towards neurosis which imagines symptoms and pathology as an attempt by the individual soul to heal itself, as this later definition of neurosis contains no "god in the disease," no dignity in the symptom, and no "alchemical gold" to be found. Giegerich takes neurosis seriously and at face value for what it is, namely, *a sickness*, with no God "preserved and waiting to be redeemed."

Second, while neurosis serves no function for the individual person, Giegerich does suggest that it maintains an inner *telos* in the life of the *objective* soul.[40] Here,

---

38 In exploring the Shoah as an example of the phenomenon of neurosis at work, I am not suggesting the Shoah was *only* neurotic. This would be a grave mistake and an attempt at producing a master narrative that by all means is impossible to arrive at within the multitudinous context of the Shoah, e.g. the contexts of anti-Semitism, obedience to authority, advanced technology, German history, religious persecution, economic turmoil, etc. Speaking of the Shoah as an expression of neurosis is thus merely a discussion of its *psychological* dimension. Second, I also do not want to confuse neurosis with genocide, as Giegerich suggests that the two are related only insofar as genocide has the potential to be expressed neurotically. He notes, for example, that the Rwandan genocide, while a truly significant tragedy, was not a product of the neurotic soul. See *Neurosis*, 279–280.

39 Wolfgang Giegerich, *What is Soul?* (New Orleans, LA: Spring Journal, Inc., 2012), 160.

40 Giegerich discusses the role of neurosis in the objective soul, suggesting that the soul created neurosis for its own purposes in order to further establish itself in modernity as subjectivity and to further differentiate itself from the mythological, religious, and metaphysical age. "The soul's purpose with the performance of the neurotic drama is to initiate *itself*, the soul, explicitly into modern subjectivity," in *Neurosis*, 351.

neurosis does not originate from within the human being, but it occurs *in the soul*, i.e., it is a product of the objective soul and one which carries an inner life of its own. This is radically different from the form of "neurotic dissociation" Giegerich discussed when he spoke about the nuclear bomb. In Giegerich's previous definition of neurosis as seen with the bomb, Giegerich understands neurosis as that which occurs between human beings and the world, between psychology and technology, between the inner and the outer. Here, we see a rather drastic change in the way neurosis is now viewed not in terms of a dissociative split on the level of physicality or positivity, but wholly on the level of the soul, or psychology. It is the objective soul, i.e., the historical and cultural soul at large, that creates neurosis, and thus neurosis is a *psychological* phenomenon, one that merely expresses itself *psychically* in human beings. Here, it is helpful to explore exactly how Giegerich understands this difference between psychology and the human being.

One of the most significant notions that Giegerich maintains in his understanding of psychology is the "psychological difference." He describes this difference as that between "psychic" life and "psychological" life, wherein psychic life includes all those aspects of the individual such as one's biology, emotions, feelings, behaviors, thoughts, and fantasies and psychological life includes the inner workings and logic of the soul. While psychic life is that which he calls the "human, all-too-human" dimension, psychological life is a speculative discipline that listens to the movements, directions, and "logic" of the soul as it expresses itself in history. This psychological difference is similar to the difference between religion and theology,[41] where the practical world emerges in religion, i.e., one's prayer life, moral duties, etc., and the nature of God emerges in theology, i.e., how to understand God as three persons in the Trinity, how to understand the incarnation of God in both man and Divine form, etc. Similarly, a difference is maintained in Giegerich's notion of psychology, where psychology is the discipline and methodology in which one is able to speculate upon the inner workings of the soul. It is thus not a soul that is defined and limited by being, for example, *inside* the person. Instead, the soul possesses its own interiority as a substance-less reality.[42]

The dissociative nature of neurosis in the Shoah

Giegerich acknowledged that one of the defining characteristics of neurosis is its self-contradiction and self-dissociation[43]—one in which two worlds coexist in the

41   David Miller, email message to author, February 16, 2016.
42
> Psychology as a modern field of study is something else. "Substance" as such is distilled, evaporated... For psychology this means that it can today only be the discipline that it is if it is nothing but a particular methodological *procedere*, an approach to (potentially all kinds of) possible experience, a mode or style of perceiving, reflecting, interpreting, and reacting, a form of consciousness
> (Giegerich, *What is Soul?*, 287–288)

43   Giegerich, *Neurosis*, 72.

same space yet remain insulated from, indeed, immunized against, each other. The left hand truly does not know what the right hand is doing.

> [This] neurotic dissociation is a disunity plus its denial. It is not neurotic to have a right hand and left hand that do different, maybe opposite things. It is, however, neurotic if the right hand must not know what the left hand is doing and vice versa. In other words, the neurotic dissociation consists in the *denial* of *itself* (of the dissociation) and, therefore, in the insistence that each of the dissociated partial truths be the whole truth.[44]

This defining feature of neurosis means that two independent worlds exist wholly exclusive from one another, the one never being influenced or affected by the other. Let us explore how this dissociative quality of neurosis might be seen in the Shoah.

Perhaps the greatest and most difficult reality to understand about the Shoah, and one which leaves many puzzled and confused, is how it is possible for a man or woman to knowingly participate in murder, and later, return home to one's family as if nothing occurred. Apart from the *individuals* in which this occurred, more importantly, how is it possible for a mass population of individuals to do the same? This question has plagued psychologists for some time after the Shoah and is perhaps most confusing when one looks to the results of the psychological tests administered to a select number of Nazi perpetrators in the aftermath of the World War II. Surprisingly, nearly all results of the Rorschach tests that were administered to these Nazi perpetrators suggested no degree of psychopathology or criminality.[45]

The preeminent 20th-century philosopher, Hannah Arendt, addresses this phenomenon with regards to Adolf Eichmann, the man who was tasked with facilitating and managing the deportation of Jews and other "undesirables" to concentration camps and death camps throughout Europe. Sent to report on the infamously publicized Eichmann trial that occurred in Jerusalem after his capture, Arendt published three literary pieces in *The New Yorker* that were later collected into what is now, *Eichmann in Jerusalem: A Report on the Banality of Evil.*[46] Upon publication, her writings provoked outrage and controversy, not only for her assertion that Eichmann was no beast or killer but rather "normal," but also because she discussed the complicity of Jewish leaders in their own deaths. Ultimately, this book became one of the most highly influential texts in Shoah literature.

In sticking with the topic of the dissociative nature of neurosis, it could be argued that the popularity and controversy that surrounded the publication of *Eichmann* was triggered by Arendt's ability to capture the very modern

44 Giegerich, *Soul's Logical Life*, 25.
45 Molly Harrower, "Rorschach Records of the Nazi War Criminals: An Experimental Study after Thirty Years," *Journal of Personality Assessment*, 40 (1976): 341–351.
46 Hannah Arendt, *Eichmann in Jerusalem: A Report on the Banality of Evil* (New York, NY: Penguin Books, 2006).

phenomenon of neurosis[47]—the heart of its dissociative nature—and force humanity to confront the "greatest moral and even legal challenge of the whole case": how could Eichmann be both a killer and an ordinary human being? She describes the conundrum of this neurotic split at length in the following passage:

> Throughout the trial, Eichmann tried to clarify … his plea of "not guilty in the sense of the indictment." The indictment implied not only that he had acted on purpose … but out of base motives and in full knowledge of the criminal nature of his deeds … [H]e was perfectly sure that he was not what he called an *innerer Schweinehund*, a dirty bastard in the depths of his heart … [H]e remembered perfectly well that he would have had a bad conscience only if he had not done what he had been ordered to do—to ship millions of men, women, and children to their death … This, admittedly, was hard to take. Half a dozen psychiatrists had certified him as "normal"—"More normal, at any rate, than I am after having examined him," … while another had found that his whole psychological outlook … was "not only normal but most desirable" … Behind the comedy of the soul experts lay the hard fact that his was obviously no case of moral let alone legal insanity.
>
> … Alas, nobody believed him. The prosecutor did not believe him, because that was not his job. Counsel for the defense paid no attention because he, unlike Eichmann, was, to all appearances, not interested in questions of conscience. And the judges did not believe him, because they were too good, and perhaps also too conscious of the very foundations of their profession, to admit that an average, "normal" person … could be perfectly incapable of telling right from wrong. They preferred to conclude from occasional lies that he was a liar—and missed the greatest moral and even legal challenge of the whole case. Their case rested on the assumption that the defendant, like all "normal persons," must have been aware of the criminal nature of his acts.[48]

Rather than facing the real question of how such a neurotic split within a "normal" human being can exist, it was avoided. In this, one might say that the neurosis which created an "Eichmann" was also at work in the very *neurotic thinking* which ultimately condemned him to death.[49] Thus, we can see that the neurosis lives on.

The phenomenon of a dissociative split in perpetrators such as Eichmann has been discussed at length in psychological literature. Robert Jay Lifton described such splitting, or as he called it "doubling," as "the division of the self into two functioning wholes, so that a part-self acts as an entire self."[50] Furthermore, it is

---

47 Arendt does not interpret Eichmann in light of a theory of neurosis.

48 Arendt, *Eichmann*, 25–26.

49 This is not a statement about the appropriateness of death for Eichmann. It is a *psychological* statement, i.e., as the question of social justice is irrelevant in terms of psychology. Giegerich notes, "Anger, fury, the wish for revenge or compensation, etc. are unpsychological, namely (if I may say so) 'sociological'." In *What is Soul?*, 246.

50 Robert Jay Lifton, *Nazi Doctors: Medicalized Killing and the Psychology of Genocide* (New York, NY: Basic Books Inc., 1986), 418.

interesting to note that in psychological and clinical research of Shoah survivors, a similar kind of phenomenon is said to occur as a result of the experienced trauma—a splitting that leaves the trauma behind and one in which *dissociation* becomes the main form of psychological defense. It is also worth noting the degree to which all modern psychological theories of trauma—most of which are based on a foundational under-standing of dissociation—arose out of the context of World War II in the attempts to treat survivors in its aftermath. The foundation of trauma theory, originally articulated by Niederland as "survivor syndrome,"[51] has its origins in the Shoah.

The goal of providing these examples above is not to substantiate a reason for the perpetrators' murderous behavior in the Shoah, nor am I looking to discuss the clinical realities and psychological defense mechanisms of dissociation on a psychic level—as these do indeed occur. I am, however, hoping to draw attention to the fantasy which plays out in the ways we have attempted to articulate the Shoah and its aftermath—both those who participated and those who were victims. Our psychological language and ideas have been consumed by notions of splitting and dissociation and further prevail in the neurotic thinking that would keep "perpetrator" and "victim" so neatly apart.[52] This truth reflects the soul's *neurotic* truth in that it mirrors the inherent dissociative logic of neurosis in modernity. It points to the notion that the underlying logical structure of the Shoah was neurotic and further highlights the soul's "Work" of neurosis in the 20th century in the field of psychology itself.

The "Absolute" of neurosis in the Shoah

We can follow the idea of the neurotic nature of the Shoah into the second aspect of neurosis, namely, the neurotic soul's capacity to inflate empirical reality with metaphysical, Absolute significance. This tendency is related to the neurotic soul's desire to maintain its innocent and "meaningful" existence as embedded within the sense of "in-ness" that one finds in the mythic, metaphysical, and religious age.[53] Let us explore Giegerich's understanding of this quality of neurosis a bit further.

---

51   William Niederland, "Clinical Observations on the 'Survivor Syndrome'," *International Journal of Psycho-Analysis*, 49 (1968): 313–315.
52   "Compare this to the idea of vicitimization in all sorts of recovery groups and psycho-logical theories today where the abstract (undialectical) difference (i.e., the split) between victim and agent is insisted upon, even celebrated, and where a ritual attempt is made to establish this split in consciousness and to establish consciousness *in* this split and *as* this split—in other words: *as* neurotic consciousness," in Giegerich, *Soul's Logical Life*, 247.
53
   But the moment the soul, under the conditions of modernity, nevertheless wants to become a present reality in life and to revive its former status of being in possession of substantial truth, it can only do so by way of simulation and thus turns into the sick soul. "Sick" because what its simulation achieves is by no means a new present reality of mythic, archetypal, or metaphysical truths, but only their imitation and thus the former truths *as* untruths.

(Giegerich, *What is Soul?*, 164)

As man had once been "upward-looking" in his nature, finding "his ground not within himself (in his body), but above in Nature, i.e., in an animated cosmic order, and ultimately in God, in the Ideas, in the divine light of reason,"[54] the advent of modernity creates a situation in which "the soul's deepest need has become in itself fundamentally *frustrated* upward-looking … bereft of its object to which it could reach out."[55] "There simply is no space anymore into which the soul could extend and ecstatically release itself."[56] Prior to this,

> a neurosis would have been impossible. It required the self-constitution of man as logically or ontologically solitary individual, that is to say, as fundamentally self-enclosed atomic I, for neurosis to become possible, because only then was the individual himself in his bodily concreteness "the battleground" of the struggle about the ultimate decisions, the venue or arena in which the opposite forces of the soul could rage and spend themselves.[57]

The consequence of such a significant change in the constitution of man's nature thus means that the ecstatic force which once had a home in the cosmic order now finds a home in concrete, earthly reality.

In taking on the quality of "Absolute" significance, the neurotic soul thus expects earthly reality to carry the weight of heaven. Giegerich notes:

> Neurosis regressively restores a sense of metaphysical upward-looking, but one that is reduced to the empty form of upward-looking per se which has nothing *to* which it could go upwards and is locked into itself. As such it is in itself the opposite of itself, frozen into rigid, hardened, even cemented fact. It is stuck and locked in the tight material reality of a concretistically enacted pathology (when as upward-looking it was actually meant to be the soul's releasement into its own infinity).[58]

With the psychological difference having collapsed, empirical reality is granted a level of inflated meaning or purpose that it heretofore had not held, thus procuring "a positively real existence for 'The Absolute' within the absolutely closed earthly phenomena."[59]

In describing this Absolute quality, it is essential to note the considerable power and force that is carried within it. Giegerich continues:

> The neurotic "The Absolute" is the internal contradiction of this absolutely pointless, hopeless, futile, but nevertheless absolutely powerful, upward-looking

54 Giegerich, *Neurosis*, 112.
55 Giegerich, *Neurosis*, 130.
56 Giegerich, *Neurosis*, 125.
57 Giegerich, *Neurosis*, 112.
58 Giegerich, *Neurosis*, 134.
59 Giegerich, *Neurosis*, 129.

that is stuck in itself ... The Absolute is a "storm in a tea cup" (or better: a storm in a sealed bottle). Like a motor idling at highest speed, it creates a free-floating, disengaged energy that can attach itself to all sorts of in themselves contingent and depleted empirical purposes and behaviors as its (in *psychological* regards more or less arbitrary) vessel and thus impart to them, fill them with, blow them up from within, with an irresistible compellingness, with that "must" and absolute conviction with which neurotic symptoms present themselves. This is what makes obsessions, compulsions, phobias and other symptoms possible, but also on a more intellectual level ideologies and fundamentalisms.[60]

It is this quality of neurosis—the demanded presence of the Absolute—that fueled the force behind the deeply ideological, highly technological, and incredibly efficient bureaucratic machine that was National Socialism. Mass murder on the scale of the Shoah (and one should note, in such abstract and sophisticated methods as a highly complex railway system and perfectly designed killing centers, to mention only a few) needs a neurotic home within which to be possible. More importantly, "as bereft of its object to which it could reach out," it needs an *object* to which it can release itself.

When one looks to the Shoah as an example of the phenomenon of neurosis at work, one can locate the "object" of the Absolute clear as day. When Hitler, for example, declared to Himmler in 1942 that "the discovery of the Jewish virus is one of the greatest revolutions that have taken place in the world,"[61] he was not just speaking in terms of traditional bigotry or racism. He was speaking from within the neurotic Absolute—that phenomenon of neurosis which inflates empirical reality with Absolute significance—or what Giegerich says "is the purpose that 'the soul' of the 19th/20th century pursues with its grand project of the production of neurosis."[62] In this sense, the Jews were the arbitrary empirical vessels that embodied such metaphysical importance—the empirically real gene that was determined a threat to the general population, *absolutely*. Where the soul had once released itself into the meaningful cosmos, here, the neurotic soul found new meaning in the "Final Solution to the Jewish Question" in which the *total* annihilation of a particular population was sought. In truth, the Jews and other "undesireables" who were transported in railroad cars to their ultimate deaths in gas chambers and burning ovens were the arbitrary victims of an Absolutely neurotic scheme.

Here, we must backtrack for a moment and see how Hitler's statement—"The discovery of the Jewish virus is one of the greatest revolutions that have taken place in the world"—was actually a true statement. He was capturing the *psychological essence* of neurosis, albeit unbeknownst to him. The discovery of the "Jewish virus"

---

60 Giegerich, *Neurosis*, 130.
61 Cited in Zygmunt Bauman, *Modernity and the Holocaust* (Ithaca, NY: Cornell University Press, 1989), 71.
62 Giegerich, *Neurosis*, 129.

was indeed a revolution unlike the world has seen, not because it was true that the Jewish people truly possessed a virus, but because the very possibility of being able to declare the Jews as virus-ridden was a revolutionary phenomenon heretofore impossible by humankind. Such inflation of human beings and biological reality is not possible without the arrival of neurosis in the 20th century. Just as the creation of the nuclear bomb (also in and through splitting!) was not possible prior to the developments within nuclear physics, so too was it impossible to have arrived at a revolutionary notion of a people as being virus-ridden and thus disposable in such unconditional and Absolute terms.

The nuclear bomb as neurotic

If we return now to the topic of the psychological nature of the nuclear bomb, we can see a neurotic logic expressed very clearly. For if we follow the bomb to its explosion, we are left with that inner contradiction and dissociative split that is a defining feature of neurosis proper. Within the idea of the nuclear bomb, we have two whole worlds which act independently of one another; indeed, they are immunized against each other. On the one hand, one idea builds the bomb for the sake of protection, and on the other, one idea seeks to destroy the entire world, thus rendering protection absolutely pointless. Indeed, what benefit could the development of the nuclear bomb be for humanity when it has the capacity to destroy humanity within a matter of minutes? If the bomb is built ultimately as a weapon of self-defense, and other countries have the same capacity to use such weapons, the idea of self-defense shows itself to be meaningless. The nuclear bomb thus renders itself absurd, as it negates the very idea for which it is built. This is the inner neurotic and dissociative logic which defines the nuclear bomb.

In such absurdity, it also echoes Giegerich's notion regarding the neurotic "The Absolute," as "only in the undignified, pathological, often silly and at any rate disgraceful form of neurotic behavior, that is, only *as stinking water*, can the neurotic soul's *highest value*, the absolute principle, become positively real."[63] He states, "the abstract principle of The Absolute at the core of neurosis can have its positive realness only negatively: only through the (*absoluteness* of the) *rejection* and *condemnation* of a real phenomenon."[64] We see this neurotic behavior most clearly expressed in the bomb's *explosion*, for when you follow the bomb to this logical end, it wipes the slate clean. Its end is *absolutely* negative, in that it means *total* and *unconditional* annihilation. With its limitless capacity to destroy, positive, empirical matter—as granted with *Absolute* metaphysical significance—finds its ultimate neurotic expression in the explosion which renders its existence absurd.

If we thus hold the "exploded bomb" as an ever-present reality *in* the nuclear bomb, we can say that the nuclear bomb is a further expression of the soul's neurotic unfolding. Even if we imagine that the bomb can be thoughtfully contained in

63 Giegerich, *Neurosis*, 298.
64 Giegerich, *Neurosis*, 298.

something like the idea of "nuclear deterrence," i.e., the bomb can perpetually remain *in potentia*, the unexploded bomb still "harbors within itself and *celebrates* the neurotic structure."[65] This is similar to the way in which Giegerich describes the difference between neurotic symptoms and neurotic theory. While in one sense, neurotic *symptoms* might take on a certain pathological character in the human person, psychological *theory* can also be "neurosis-syntonic,"[66] meaning that the underlying neurotic structure of both are the same despite their expressions being different. In this, the exploded bomb and the bomb *in potentia* express the same logic. There is no real psychological difference between the two.

Indeed, the nuclear bomb, like a neurosis, is itself a *real* "storm in a tea cup"—a storm created by a nuclear splitting, i.e., a nuclear "dissociation"—with a "disengaged energy" that could destroy the very hands that created it. It follows the motto that Giegerich says defines neurosis—"*Fiat absolutum et pereat homo*: May the Absolute happen even if it means that the human being perishes."[67] This is nothing less than the idea embedded in the inner nature of the bomb. It, along with the Shoah, is the neurotic soul's self-expression in the cultural achievements of Western mankind.

Revisiting the imaginal interpretation of the bomb

With the neurotic nature of the bomb in mind, we can see how Giegerich's original imaginal interpretation of the nuclear bomb is flawed. While we can see how his interpretation of the bomb was correct in speaking of the bomb as symptom, it had not made its way to being truly *neurotic* because it had not confronted its *explosion*—both the literal explosion of the bomb *and* the "explosion" that would be caused by true psychological thinking. His initial attitude toward this symptom did not recognize the "true sickness" present within it. In maintaining an imaginal approach, he saw the bomb as compensatory, containing "dignity," the riches of the imaginal, a "spiritual" reality, and an inner "meaning." As he once noted, "We have to ask with Jung (who asked about the content of neurosis, the content of psychosis) what the essential content or imaginal substance of the Bomb is",[68] we can see that Giegerich was focused on the *contents* of the inner bomb, and thus his view of the bomb did not live up to his later, more distilled vision of psychology that would recognize the need for such contents to be further dissolved. If Giegerich *had* seen the bomb as neurotic, these "contents" of the bomb would have been recognized as *simulated* phenomena of an era dead and gone, connected to the *Absolute* quality of neurosis. We would be left with only the logical shell of the bomb, i.e., its neurotic logic, wherein the bomb would by no means be "legitimate" and "indispensable," but actually *disposable*.

65 Giegerich, *Neurosis*, 59n.
66 Giegerich, *Neurosis*, 59n.
67 Giegerich, *Neurosis*, 300.
68 Giegerich, *Technology*, 63.

Giegerich's bomb was thus not a bomb that was truly sick. In its imaginal stance, it was a bomb simulating the presence of God—a God who was "preserved" and "waiting" to be redeemed. In wanting to instantiate the bomb *as* God, Giegerich inflated the bomb with metaphysical importance. It was thus a neurotic interpretation of neurosis,[69] one that is in union with the thinking that would inflate empirical reality with that Absolute and unconditional quality that is a defining feature of neurosis proper. In truth, the bomb holds the original *place* of God, as it indeed can destroy the world many times over, but such place is merely the *neurotic form* in which such Absolute presence might now exist in modernity. In this, Giegerich's imaginal stance confused the presence of the neurotic Absolute and unconditional power of the bomb for the *actual* reality of God.[70]

With regards to the psychological difference, we must add that Giegerich's imaginal stance towards *neurosis* in particular also *collapsed the psychological difference*. Because his original understanding of neurosis used to interpret the nuclear bomb did not occur *in the objective soul*[71] but rather, in the realm of physicality and positivity, i.e., between human beings and nature, Giegerich was unable to reach the inner nature and logic of the neurotic bomb itself. While the seeds of Giegerich's theory of neurosis were clearly sown, for example, in discussing the dissociative *split* that occurred in God as well as speaking of the return of God to "earthly reality," this is a fundamentally neurotic way of speaking about the bomb that denies the psychological side of the psychological difference. In all, neurosis—*as a genuine soul phenomenon*—was imagined solely in its personalistic, psychic, or positivistic expression. He thus worked within one side (the psychic) of the psychological difference. Ultimately, then, one can see that Giegerich misplaced the true neurotic dissociation: it is not the one that occurs between me as human ego and the bomb as material, technological, and physical other. *It is the one that occurs in the inner soul of the bomb itself.*

Conclusion

There is a common tendency to view the Shoah as too far removed from the psychological condition which allowed it. Take, for example, the fact that the United States constructed a museum dedicated to the Shoah prior to any museum dedicated to African slavery, Native American genocide, Hiroshima, or Nagasaki.[72] There is a profound dissociation here, one which attempts to maintain the innocence of America's ways of knowing, behaving, and seeing. So long as it keeps the bomb

---

69 See Giegerich, *Neurosis*, 80.
70 I say "actual" here with recognition of the fact that Giegerich saw the bomb imaginally, not literally. He notes, "The statement, 'The nuclear bomb is God,' cannot be taken literally." in Giegerich, *Technology*, 98.
71 Giegerich does acknowledge that the bomb's invention cannot be separated from the soul of the Christian West, i.e., it is a product of *history*. However, his theory of *neurosis* in particular stayed within the collapsed version of the psychological difference.
72 Christine Downing, email message to author, February 7, 2013.

away and distracts itself by focusing upon the "evil" it defeated in the Shoah, it does not have to be confronted by the hugely frightening and complicated reality of our neurotic and atomic age. However, if we see the bomb as neurotic and as connected to the Shoah, this means that it might be possible to see the shadows within our own ways of knowing. It means recognizing that a fundamental neurotic logic lay at the ground of modern civilization—expressed in the most individual neuroses in the consulting room, extending all the way into modern genocide and nuclear weaponry. In this, we might see our*selves* as not so far removed from the neurotic symptoms of society.

This is why the notion of the psychological difference is so important, as it points to the idea that discussion on matters related to neurotic symptoms transcends the embodied forms in which they express themselves. In this, then, we have not only been talking about the *literal* exploded bomb, the *literal* Shoah, Hiroshima, or Nagasaki, but we have also been talking about a specific moment in *history*[73]—a specific *psychology* from which these creations originated. We might think of the bomb and the Shoah as two separate rocks that were split in half—originally belonging to the one same rock. They share, so to speak, the same neurotic DNA. Our job has been to piece these rocks back together to form the original unity so that we might understand what they share in common, further delineating the neurotic nature of the bomb. In this, it is as if the bomb and the Shoah are twins, though not identical, sharing one common neurotic denominator. The same dissociation and splitting which defines the Shoah, along with the rise of the Absolute in empirical, physical form as discovered in the "Jewish gene," is the same psychological occurrence to be found in the use of nuclear fission for the purposes of weaponry and the manipulation of nature and matter to produce *total* annihilation. In this sense, the Shoah and the nuclear bomb originate from out of the same neurotic (or atomic) ground—the same contemporary situation. They are the lasting imprint of the "Work" of neurosis in the 20th century. The nuclear bomb, like the Shoah, is in fact the representation of neurosis proper.

This is not the first time such parallels have been drawn. Elie Wiesel, for example, echoed this truth long ago. On November 20, 1983, Wiesel was invited (amongst many other notable guests) by ABC News to address the prospects of nuclear war and deterrence after the premiere of *The Day After*,[74] an ABC television film which postulated a fictional nuclear war between the United States and the Soviet Union. Upon seeing the film, Wiesel was asked for his response. He replied:

> I am scared. I am scared because I know that what is imaginable can happen. I know that the impossible is possible ... I had a strange feeling that I had seen it

---

73 With the discovery of nuclear fission in 1938 in Berlin, the race to develop the first atomic bomb began shortly thereafter. Leo Szilard, the famous Hungarian physicist who is known for first imagining a "nuclear chain reaction," along with Albert Einstein, strongly urged President Roosevelt to begin development of the nuclear bomb for fear that Hitler might develop it first, thereby using it for world domination. In this, the bomb and the Shoah are intimately related.

74 *The Day After* (Burbank, CA: ABC Circle Films, 1983).

before. Except once upon a time it happened to my people, and now it happens to all people. And suddenly I said to myself, maybe, the whole world, strangely, has turned Jewish. Everybody lives now facing the unknown. We are all, in a way, helpless.[75]

We might speculate that Wiesel was confronted with the terrifying neurotic truth of the modern world in this moment—present in both the Shoah and nuclear holocaust—which recognized the inherent powerlessness of humanity in the face of such absolute terror. Such feeling of helplessness is indeed a genuine and honest response to the frightening reality that both the bomb and the Shoah embody. But are we still helpless, today, more than 71 years after the nuclear bomb was first dropped and the Shoah ended?

Norris Bradbury, the American physicist who succeeded Robert J. Oppenheimer as the director of the Los Alamos National Laboratory, once stated, "Most experiences in life can be comprehended by prior experiences, but the atom bomb did not fit into any preconceptions possessed by anybody."[76] Similarly, Auschwitz shattered the mind's capacity to place this reality within a framework which could understand it. In the face of these unknowns, humanity was certainly helpless; any modern psychologist or philosopher who has truly lingered with and confronted the reality of death camps and nuclear weaponry is aware of this fact. However, with Giegerich's thought, particularly his revolutionary work, *Neurosis*, we now have a conceptual framework within which to understand these unknowns. While as humans, we might remain *psychically* helpless, *psychologically*, we can now actually conceptualize two of the most catastrophic "creations" of contemporary life. Is it not amazing, that with *Neurosis*, Giegerich wrote an entire book about the nuclear bomb and the Shoah without ever once addressing them directly? It is an achievement that cannot be understated, and one that makes his work of dire significance for the 21st century.

Giegerich's theory is a *modern* theory, meaning it carries the atrocities of the 20th century as realities already sublated within it, as already fully thought. His theory of neurosis has captured the underlying logic of our atomic age. Before, it was inconceivable. Now, it *is* conceivable. Is this not remarkable, that we are now no longer *only* helpless? We have the capacity to *think* the underlying neurotic logic of our present human condition.

75 Wiesel, *Viewpoint*.
76 Cited in Rhodes, *Atomic Bomb*, 674.

11

"ONE SMALL STEP FOR A MAN…"

The moon landing and "the psychological difference"

John Hoedl

Neil Armstrong, after taking his final step from the spaceship onto the moon declared, "That was one small step for a man, and one giant leap for mankind."[1] Comprehended psychologically, this statement speaks to what Wolfgang Giegerich calls the "psychological difference"—the distinction between two expressions of consciousness that is a foundational concept for Psychology as the Discipline of Interiority. If we examine the moon landing within the context of this psychological difference, our focus is not on the ordinary event but rather on the meaning "behind" this achievement, its syntactical or psychological dimension. It is concerned with what Giegerich calls the syntax of the observable, similar to what Jung describes as the reality "behind the impressions of daily life … covered by a thin veil of actual facts."[2] There can therefore be a difference between what the general, collective human understanding of a phenomenon or event is and what it may reveal in terms of objective consciousness, the objective psyche (Jung), or "soul."[3] For example, Giegerich states, "we usually think in all earnest that technology serves our practical purpose, that it exists for our sake and ought to be there for our benefit. This is ego-psychology. Its true purpose, however, is a soul

---

1 After acoustic analysis, it seems to have been concluded that there was indeed an "a" between "for" and "man" in Armstrong's statement. He himself had always maintained he said, "for a man."

2 "… behind the impressions of daily life—behind the scenes—another picture looms up, covered by a thin veil of actual facts," in C. G. Jung, *The Visions Seminars: Book One* (Zürich: Spring Publications, 1976), 8.

3 In Psychology as the Discipline of Interiority, the word "soul" is here placed in quotes to clarify the fact that it is not a positivity. The inverted commas encourage the reader to avoid the common error of hypostasizing what is a form of consciousness *per se*, and *ipso facto* negativity. Whether or not the word is in quotes, this qualifier always applies. In fact, the act of pushing off from a literal conception of "soul" and conceiving of it as a dynamic or a negativity, supports an awareness of the "psychological difference."

purpose."[4] That there is a "soul purpose" present in humanity reaching the moon comes out in Armstrong's announcement, which in effect, is an expression of the psychological difference writ large for humanity. It is an acknowledgement of both the personal ("a man") and the collective ("mankind"), in other words, the human and the soul present in this one event.

Bearing this in mind, this essay will examine the nature of the psychological difference as understood within the development of technology and the moon landing. Tracing Giegerich's steps, it will explore the evolution of human technology in its various forms beginning with archaic hunting and sacrificial killing before proceeding into the development of the technology that led to the moon landing. Ultimately, this essay will show how the moon landing, as a technological achievement, is one giant leap for mankind in that it reveals the soul's move to firmly establish itself as reflective consciousness and thought, over and against instinctual life.

Archaic "technology" and soul making

Recognition of the above mentioned psychological difference acknowledges that due to the inherent structure of consciousness, two different ways of comprehending phenomena are possible, thus allowing for a fundamental "depth" to the world. This depth manifests in a manner specific to and consistent with the general form of consciousness operative at a given time in history, for example, as in the mythological, metaphysical, theological, scientific, and now in modern times, psychological ages.[5] Jung's psychology of the unconscious is a psychology with depth, observed in symbols, dreams, archetypes, etc., but he did not go so far as to seriously explore the psyche's possible manifestation in technology. Giegerich, however, makes the case for technology being a "tool" for the soul to move itself forward, taking humans, so to speak, along for the ride.

Technology is obviously designed for the practical purpose of helping humans get things done in the world. However, in addition to this straightforward and basic purpose, it can have a *psychological* function as well. In other words, technology can be used by consciousness as a kind of pushing off point for its own purposes, i.e., to leverage itself towards a deeper, more complex structure or self-understanding. This is obviously a much more complicated and difficult function of technology to comprehend. Even the notion that "soul" can have its own self-understanding might lead us to think of it as having an existence separate from human consciousness, but we must not fall into the trap of reifying or substantiating it,

4 Wolfgang Giegerich, *The Soul Always Thinks (Collected English Papers, Vol. IV)* (New Orleans, LA: Spring Journal, Inc., 2010), 45. Heidegger wrote, "For the essence of technology is not anything human. The essence of technology is above all not anything technological," in Martin Heidegger, *What Is Called Thinking* (New York, NY: Harper Perennial, 1954/2004), 22.

5 See Wolfgang Giegerich, *What is Soul?* (New Orleans, LA: Spring Journal Inc., 2012), 74–86.

thinking of it as "out there" somewhere. Consciousness as "soul" in the way Psychology as the Discipline of Interiority conceives of it is truly objective, as in Jung's idea of the "objective psyche," and has its own movement and development separate and even at times opposed to that of humans, however it always manifests in, or better, *as* human consciousness.[6] Comprehending and discerning the distinction between these two forms of consciousness—practical vs. psychological, human vs. "soul"—is bringing the psychological difference to bear on phenomena, and, according to Giegerich, is the work and challenge of depth psychology today.

While there is a significant difference, psychologically speaking, between ancient tools and modern technology, the psychological difference can still be seen in some of the oldest known hand axes, roughly 400,000 years old. These symmetrically beautiful stone axes that are curiously much too large to be practically useful are thought to have been tools built strictly for symbolic reasons, despite the fact that their shape followed more or less exactly that of a regularly used hand axe.[7] We could say that these stone axes were a *psychological* tool, in that their action or function were not intended for the person or people who made the tools, but rather for consciousness *per se*, or "soul." With these symbolic axes, consciousness was able to "go to work," in effect, on itself.[8]

Giegerich devoted much attention to both ancient rituals and modern forms of technology, speculating upon their psychological significance and function. In his well-known essay "Killings,"[9] for example, in a discussion of archaic hunting and

6   This brings to mind Jung's notion that we are in the psyche, the psyche is not in us! "As I see it, the psyche is a world in which the ego is contained," in Jung, *CW* 13, § 75.

7   The Furze Platt Axe from Maidenhead, England, is one example. There is currently debate among archaeologists over the "meaning" of very old hand axes since many are found to have an elegant aesthetic that goes beyond immediate function, and many seem not to have been used. See, for example, Penny Spikins, "Goodwill Hunting?: Debates Over the 'Meaning' of Lower Paleolithic Handaxe Form Revisited," *World Archeology*, 44:3 (2012): 378–392. However, the point here is that the function of these axes was not practical, but psychological.

8   In the technological developments at the beginning of the space program in the late 1950s, the astronauts, all of them former pilots, began complaining at one point that there was not much "flying" left up to them. The spaceship, they said, almost flew itself. Mailer picked up this theme when he wrote: "in NASA-land, the only thing open was the technology—the participants were so overcome by the magnitude of their venture they seemed to consider personal motivation as somewhat obscene. [I] had never before encountered as many people whose modest purr of efficiency apparently derived from being cogs in a machine," Norman Mailer: *Moonfire, The Epic Journey of Apollo 11* (Cologne, Germany: Taschen, 1969/2010), 220. The process was so auto- mated that the flight engineers used to boast, to the astronauts' annoyance, that given a year they could instruct anyone off the street how to fly a rocket to the moon. The human element was being reduced, or *sublimated*, almost to the point that it was the machines, the computers, that were "flying" the human, and not the other way around. This is an example of the idea that consciousness as technology uses humans to achieve *its* goals, further suggesting the reality of an objective "mind" by which psychological life unfolds.

9   Wolfgang Giegerich, *Soul Violence (Collected English Papers, Vol. III)*, (New Orleans, LA: Spring Journal, Inc., 2008), 189–265.

blood sacrifices, we see how a spear or club functions in both the practical human domain as well as that of the psychological. We can think of the spear thrown by early human hunters as serving two purposes: naturally, it was intended to find its target—pierce and kill the hunted animal for food, clothing, etc.—but *unnaturally*, that is, to the extent that for early humans, hunting itself was contra-instinctual and therefore an "incursion" of the objective psyche, or "soul" into the human world, the spear's function was strictly psychological, unrelated to the needs of the hunters as humans. Giegerich hypothesizes that hunting was not an instinctual action of archaic humans. The first hunters were therefore *compelled* to overcome the natural instinct to flee from big game and instead track and kill them. This compulsion, concludes Giegerich, was the incursion of something *contra-naturum*; for him, archaic hunting was a sacrificial (religious) act. Citing Baudler, Fromm, and Eliade, Giegerich writes:

> It would be a fundamental mistake to consider the primordial hunt as man's animal heritage. This is precisely what it is not. … Man is not naturally equipped with an instinctual apparatus enabling him to prey on other animals. … Human killing is, from the outset, an undertaking having its origin, not in biology and nature, but in soul and mind.[10]

In this case then, the spear's function was strictly psychological, unrelated to the needs of the hunters as humans.[11] Keeping in mind the psychological difference, we can view the same spear with the same action, but having different consequences within entirely different realms—one human, the other psychological.

What was the psychological function of the spear? Giegerich insists that the penetrating of the spear was, for consciousness, the establishment of a difference between the "biological" and the imaginal, or the "physical" and the noetic. Here the spear was the soul's tool that, in finding its target, pierced into its *own* biological, instinctual form in order to force an opening for a new kind of consciousness to emerge. Giegerich states:

> The killing thrust of the spear or blow with the ax is a thrust or blow into the dullness of animal life. It was the soul itself that with the shock of the killing blow shocked itself out of the darkness of merely-biological existence. Amidst this darkness and from within it, it violently opened up for itself for the first time the luminous soul-space as a small island.[12]

The animal "out there" became more than a simple other or object the way consciousness had perceived objects for millennia. The ordinary other now became, as well, consciousness' *own* other, a "symbol" of its instinctual, undialectical position.

10 Giegerich, *Soul Violence*, 198.
11 The "technology" used here was not always a spear. As Giegerich points out, axes, clubs, and the like were also used.
12 Giegerich, *Soul Violence*, 203.

Consciousness now saw *itself* as the animal.[13] In other words, at the same time that consciousness perceived the biological animal pierced by the spear, it also conceived of *itself* being penetrated, that is, a "natural," naive, insular expression of itself. And just as the living animal is finally killed and becomes a corpse, natural consciousness is negated, its "corpse" sublated, and the resulting, refined, reflective consciousness is established. The soul, says Giegerich, kills itself into being.[14]

Giegerich suggests that this killing continued until the soul had sufficiently established itself as distinct from its instinctual (Jung would say "unconscious") heritage. It is fair to assume with Giegerich, pointing to cave paintings of what seems like ritualized hunting, as well as evidence from hunting cultures that exist today, that archaic hunting morphed into elaborate ritual sacrifices.[15] Over the millennia, these sacrifices kept the space or "clearing" produced by the penetrating spear open, thereby allowing culture to generate and develop.[16] In modern times these rituals have all but ended except in anachronistic forms such as bullfighting in Spain, Mexico, and other countries, or in the highly sublimated Eucharistic body and blood of Jesus Christ in the Catholic Mass.[17]

So, we have examined how ancient rituals and tools, in particular the spear, were used by the soul to further itself with the act of killing. However, as with the early stone axes that were not used in a practical sense but only in a symbolic one, the use of tools in relation to ancient rituals was already a movement of consciousness out of its primordial existence. Therefore, the axe and spear and in a sense all subsequent technology, carry the original echo of the soul lifting itself away from instinct to mindedness, from raw material to tools, and from an embeddedness in the natural world to the scientific achievements needed for modern technology and space travel.

From spear to rocket

In Stanley Kubrick's film *2001: A Space Odyssey*,[18] released in 1968 one year before the moon landing, there is a scene in which some kind of early hominid

13 Because consciousness does not exist as a positivity, it can only "see" itself, or establish a reflective position, by positing itself *as* a real object already present in the world.
14 "In a kind of self-bootstrapping, the soul first made itself through killing, it *killed itself into being*, and this is why I consider sacrificial killings as the primordial soul-making," in Giegerich, *Soul Violence*, 205.
15 "Hunting behavior became established and, at the same time, transferable through ritualization. In this way, it was preserved long after the primitive hunter," in Walter Burkert, *Homo Necans: The Anthropology of Ancient Greek Sacrificial Ritual and Myth* (Oakland: University of California Press, 1983), 35.
16 "Through solidarity and cooperative organization, and by establishing an inviolable order, the sacrificial ritual gave society its form," in Burkert, *Homo Necans*, 35.
17 During special celebrations in the Greek Orthodox Church, the body of Christ is presented as a consecrated loaf of bread that is ceremonially pierced several times by a priest with a sacred lance.
18 *2001: A Space Odyssey*, directed by Stanley Kubrick (1968; Burbank, CA: MGM, 2001), DVD.

uses a large bone as a weapon to strike repeatedly and eventually kill another member of its species. It then flings the weapon into the air, and as the camera follows it up, turning and soaring, the image of the bone transforms into a space ship. Here a direct link is established for the viewer between ancient tools and modern technology: the pre-modern bone used to kill, and the modern (or futuristic) vehicle used to explore outer space. There is also a connection here between the notions of "killing" and "exploring" that comes out, for example, in the original Latin word for exploring, *ex-plōrāre,* which refers to hunters crying out as they spot their prey and move in for the kill. From the perspective of the soul, we could say that "killing" is "exploring" and "exploring" is a "killing." Inherent in both actions is the negation of a previous position which is the *ipso facto* development of discovery of a new one.

The significance of the image in the Kubrik film is that it highlights the evolution of technology and its psychological function; the process that originally began with the bone (or spear) used to kill and open up a reflective space for consciousness, continues with the rocket. Now the rocket carries consciousness further into itself—*a deeper exploration*—opening and penetrating an "outer" space that furthers consciousness and makes the original movement more comprehensive and explicit. Killing and exploring thus go hand in hand. Psychologically, we might speculate that the rocket is the inevitable psychological continuation of the ongoing unfolding of the soul's self exploration that originally began with the spear. Just as the rocket, as technological tool, launches humans into outer space, the soul pushes off from its known established base, its "earth," into unexplored regions of itself.

This journey from psychological spear to rocket took a great deal of development in the history of the soul. This movement is vital in that for Giegerich, "the soul is fundamentally historical, historical process … in the sense of the history of culture at large—this is the soul's *opus magnum.*"[19] The notion of objective consciousness evolving over time was also noted by Jung when he discussed how the location of the psyche migrated from "outside" in former times, to "inside" in modern times. He writes:

> It is of course only from my own experience with other persons and with myself that I draw my knowledge of the spiritual problem of modern man … No doubt I can only draw a one sided picture, for everything I have described lies in the psyche—it is all *inside.* I must add at once that this is a remarkable fact in itself. For the psyche is not always and everywhere to be found on the inside. There are peoples and epochs where it is found *outside,* because they are wholly unpsychological. As examples we may choose any of the ancient civilizations, but especially that of Egypt with its monumental objectivity and its naive confession of sins that have not been committed. … Whenever there exists some external form, be it an ideal or ritual, by which all the yearnings and hopes of the soul are adequately expressed—as for instance in a living

19 Giegerich, *What is Soul?,* 73.

religion—then we may say that the psyche is outside … just as there is then no unconscious in our sense of the word.[20]

Giegerich describes the process of the soul's movement in time in more detail explaining that consciousness pushes off from each stage or level of its self-expression by going deeper into itself and revealing more of its complexity. The establishment of a new base, or new status for consciousness, comes about through the full comprehension, negation, and sublation of the previous one. For example, when myths were being written down and discussed objectively as narratives, one must conclude that the age of myth had been spent, for it is not possible to be enveloped in a mythological orientation to the world when it is an "object" to be studied. Following Giegerich, one would say that the soul had then advanced to a higher, or deeper form of expression as seen, for example, in the transition from *mythology* to *philosophy* in ancient Greece. Keeping the psychological difference in mind, we would say that this shift was the soul's need to move from its previous status, and the philosophers gave expression to and developed this newly established position in the soul.

For both Giegerich and Jung, an indispensable phase of the soul's movement toward modernity was Christianity. Psychologically speaking, Christianity was the soul's process of radical transformation, its leap from a mythic mode of consciousness toward a more modern, i.e., differentiated and abstract, relationship to nature and eventually to what we would call the modern "ego." Jung wrote,

What Christianity really struggled against was that clinging to the object, to natural reality. Christianity has brought about a higher level of consciousness by stressing the autonomy of the idea. There was mind independent of matter … One came to understand that God is different from the world, that He is neither the storm nor the fire; that logos is not an object, but autonomous; … that a thought can exist by itself and does not necessarily depend on physical life—that was the decisive achievement of Christianity.[21]

Giegerich concurs. For him, before Christian consciousness had taken hold, "primitive man's essential knowledge [was] not derived from rational argumentation and from empirical observation, but from immediate 'identity with the world,' epiphanic and visionary experience, from immersion into the 'dream-time'."[22] But this changed drastically when

Christianity catapulted the psyche onto a very different niveau, and it is on that niveau where the psyche actually is today… Nature is nothing but a kind

20 Jung, *CW* 10, § 158–159.
21 C. G. Jung, *Dream Interpretation Ancient and Modern: Notes from the Seminar Given in 1936–1941* (Princeton: Princeton University Press, 2014), 112.
22 Wolfgang Giegerich, David L. Miller and Greg Mogenson, *Dialectics and Analytical Psychology: The El Capitan Canyon Seminar* (New Orleans, LA: Spring Journal, Inc., 2005), 52.

of machine, a system of abstract, formal laws, a set of mathematical formulas. This is the Christian soul's truth about nature … As far as the natural world is concerned, all the *passion* of the soul [that was once located there, now] seems to go into physics and technology. *This* is where the real action is.[23]

Jung also discussed the movement of soul in history being preceded by what he called a "psychological necessity."[24] He recognized, for example, that despite the Romans having sufficient engineering capability to be able to build a steam engine, all that came of it was the toy of Hero of Alexandria (c. 10–70 AD).[25] In other words, there was not the need in the soul at that time to advance *itself* further, which would have then resulted in a development of, in this case, technological culture. The soul has to, so to speak, open the door first. The "objective mind" has to have already been there before we can conceive of taking up the project. We can take the old saying attributed to Confucius, "Wherever you go, there you are," a step further and say, "Wherever you go, the soul has already been." The physical, explicit accomplishment of something in the world, such as reaching the scientific age or landing on the moon, is the following through or "making complete" *vollig machen* (Jung) of an already established, *in the soul*, position.

In this light, we can say that in order for humans to be able to travel into outer space and land on the moon, the soul had to first create, or conceptualize an inner "outer" space. The soul must have had the "necessity," to use Jung's term, to experience itself now from an entirely new, even alien, vantage point—negating what it had up until now created for itself as "world," thereby entering an entirely new realm. To achieve this, consciousness had to leave behind its mythological and religious notions of heaven and earth, because the sky or the heavens had always been the domain of the gods or God—the place where humans by definition could not go. Metaphysically, there was no ontological allowance for humans to venture up into the heavens. There was earth, and then on the other side of an impenetrable logical barrier, there was heaven. At this level of consciousness, the human spirit or soul was able to reach heaven, but the corporal, fleshly self could not.

Describing how in modern times we are bereft of symbols, myths, and religion and live in "spiritual poverty," Jung, in a rather foreboding tone, states that one must "dwell with oneself alone, where in the cold light of consciousness, the blank barrenness of the world reaches to the very stars."[26] We could here say that what

---

23 Wolfgang Giegerich, *The Flight Into the Unconscious: An Analysis of C. G. Jung's Psychology Project (Collected English Papers, Vol. V)* (New Orleans, LA: Spring Journal, Inc., 2013), 333.

24 Jung, *CW* 10, § 159.

25 Hero's "toy," called an aeolipile, was basically a metal ball, perhaps a foot in diameter, with water inside placed over a heat source. When the water was heated to boiling, the steam rose and was forced out of two attached curved pipes causing the ball to rotate. Hero himself considered his invention a novelty and as having no practical use (Smith College Museum of Ancient Inventions, accessed March 28, 2016 from http://www.sm ith.edu/hsc/museum/ancient_inventions/hsclist.htm).

26 Jung, *CW* 9i, § 29.

Jung was (perhaps unconsciously) observing was the fact that the development of the soul had now cleared the way, so to speak, for a physical rocket to travel to the moon. The space above us was now physical, secular space, governed and navigable via the laws of science and rationality, *not* an imaginal heaven. The moon was no longer the abode of the dead or the gateway to heaven or hell. It had become a physical body ready to be discovered and explored.

Now, it's a long way from a bone or a spear in the hands of an early ancestor to a modern rocket carrying humans to the moon. But we must recognize that it's *also* a long way from experiencing the soul in physical nature, i.e., sensually and mythologically as our ancestors did, to the modern comprehension of soul as reflective and psychological, i.e., a theory about archetypes (Jung) or the logical life of the soul (Giegerich). For the soul, landing the rocket on the moon is to touch down on, *in the Real*,[27] a deeper strata of its own nature, its absolute-negative or logical truth. As Giegerich describes, this is the soul's existence as sublated image and emotion. It bears little resemblance to the natural world. Moonscape has, for example, no blood, no flesh, no warmth, no "atmosphere," no *nature*. Like the moon, the modern soul emphasizes the cold, conceptual, abstract, nonhuman side. The images of the moon are stark and grey—negative and other-worldly. They are akin to a pushing off from the sensual to the abstract and formal. The moon is *not* earth; it is an image of a *negated earth*. Buzz Aldrin, standing on the moon, described it as a "magnificent desolation."[28]

Touching down on the moon: one small step, one giant leap

We have brought up the twofold idea that the tool, in our case a bone or a spear, carries with it *per se* the notion of consciousness having "lifted" itself from its natural state. In addition to this, as Giegerich has shown, psychologically the tool "goes to work" *for* consciousness in, for example, the act of sacrificial killing. With the sacrificial killing of a real animal, consciousness pushes off from itself as instinctual life into mindedness. With the rocket (or sublated spear, if we can call it that), we see that it pushes off from, or negates, the entirety of nature on planet earth. What is important to note here is that consciousness' movement deeper into itself via the rocket is a "leaving," even a "blasting off from," not only instinctual life, as with the spear's cut into the biological, but the entire earth itself and into a space very different from what was left behind. What does this mean for consciousness, for the soul? What does it mean for the soul that humans now explore outer space and land on the moon?

Six hours after landing, Neil Armstrong was ready to leave the lunar module and step on the moon. Back on earth, six million people were fixed to their TV screens

27 For Giegerich, the "Real" coincides with the notion of the "existing concept" which, unlike an *abstract* concept, is the concept's availability to the perceiving mind as a phenomenon in the world.

28 Buzz Aldrin, *Magnificent Desolation: The Long Journey Home from the Moon* (New York, NY: Three Rivers Press, 2010).

in awe and anticipation. Norman Mailer[29] had an inspired insight into the moment Armstrong was climbing down the ladder outside the spacecraft: "Man was descending into this kingdom of death itself."[30] Seen psychologically, one might speculate that the "kingdom of death" is the *negation* of the entire level of consciousness that had been inspired by and symbolized as the moon's image in the heavens. Now, by stepping onto a substantiated, physical, geological reality, this status of consciousness was confirmed and even celebrated as (logically) dead. Just as the spear had sacrificed the animal, the biological, to provide space for the soul to come into being, now the rocket as sublated spear allowing the astronauts to touch down on the moon killed all lingering *imaginal* ideas clinging to the *now* factual moon. On a collective level, the moon was no longer Aristotle's "perfect sphere" or Dante's "eternal pearl to magnificently ascend into the heavenly empyrean." For the astronauts and the six million people watching Armstrong on earth, the moon became, in that instant, explicitly part of the modern, alienated, and secular world. For the soul, setting foot on the moon was its way of solidifying its own internal movement of negating once and for all any tendencies toward re-enchanting the world.

Christ foreshadows this thought in claiming that his kingdom is NOT of this world, alluding to an understanding of heaven as a psychologically *negated* world, or a world of absolute negativity.[31] It has taken mankind a long time to see through the natural, imaginal understanding of heaven as a positivity somewhere up above the earth. Armstrong's stepping onto the moon confirmed a *psychological* comprehension of heaven. In effect, this action said, "There is no mythological or divine heaven. There is only one physical universe, and, along with it, the psychological or the realm of the soul."[32] The "small step for a man" is, of course, the three foot distance from the last wrung on the ladder to the surface of the moon. The "one giant leap for mankind," *homo totus,* is the journey of the soul from occlusion in instinct and image to finally coming home to the comprehension of itself as the logic or syntax of life. "Then I saw a new heaven and a new earth, for the first heaven and the first earth had passed away."[33] Psychologically, this new heaven

---

29 Two time Pulitzer Prize winner Norman Mailer was hired by *Life Magazine* to put his personal reflections on Apollo 11's lunar voyage into an article. Mailer wrote most of the article while the event was happening.

30 Mailer, *Moonfire*, 8. Mailer also wrote, "One of the reasons why the moon is so romantic to us is that it is the great symbol of the dream of death … Something very deep in the unconscious comprehension of all of us recognizes the moon as an avatar of the dream of death," in Mailer, *Moonfire*, 8.

31 According to Giegerich, when Jesus says to his tempter, "My kingdom is not of this world," we are witness to "the first time conquest or birth of this new objective soul dimension, the dimension of spirit as logical negativity, through the process of negating the natural desire or the naturalistic understanding of the desire," introducing consciousness to its truth as absolute-negative. See Wolfgang Giegerich's "Christ's Initial Meeting with the Tempter" in *Spring # 84 A Journal of Archetype and Culture: God Must Not Die! (Or Must He?): Jung and Christianity* (2010): 16–19.

32 This statement is not meant to disparage any religious belief in heaven but is made from a psychological, not theological position.

33 *Revelations* 21: 1.

and earth is the realm of logical negativity. It is earth in its reflected, logical form. Understood psychologically, man's stepping onto the moon is the soul's action of explicitly, in the Real, demonstrating its having now consciously touched down in the realm of "magnificent desolation" or absolute negativity.[34]

In truth, humans long ago left the natural world as a consequence of the soul's movement from instinct to reflective consciousness and thought. We have lived encapsulated in the mind since the time of the spear, so that all we experience is psychic.[35] In modern times, with the act of landing on another heavenly body, the soul truly and in the Real caught up with the throw of the spear. It was able to consciously and technologically push off from *terra firma* (solid earth). As Giegerich put it, "Nature and the world have become obsolete ... The soul has overcome the world and thus come home to itself."[36]

---

34 After having been on the surface of the moon for a few hours completing all the technical duties and before venturing out of the capsule, unknown to the public back on earth, Buzz Aldrin celebrated Holy Communion. He had brought up a small amount of consecrated wine and communion wafers (the body and blood of Christ), and a small chalice. He performed the ritual of the Last Supper on the moon and read the words from the Gospel of John: "I am the vine, you the branches. You who dwell in me as I in you Bear much fruit, But without me you can do nothing" (*John* 15:5). Armstrong, with his feet planted firmly in the modern world, apparently, "looked on, an expression of faint disdain on his face (as if to say, 'What's he up to now?') while Aldrin went on with his ceremony," in Andrew Chaikin, *A Man on the Moon: The Voyages of the Apollo Astronauts* (USA: Penguin Books, 1994), 205.

35

> We are in truth so wrapped about by psychic images that we cannot penetrate at all to the essence of things external to ourselves. All our knowledge consists of the stuff of the psyche which because it alone is immediate, is superlatively real. Here, then, is a reality to which the psychologist can appeal—namely, psychic reality.
>
> (Jung, *CW* 8, § 680)

36 Giegerich, *What is Soul?*, 285.

12

THIS LOSS IS NOT AN INTERLUDE

Entering the radical ecopsychology project[1]

Jordan Dessertine

Introduction

A guiding assumption of this chapter is that there are many ways into Wolfgang Giegerich's writings. One need not be a "Jungian" to appreciate the simple yet tremendously challenging message that pervades Giegerich's oeuvre (though it helps to know something of Jung's work). This is an assumption that I have come to appreciate by virtue of my particular background, which unlike most other authors in this collection does not revolve around the particular brand of psychology arising from the life and works of C. G. Jung. Rather, my orientation might better be described as that of a cultural critic, and more precisely as one who stands at the crossroads of philosophy and ecology.

The motivation behind my inclusion in the present collection is, as far as I can tell, twofold. Firstly, it is an occasion to include a voice from outside the confines of the Jungian community, a voice which, although actively engaged in the ongoing conversation surrounding Giegerich's writings and psychology, is neither Jungian nor even psychological in the strict sense of being a practicing analyst or therapist. Secondly, by virtue of my particular background, my inclusion may also be seen as an opportunity to form a bridge between what is going on within the small and relatively insular community gathered around Giegerich's works and the blossoming field of ecological thought: a field that includes a growing list of disciplines, from scientific ecology, deep ecology, social ecology and human ecology to ecofeminism, ecopsychology, conservation psychology and environmental activism—to name only a handful of ways in which "ecology" in the broad sense has come to pervade our thinking today.

From within this wide array of ecologically inspired fields of inquiry, I have chosen to focus the present chapter on one in particular: ecopsychology, and more precisely the "radical" conception of ecopsychology put forward by Andy

---

1 The title of this chapter, "This loss is not an interlude," is taken from Giegerich's essay "The End of Meaning and the Birth of Man" (CEP 4, p. 209). Here the modern loss of meaning is characterized as an irrevocable, logical one – as opposed to a mere "interlude" awaiting the arrival of Nietzsche's utopian overman.

Fisher.[2] There are two reasons for this decision. The first reason is that there is no way to speak to "ecological thought" as a whole. This is due in part to the limited space allotted here and to the limits of my own knowledge, which together fail to provide the breadth and depth required for such a massive endeavour. It is also due to the fact that "ecological thought" embraces a wide and in many cases inconsistent variety of views that elude any attempts to be treated as a single coherent whole. There is no way to address "ecological thought" without falling into a series of unfair generalizations. For instance, how does one address the activism of the Sierra Club, Pope Francis' most recent encyclical *On Care for Our Common Home*,[3] Slavoj Žižek's commentaries on nature's inexistence,[4] and David Abram's animistic phenomenology[5] in a single breath? One simply cannot—at least not without recourse to an aggressive form of reductionism.[6]

The second reason I have chosen to focus this chapter on Andy Fisher's radical ecopsychology is very similar to the reason why I assume Giegerich chose an article by Robert Romanyshyn to be the object of his critique of ecopsychological thought in his 2009 article "The Psychologist as Repentance Preacher and Revivalist."[7] Fisher's particular brand of ecopsychology displays a high level of sophistication and historical awareness, similar to Romanyshyn's, one that is far superior to a great deal of the thinking I have encountered in the course of my research. This, in my

2 Andy Fisher, "What is Ecopsychology? A Radical View," in *Ecopsychology: Science, Totems, and the Technological Species*, ed. Peter H. Kahn Jr. et al. (Cambridge, MA: The MIT Press, 2012), 79–114. I sometimes refer to Fisher's particular brand of ecopsychology simply as "ecopsychology." Unless otherwise specified (as in the section "A brief prehistory of ecopsychology"), the term "ecopsychology" refers to Fisher's particular definition, and not ecopsychology at large.

3 Francis, *Laudato Si* [Encyclical Letter on Care for Our Common Home], accessed December 20, 2015, http://w2.vatican.va/content/francesco/en/encyclicals/docum ents/papa-francesco_20150524_enciclica-laudato-si.html

4 Slavoj Žižek, Nature does not exist [Video]. (2011). www.youtube.com. Accessed December 18, 2015, https://www.youtube.com/watch?v=DIGeDAZ6-q4

5 David Abrams, *The Spell of the Sensuous* (New York, NY: Vintage Books, 1997).

6 That said, a number of authors have made remarkable attempts at addressing ecological thought from a broad standpoint. I think, for instance, of Timothy Morton's *Ecology without Nature: Rethinking Environmental Aesthetics* (Cambridge, MA: Harvard University Press, 2007), in which he critically assesses the genre of ecological writing from a literary-critical perspective; and of Sean Esbjörn-Hargens and Michael E. Zimmerman, whose *Integral Ecology: Uniting Multiple Perspectives on the Natural World* (Boston, MA: Integral Books, 2009) offers a sweeping and cutting-edge approach to ecology that, as its name attests, offers an impressive synthesis of existing ecological perspectives.

7 See Wolfgang Giegerich, "The Psychologist as Repentance Preacher and Revivalist: Robert Romanyshyn on the Melting of the Polar Ice," *Spring* 82 (2009): 195–221, which Giegerich wrote in response to Robert D. Romanyshyn's article "The Melting Polar Ice: Revisiting Technology as a Symptom and Dream," *Spring* 80 (2009): 79–115. Giegerich's response to Romanyshyn features an approach and particular subject-matter that differ somewhat from mine in the present chapter. That said, insofar as this chapter offers a critical consideration of ecopsychology from the standpoint of Giegerich's psychology of soul, this chapter can be seen to largely reaffirm many of the same points that Giegerich raised in his earlier article.

view, places his radical ecopsychology on the crest of the ecological wave—while by no means making it representative of the wave as a whole. Moreover, Fisher's radical ecopsychology is expressive of certain prevailing trends in ecological thought (though, again, without making it a figurehead for ecological thought as a whole). His vision of ecopsychology provides an articulate example of the counter-cultural eco-critique of modernity, as well as the dualistic treatment of the ecological crisis which manifests as a desire to overcome dualism. Insofar as Fisher's theory of ecopsychology presents a high-level instance of "ecological thought" that is expressive of some of its major trends and assumptions, I consider Fisher's essay "What is Ecopsychology? A Radical View," a prime topic for an essay of this length and breadth.

The psychological method

One objective of this chapter, as was stated earlier, might be to form a theoretical bridge between Giegerich's psychology of soul and ecological thought, by way of ecopsychology. But as will be seen, my objective here, insofar as it is to stay true to the spirit of Giegerich's thinking and to the notion of psychology he elaborates, cannot be to form a bridge of this kind, let alone of any kind. In the land of disciplines, fields, and specialties, bridges are erected in the spirit of *interdisciplinarity*—a fashionable approach which nonetheless, if we are to do justice to the notion of psychology inherent in Giegerich's work, has no place in psychological thinking.

On the subject of interdisciplinarity, Giegerich has written that psychology, by its very nature, is incapable of taking part in interdisciplinary work.[8] The reason for this lies at the heart of psychology and of the contemplative task that distinguishes psychology from all other sciences. Each science, from physics to biology to sociology to anthropology, is defined by the portion of the taken-for-granted natural-empirical world which is assigned to it "as its own 'delimited field of work' and sphere of competence."[9] In contrast, psychology's "sphere of competence" (the psyche or soul) is of a distinctly different order. Far from being a mere "portion," "field" or "sphere" of the natural-empirical world that is the common object of the sciences, the object of psychology is *that which gives rise to* every portion, field, or sphere of scientific inquiry. In Jung's words, it is "the very subject that produces all science."[10] Jung recognized that the psyche "has a share in all the sciences, because it forms at least half the precondition of the existence of them all."[11] The psyche is the *I*, the scientific observer and *"doer,"* the process by and as which (scientific) thought occurs. In psychology, however, the psyche is not only the "I,"

---

8   Wolfgang Giegerich, *Technology and the Soul: From the Nuclear Bomb to the World Wide Web*, (*Collected English Papers Vol. II*) (New Orleans, LA: Spring Journal Inc., 2007), 11–12.
9   Giegerich, *Technology*, 11.
10 Jung, *CW* 8 § 429, cited in Wolfgang Giegerich, *The Neurosis of Psychology (Collected English Papers, Vol. I)* (New Orleans, LA: Spring Journal, Inc., 2005), 3, transl. modif. by Giegerich.
11 Jung, *C.W* 16, § 209, as cited in Giegerich, *Technology*, 11, transl. modif. by Giegerich.

but is also "It," the object being observed. Psychology's object, in other words, is itself the scientific *I*, "the very subject that produces all science."

The consequence of this for psychology (what Jung called its "fate—its distinction as well as misfortune"[12]) is that it operates on a wholly different level from other sciences. To the extent that psychology's object cannot be said to be different from itself, psychology is not a science but a *"sublated* science":

> The opposition basic to the sciences of subject and object, theory and nature, does not exist in and for psychology. […] The clear distinction between psychology and its subject-matter, the soul, cannot be maintained: psychology is itself soul and soul is interpretation of itself (psychology).[13]

Soul and the "science" whereby it acts out its self-reflection (psychology) follow a "uroboric" logic—the logic of the *uroboros*, the tail-eating snake that provides its own sustenance and is therefore absolutely self-contained. Another way of putting this is to say that psychology is *methodologically restricted* to itself alone. It does not partake in the ground of the other sciences, the taken-for-granted natural-empirical world beheld by the ego-subject. Psychology, rather, has only itself as ground. Its "ground" is the groundless ground of self-reflection. For this reason, Giegerich writes:

> psychology is not on the same level with all the other sciences; it is logically above or beneath them. There cannot be a kind of simple "collegiality" and collaboration on an equal footing between psychology and the sciences because psychology is not defined by a particular section ("field," "specialty") of reality as its subject-matter.[14]

In light of this, one can see that even if it *were* my goal, I would be hard-pressed to construct a theoretical bridge between psychology and ecology. The only way to make such a bridge is to impose upon psychology the profoundly unpsychological standpoint of common-sense thinking with its implied opposition between subject and object and its taken-for-granted (i.e., uncritical) ground in natural-empirical reality, where reality is that which is "out there," independent from the thinking *I*. In other words, I would have to depart psychology altogether—while nonetheless retaining the *word* "psychology" to refer to that science which is responsible for the study of the "psyche." And the "psyche" here would correspondingly not be understood as "the very subject that produces all science" (a thought which inevitably leads to the notion of psychology outlined in this section). Rather, "psyche" would become a mere *content* of the natural-empirical world, a content which although identified with the thinking process underlying its own study is

12 Jung, *CW* 16, § 209.
13 Giegerich, *The Neurosis of Psychology*, 3.
14 Giegerich, *Technology*, 12.

methodologically treated as an external object, something "out there" to be studied and perhaps even modified or corrected.

I could do this, and indeed in doing so I would be aligning myself with a dominant attitude in psychology.[15] But in so doing I would also be exiting the notion of psychology that Giegerich puts forward in Jung's stead. This notion is to my mind irrefutable in the sense that it is self-evident. All it does is carry to its logical end the obvious statement that there is no way to view the soul from the outside: that "no explanation of the psychic can be anything other than the living process of the psyche itself."[16] To carry this thought to its end is to find that one has exited the familiar territory of scientific, phenomenal, or common-sense thinking with its literal interpretation of the subject–object opposition and entered the groundless territory of self-reflection and self-relation—not in the sense of my ego or personality's reflection or relation to itself, but of *soul's* self-reflection, the relation of *soul* with *it*self as both the subject and object of psychology. In this territory, the soul is no longer treated as a mere content of empirical reality, something to be studied "out there." It has risen to an awareness of itself as "the very subject that produces all science." This awareness gives rise to a uroboric methodology that drastically differs from the scientific or phenomenal method, firstly in that it is oriented, from the outset, towards itself, and secondly in that it recognizes from the outset that that which it beholds is itself. Psychology cannot be interdisciplinary because it is from the outset *trans-* (or *pre-*) disciplinary. It is indifferent to the disciplinary categories of science, for these disciplines are merely by-products of psychology's true object, the soul.

The fact that psychology has itself for its object therefore means that it cannot be involved in interdisciplinary studies. Psychologically speaking, there is no other discipline to speak of, only psychology, soul's uroboric activity of self-reflection. This statement about the soul and psychology holds another implication that I would like to briefly touch upon before moving forward. This implication concerns the orientation or attitude that inevitably results from our having recognized psychology's uroboric orientation (i.e., that in it the soul reflects *itself*, not some external reality).

The sublation of the opposition between subject and object, or theory and nature that has to take place in order for psychology to happen necessarily incurs a shift in the agency of the psychological subject in relation to its object. If in psychology subject and object are ultimately indistinguishable—both "moments" (in the dialectical sense) of soul's self-reflection—then the psychological subject is different from the so-called "Cartesian" ego that views itself as fundamentally distinct from its object. The latter "Cartesian" ego, in viewing its object as wholly external to

15 "And what is the widespread desire even among analytical schools of psychology to set themselves up as 'science' other than a fraternization with the ego and its common sense mentality, what else but an insistence on the unbroken, not to be broken continuity of 'natural consciousness'?" in Wolfgang Giegerich, *The Soul's Logical Life: Towards a Rigorous Notion of Psychology* (Frankfurt am Main; New York: Peter Lang, 1998), 20.

16 Jung, *CW* 8 § 429, cited in Giegerich, *The Neurosis of Psychology*, 3.

itself, is likely to develop the attitude that such an object exists at its (the subject's) pleasure, for it to understand, take apart, put back together, make use of as it sees fit. More importantly, such an ego-subject naturally develops the inflated idea that it is in charge. Since it does not recognize its role as one "part" or "moment" in the psychic process, it claims all thought and meaning for itself.

The psychological subject, in contrast, can hold no such presumption. The relation of the psychological subject (soul) to its object (also soul) is not governed by time, space, and causation in the formal sense. Rather, the logic that relates the subject and object of psychological thought is uroboric, dialectical.[17] According to this dialectical logic, the very idea of a subject *acting upon* its object "from the outside" makes no sense. Instrumental reason must give way here to *absolute* reason, the logic of the soul's self-relation according to which subject and object have been "ab-solved" of their difference. The observer is the observed. Both are psyche, psychic activity, soul.

In this context, the psychological context of self-relating soul, the work cannot be to study the soul with the intention of modifying, correcting, healing, or curing. That which is studying the soul is the soul itself. And the soul is always already whole. "Only the ego wants solutions."[18] The task of psychology, its "opus," must shift accordingly, away from the curative projects of the ego that wants solutions, in favour of the standpoint of soul. Once all such curative projects and agendas, the ego's hopes and dreams, have been abandoned, only one task remains: to bear witness to the soul as it is for its own sake. Psychology can do nothing else, for it is no longer bound to the sort of instrumental logic that defines other sciences. In Giegerich's words,

> The therapist is not a healer. Therapy does not *want* anything of its own accord. It does not have a program. All it wants is in each case to release whatever *is* into its depth, its truth. This is its *opus*. This is how it reaches soul, the soul in the real.[19]

What does this mean for the present chapter? Insofar as its objective is not only to speak *about* the soul but also, and perhaps more importantly, to be reflective of the mode or style of thinking as which psychology is, a particular task lies ahead of us. This task might be described as the need to psychologically "*enter*" radical ecopsychology: to view ecopsychology "from the point of view of soul—that is, as the soul's own further development, its further-determination, its advancing to new statuses of

17
> It needs no saying that the *kind* of abstract thought that psychology has to let itself in for cannot be physics' abstract thought. It is not mathematical and formalistic, and the logical "laws" governing it are not those of formal logic. They are rather those of a much more complex dialectical logic, such as developed by Hegel in his *Science of Logic*, which might serve as a model for the kind of abstract thought required to do justice to the complexities of the plight of the modern soul.
> (Giegerich, *Soul's Logical Life*, 26)

18 Giegerich, "Repentance Preacher," 211.
19 Wolfgang Giegerich, *The Soul Always Thinks (Collected English Papers, Vol. IV)* (New Orleans, LA: Spring Journal, Inc., 2010), 21.

itself"[20]; "to let each new event and manifestation of soul teach us afresh what 'soul' and 'soulful' means"[21]; to "let it be and expose myself to it. In full awareness, [to] allow Pandora's box to be opened."[22] The objective is not only to speak about how the psyche is theorized in Andy Fisher's ecopsychology but to see the latter as an event and manifestation of the soul in which the soul is articulating something about itself. To do this means to view ecopsychology exactly as it is, while also simultaneously seeing it as more than what it professes to be: namely, as a positive manifestation of soul. This involves a kind of deconstructive exercise whereby ecopsychology is unpacked all the way down to the level of its innermost constitution, the "syntax" or "logical life" that inheres not only in its view of the psyche and the many presuppositions informing this view, but also in that which does the "viewing," namely, the ecopsychological *I*.

Before we initiate this "entrance" into radical ecopsychology as a psychological phenomenon in its own right, however, some historical context is needed. The following section provides such a context through a brief prehistory of the field of ecopsychology.

A brief prehistory of ecopsychology

Ecopsychology is the relatively young progeny of what might be called a later development in the modern ecology movement. Rachel Carson's seminal book, *Silent Spring*,[23] is famously known for having spurred the modern ecology movement to life in the 1960s. It is true that Carson's work was preceded by the remarkable achievements of conservationists like John Muir, Gifford Pinchot, and Aldo Leopold (to name only three), but it was really in the 1960s and 1970s that the ecology movement finally acquired its mainstream status with the enactment of federal environmental policies and the establishment of the Environmental Protection Agency in the United States, the foundation of Earth Day in 1970, and the worldwide proliferation of ecologically inspired activism and writing—both in the natural sciences and in a growing number of fields ranging from social justice and feminist theory to philosophy, psychology, and religion. It is in the midst of this proliferating interest in ecology, not only as a science but also as a vehicle for social and critical thought, that a number of influential voices set the stage for the later emergence and development of ecopsychology.

In 1973, the Norwegian philosopher Arne Naess published a short article outlining what he called the "deep, long-range ecology movement."[24] This movement, which would later come to be known simply as the "deep ecology movement," sought to both widen and deepen the purview of the mainstream ecology

20 Giegerich, "Repentence Preacher," 198.
21 Giegerich, "Repentence Preacher," 205.
22 Giegerich, "Repentence Preacher," 196.
23 Rachel Carson, *Silent Spring* (Boston, MA: Houghton Mifflin, 1962).
24 Arne Naess, "The Shallow and the Deep-Long Range Ecology Movement: A Summary," *Inquiry: An Interdisciplinary Journal of Philosophy* 16 (1973): 95–100.

movement. Despite earlier efforts by individuals like Leopold and Carson who brought attention to the cultural and ideological roots of ecological problems, the mainstream ecology movement had remained, and in a significant sense remains, largely characterized by a palliative approach to problem-solving.[25] According to Naess, the ecology movement could be "widened" by first recognizing its connection to the two other major social movements of the 20th century, namely the peace and social justice movements, which had the shared objective (along with the ecology movement) of eradicating the various forms of self-destructiveness that plague human society.[26] As for the "deepening" of the ecology movement, this could be achieved through the recognition that our ecological problems are ultimately rooted in cultural and ideological assumptions concerning the world and humanity's relationship to it. Only by addressing such problems on the level of the values and assumptions that engender them, and not simply on the level of their material manifestations, can we hope to make a lasting difference. The deep ecology movement thus called for "a deep questioning process"[27] that went beyond strictly technical solutions to ecological problems and engaged with the human modes of thinking and acting at the roots of the problems we face.

Around the same time that Naess helped establish and identify the deep ecology movement, the environmentalist and author Paul Shepard put forward a theory concerning the relationship between modern society and nature that would prove to be of central importance to ecopsychology and to the (deep) ecological critique of modernity. Shepard claimed that "the human species came of age with daily connection to an abundantly diverse and wild nature and that modern times are diseased because we are disconnected from that diversity and wildness."[28] This theory and its underlying sentiment were carried forward by a number of thinkers in the ecology and deep ecology movements, and by the 1990s, "these ideas had coalesced in a growing body of work called 'ecopsychology'."[29]

The term "ecopsychology" was coined by Theodore Roszak in his 1992 book *The Voice of the Earth*.[30] The goal of this book, in Roszak's words, was "to bridge

---

25 Leopold famously wrote, "No important change in ethics was ever accomplished without an internal change in our intellectual emphasis, loyalties, affections, and convictions," in Aldo Leopold, *A Sand County Almanac* (New York, NY: Ballantine Books, 1966), 246. As for Carson, Naess suggests that *Silent Spring* was not just about publicizing the abuses of a hubristic chemical pesticide industry, but that it also "revealed political, economic, and technological forces that could engender future silent springs. Rachel Carson went deep and questioned the premises of her society," in Arne Naess, *The Selected Works of Arne Naess, Vol. 10* (Dordrecht, The Netherlands: Springer, 2005), 89.

26 Arne Naess, *The Ecology of Wisdom: Writings by Arne Naess* (Berkeley, CA: Counterpoint, 2008 [1992]), 99.

27 George Sessions, "Arne Naess and the Union of Theory and Practice," in *The Deep Ecology Movement: An Introductory Anthology*, ed. Alan Drengson et al. (Berkeley: North Atlantic Books, 1995), 59.

28 Kahn Jr. et al., *Ecopsychology*, 3.

29 Kahn Jr. et al., *Ecopsychology*, 3.

30 Theodore Roszak, *The Voice of the Earth: An Exploration of Ecopsychology* (Grand Rapids, MI: Phanes Press, 1992).

our culture's longstanding, historical gulf between the psychological and the eco-logical, to see the needs of the planet and the person as a continuum."[31] We find in Roszak's words a combination of Shepard's anti-modernist attitude and the desire to address ecological problems on the "deepest" possible level: the level of "psyche" and "consciousness," of the cultural and ideological roots of modern society, which (according to its critics) range from the Cartesian dualism of mind and matter through the scientific method to our present-day industrial and consumerist practices.

Radical ecopsychology

To the extent that this anti-modernist attitude and the desire to address ecological problems at their "roots" are the two primary drivers of ecopsychology, Fisher's "radical" ecopsychology presents a wholehearted extension of the ecopsychology project. In qualifying ecopsychology as "radical," Fisher means to draw attention to two senses of radicalism. First, in the spirit of his deep ecological peers and predecessors, he means to draw attention to "the most straightforward sense of radicalism, which holds that the problems of the world are best addressed at the root, base, or ground level."[32] This root, base, or ground level, according to Fisher, is best expressed by means of "the nondual spirit of ecology," which professes the interrelatedness and oneness of all things.[33] All things are, at base, one. Modern society, in contrast, with its industry, technology, consumerism, and urban life, fragments and alienates the individual from her roots in the web of life. Modern society causes "the forgetfulness of our earth-bound nature."[34] It inflicts "a deep wound in the modern psyche" that in turn gives rise to an "earth-alienated mind."[35] The radical who, by virtue of his radicalism, has recognized the root, base, and ground level of existence as being its fundamental interrelatedness, unity, and oneness, is by definition opposed to the earth-alienating tendencies of modern society. In this way radicalism implies a revolutionary impulse: "Radicals seek change in social institutions and practices, psychological structures (such as person-ality, identity, consciousness, and needs), root metaphors, philosophical premises, worldviews, and so on. When change occurs on this level, we call it *revolutionary*."[36]

Radical ecopsychology thus carries a twofold function. In the first place, it is "recollective": "it involves recalling the unity of humanity and nature. [...] Such recollection is radical because it overcomes the forgetfulness of our earth-bound nature, healing a deep wound in the modern psyche and opening up a rich world

31 Roszak, *Voice of the Earth*, 14.
32 Fisher, "What is Ecopsychology?", 80.
33 Fisher, "What is Ecopsychology?", 80–81, 91.
34 Fisher, "What is Ecopsychology?", 81.
35 Fisher, "What is Ecopsychology?", 81.
36 Fisher, "What is Ecopsychology?", 81.

of more-than-human relations unimaginable to the earth-alienated mind."[37] In the second place, ecopsychology has the "critical" task of "questioning [...] our entire social formation insofar as it generates ecological and psychospiritual crises through the domination of nature."[38]

It should be noted that Fisher does not use the word "critical" in its original and proper definition as "a form of criticism that bends back upon itself."[39] This is the definition of critique that was developed by the Frankfurt School in the 20th century, and it is the sense which Giegerich intends when he refers to psychology as "critical,"[40] thus tying critique to psychology's uroboric methodology. Fisher, in contrast, uses the word "critical" in the sense of "finding fault." Ecopsychology's "critique" does not bend back upon itself but rather moves ever outwards, assessing modern society from the perspective of the principle of unity and interrelatedness, which it has erected as an external vantage point from which to see more clearly the failures of modernity.

As we can see, the major aspects of Fisher's ecopsychology, its radicalism as well as its recollective and critical functions, all emerge from a single presupposition, what Fisher calls "the nondual spirit of ecology."[41] This presupposition is ecopsychology's center of gravity, and as such constitutes the primary concern of this chapter. Although a number of theories are introduced into ecopsychology to further elaborate its theoretical grounding, from hermeneutics to Alfred North Whitehead's concept of internal relations, these can be said to be introduced only to the extent that they serve ecopsychology's initial presupposition, its claim that at base all things are one (and that therefore we must correct modernity's nefarious influence on our way of seeing and being in the world). I will now focus the remainder of this chapter on this presupposition as a way of coming to a clearer understanding of the logic underlying radical ecopsychology's claims about nature, modernity, and the soul.

The death of nature and the birth of psychology

The presupposition of unity and oneness that anchors Fisher's radical ecopsychology becomes problematic, and actually falls into fatal contradiction, when considered in light of the historical context of modernity—a historical context which, curiously, is insightfully assessed by ecopsychologists like Fisher. Already in Roszak, we discover an author who writes from a full awareness that "we are long past the time for pretending that the death of God is not a political fact."[42] Fisher, for his part, acknowledges that the "death of God" was the precondition for psychology's

37 Fisher, "What is Ecopsychology?", 81.
38 Fisher, "What is Ecopsychology?", 81–82.
39 Morton, *Ecology Without Nature*, 13.
40 Giegerich, *Neurosis of Psychology*, 58–59.
41 Fisher, "What is Ecopsychology?", 80.
42 Theodore Roszak, *Where the Wasteland Ends: Politics and Transcendence in Postindustrial Society* (Garden City, NY: Anchor Books, 1973), xv.

historical emergence, or, as he puts it: "Psychology [...] was born with the death of nature."[43] The "interiorization" of soul, the correlative of which was the end of that process by which the natural world was imbued with numinous significance (nature's "irrelevantification," as Giegerich has put it[44]), was a necessary precursor to the invention of psychology.

By recognizing this, ecopsychology grounds itself in a historical perspective that acknowledges the fundamental rupture of modernity: "the great historical rupture that separates all the ages in the Western tradition prior to the nineteenth century from the modern world."[45] This rupture is a key premise of Giegerich's psychology of soul, whose understanding of the soul as logically negative arises from the recognition that the "rupture" incurred by modernity is "a *real phenomenon* or *development* of the soul."[46] To see the rupture in this way, as a "*real* phenomenon of the soul," is a natural consequence of Giegerich's notion of the soul, which I do not have time to expose fully here but will provisionally define as "the self-articulation of the inner truth of the changing logical constitution of the particular societies' actual mode of being-in-the-world."[47] In its positive manifestation this "self-articulation" takes the form of history, which psychologically speaking is the record of the soul's development through time, its "own further development, its further-determination, its advancing to new statuses of itself."[48] As Jung aptly put it, "[W]ithout history there can be no psychology"[49]; not only because psychology has to conduct its inquiry of the soul from within a historical understanding of the ways in which our modes of being-in-the-world have changed, but because history is *itself a manifestation of soul*. Here we find a definite instance of Hegel's influence on Giegerich's thinking. The soul expresses itself through history. History, in other words, *is* soul, the soul's logical unfolding expressed in narrative form. Therefore, a historical rupture such as that experienced in the 19th century (a rupture whose historical reality is widely accepted by thinkers including Giegerich, Roszak, and Fisher) *must* be seen as a *real* phenomenon of soul, *must* be seen as the expression of a real (and therefore *irrevocable*) shift in the logical constitution of our particular society's actual mode of being-in-the-world. The Industrial Revolution, the collapse of metaphysical philosophy after Hegel and the rise of materialism, Romanticism, Kierkegaard's "leap of faith" and the "death" of God proclaimed by Nietzsche (and Hegel and Dostoevsky before him)—these were not merely expressions of individual whims but indicative of a radical shift on the level of soul, the level of the changing logical constitution of the West's prevailing mode of

43 Fisher, "What is Ecopsychology?", 86.
44 See Giegerich's essay, "Irrelevantification or: On the Death of Nature, the Construction of 'the Archetype,' and the Birth of Man," in *Soul Always Thinks*, 387–442.
45 Giegerich, "Repentence Preacher," 203.
46 Giegerich, "Repentence Preacher," 207.
47 Wolfgang Giegerich, *What is Soul?* (New Orleans, LA: Spring Journal, Inc., 2012), 58ff.
48 Giegerich, "Repentence Preacher," 198.
49 Jung, *MDR*, 205, cited in Giegerich, *Technology*, 17.

being-in-the-world. To the extent that Fisher's ecopsychology is erected on a recognition of this historical rupture, it lives up to its claim of radicalism.

Fisher's assessment of modernity as a shift in the logical status of the psyche or soul—a shift expressed in such phenomena as the "death of God" and the "irrelevantification" of nature—aligns to a large extent with the assessment informing Giegerich's psychology of soul. Where Fisher's ecopsychology diverges from the psychology of soul, however, is in its response to this assessment. Giegerich describes two possible lines of reaction to the realization that modernity has brought about an irrevocable rupture in the soul's logical constitution:

> One can *either* try to hold on to and defend the truth of the past *against* the real situation produced by historical developments *or* own up to the new situation into which history has placed us and allow oneself to be taught by it about how to think.[50]

This distinction rightly captures the essential difference between Giegerich's and Fisher's approaches. While Giegerich's work tends to convey the latter line of thinking, Fisher's ecopsychology is wholeheartedly committed to the former of the two responses. The task of ecopsychology, Fisher writes, is to "radically *reinterpret* the human animal in a way that integrates us into a living earth"[51]; ecopsychology is "a psychology whose goal is to *reverse* the alienation from nature that gave rise to psychology itself"[52]; "a hallmark of ecopsychology is the commitment to *fill* the world with interiority" along with its recognition "that the modern view of reality fails conceptual examination"[53]; "ecopsychology is about overcoming the human–nature dissociation at the base of modern philosophy."[54] All these things in turn demonstrate, in Fisher's eyes, "the inherent radicalism of ecopsychology, which must challenge the modern worldview at its roots to be truly a psychology of the human-nature relationship."[55] But this is not the same radicalism that characterized Fisher's assessment of modernity, the radicalism of addressing problems "at the root, base or ground level"[56]—which, as it happens, is the radical definition of radicalism. No, this latter "radicalism" is the radicalism of staking oneself against the current of the age, of bravely affirming unity and harmony in the face of a modern consciousness for which cosmic oneness and spiritual unity with nature are clearly no longer lived realities.

This latter form of radicalism and the response it implies to the situation of modernity inevitably leads one to question: Is ecopsychology a psychology? Fisher claims that it is ecopsychology's "radicalism" (in the latter sense) that makes it

---

50 Giegerich, *Soul Always Thinks*, 203.
51 Fisher, "What is Ecopsychology?", 83, my italics.
52 Fisher, "What is Ecopsychology?", 86, my italics.
53 Fisher, "What is Ecopsychology?", 87, my italics.
54 Fisher, "What is Ecopsychology?", 87.
55 Fisher, "What is Ecopsychology?", 88.
56 Fisher, "What is Ecopsychology?", 80.

"truly a psychology." Ecopsychology is psychological precisely because it challenges modern thinking and offers a holistic alternative. But if we accept what was stated at the start of this chapter concerning the nature of psychological thinking, we have to conclude that Fisher has it backwards. Ecopsychology's "radicalism," its stance vis-à-vis a modern reality that it seeks to criticize and correct, is the very reason that it has *not* achieved a psychological mode of thinking.

When considering ecopsychology's assessment and critique of modern consciousness, one has to ask the question: *Who* (or *what*) is delivering the critique? *Who* (or *what*) is speaking? As we saw at the start of this chapter, a psychology that has recognized its object to be "the subject that produces all science" naturally comes to the conclusion that that which is speaking in psychology, the subject of its psychologizing, is the psyche itself. In psychology, observer and observed are one and the same. Psychology therefore implies a methodology of uroboric self-reflection that does away entirely with the concept of a subject distinct, divided, and independent from its object. What remains for psychology after it has given up the personalistic stance of the ego over and against the world (and the curative projects that derive from this stance) is the task of releasing "whatever *is* into its depth, its truth."

Considering what I noted earlier about the relationship between history and the soul—namely, that history *is* soul—the only way that ecopsychology can here stake itself against modern consciousness, claiming to be a corrective against it, is by *removing* itself from (or rather never descending to) the uroboric self-reflectiveness of psychological thinking. Instead, it establishes itself in the standpoint of ego: the ego that stands heroically before its own history and culture and affirms that it knows better. Ecopsychology thus establishes an undialectical opposition between itself and its object. Although its object is the psyche, ecopsychology contents itself to only speak *about* this psyche, never rising to the awareness that it (ecopsychology) is also the psyche speaking about itself (bringing itself into being). By dualistically staking itself against its object, the ecopsychological stance prevents the *I* from recognizing itself as its own object, that is, *as* dualistic modern consciousness, "earth-alienated mind." The unity it proposes is therefore a strictly semantic and superficial one, an exercise in academic wordplay, while syntactically the opposition between subject and object, theory and nature, *I* and soul, is actually preserved in an ever more sophisticated form whereby it claims to be the opposite of itself, the solution to end all dualism. While it preaches oneness and nondualism, ecopsychology embraces (indeed is contingent on) a methodology of division and opposition. To the extent that it reaffirms the opposition between the ego (albeit an ego that espouses holistic ideas about the world) and modern consciousness, ecopsychology perpetuates a dualistic logic of opposition.

The neurosis of ecopsychology

The takeaway from the previous section is twofold. Not only is ecopsychology not a psychology at all, but its unpsychological way of thinking leads it to undermine its own project.

At first one might attribute these problems to the confused or at the very least unclear notion of the psyche informing ecopsychology. Indeed, despite his pre-occupation with the psychic and the subjective, Fisher never takes the time to actually define what the psyche is, leaving it at the mercy of common-sense conceptions of the term. The closest Fisher comes to defining the psychic in his article is in his discussion of Alfred North Whitehead's concept of internal relations.[57] But this definition of the psyche is subject to the same shortcoming that besets White-head's theory, namely, that it speaks about the psyche as the subjective dimension of reality without rising to the insight that it is the psyche doing the speaking.

But even this is too gentle an assessment. For it is not the case here that ecopsychology suffers merely from the fairly straightforward problem of having a confused or unclarified notion of the psyche. If this were the problem, the solution would be quite simple: ecopsychology needs to develop a more clarified notion of the psyche, after which it can go on "filling the world with interiority" from the solid ground of a rigorous understanding of its object, the psyche. But it is clear from reading Fisher that the problem runs deeper than this. Developing a clear notion of the psyche would not solve the real problem because the real problem is not that ecopsychology lacks a clear notion of the psyche. The real problem is that ecopsychology is not psychology at all.

Fisher himself writes that "in re-ensouling the world, ecopsychology becomes a sort of psychology before and after psychology."[58] As we saw in the previous section, ecopsychology's mission to "re-ensoul" the world is precisely what makes it unpsychological. To the extent that ecopsychology stands "before" psychology, it seeks to recall and revive what was lost with the historical rupture of modernity (i.e., a sense of cosmic belonging, Meaning with a capital M). To the extent that it stands "after" psychology, ecopsychology views this historical rupture as a mere interlude, something to be overcome, a dark night of the soul that will soon give way to day. In both instances ecopsychology distances itself from and disavows its present reality, the historical rupture which—and on this Giegerich and Fisher agree—is the precondition for psychology. But the split produced by this disavowal must also be disavowed, since it does not align with ecopsychology's "nondual spirit." Ecopsychology's claim of nondualism is consequently premised upon the denial of the split that it incurs between itself (the I segregated from its historical context, which is not so unlike the "Cartesian" ego criticized by ecopsychology) and the soul, which as we have seen cannot be comprehended in isolation from the historical rupture of modernity.

In *The Soul's Logical Life*, Giegerich defines neurosis in one instance as "a disunity plus its denial."[59] In light of what was just stated above, we can state with relative confidence that ecopsychology is constituted by a neurosis, in that it harbors within its way of thinking a disunity accompanied by the denial of said disunity.

57 Fisher, "What is Ecopsychology?", 91–92.
58 Fisher, "What is Ecopsychology?", 86.
59 Giegerich, *Soul's Logical Life*, 24.

Ecopsychology's wholeness and nondualistic stance is achieved through a splitting off from its constitutive "truth" (the "truth" of the soul in its modern form *as* rupture, absence, emptiness) followed by a denial of the split.

At the heart of ecopsychology lies a deception: "a program, intentional, in fact a devious plot."[60] This "devious plot" is not of Fisher's design, nor is it *his* intention. Rather, the program is "intended" on a deeper level and acted out at his expense. The neurotic deception is enacted at the expense of ecopsychologists like Fisher who genuinely affirm that they are contributing to a renewed state of wholeness when they are really, by virtue of the tacit logic of their thinking, perpetuating the exact opposite. This, the logic of opposition inherent in their thinking, is the *real* mission of Fisher's ecopsychology—not the mission he professes, but the one that is being conducted through his words and at his expense, possibly without his knowing. As Giegerich writes, "It is crucial to see that in neurotic symptoms and complexes, although they belong to subjective, personal psychology and to the modern ego-personality, nevertheless *the soul* expresses itself."[61]

The logic of opposition, whereby the I segregates itself from and immunizes itself against the "truth" of its own age, ultimately serves the *soul's* interests, not the individual author's, who in this instance is being (in a sense) manipulated for interests not his own. This recalls Giegerich's statement that

> our ultimate purposes are not really "ours." The real decisions and the real action occur on the level of the logic of soul "behind our back," not on the empirical level of our behavior and feeling. And the interests pursued are not our personal and practical life interests, as we deludedly tend to think. We are the place of action or manifestation for interests that do not necessarily have *our* better in mind.[62]

To begin to understand what (or whose) "interests" are being fulfilled via ecopsychology's neurosis, we need to look at what is being professed: What is being placed before us by means of the neurotic split-plus-denial? In this case, the neurosis is a way of affirming a recollective vision of a unified world in which the unity of all things, of humanity and nature, may once again be a lived reality. In other words, a nostalgically charged revival of the "enchanted" or "ensouled" mode of being-in-the-world that came to an end with the emergence of modernity in the 19th century.[63] Since the reinstatement of this mode of being-in-the-world as a

---

60 Giegerich, *What is Soul?*, 165.
61 Giegerich, *What is Soul?*, 158.
62 Giegerich, *Soul's Logical Life*, 229.
63 See section above "The Death of Nature and the Birth of Psychology." In his essay "The End of Meaning and the Birth of Man: An essay about the state reached in the history of consciousness and an analysis of C. G. Jung's psychology project," in *Soul Always Thinks*, 189–283, Giegerich describes modernity as a historical rupture in the logical status of the European soul that culminated in the 19th century. This rupture brought about the definitive collapse of the *Axis Mundi* (and of its metaphysical equivalent, the *copula*) as well as the end of man's mythical containment within the

shared reality is not an option—the historical rupture is real and therefore irrevocable—the *actual* "intention" of the ecopsychology project must be of a different order. Nor can its "intention" be to overcome the dualistic presuppositions of modern thought, since we have already seen that ecopsychology's fixation on unity and nondualism is premised on a dualistic split of its own.

One possible explanation of the "interest" fulfilled in neurosis is presented to us by Giegerich when he writes of the soul's "need" to dialectically present before itself the forms of thought ("statuses") which it has outgrown and shed, in order to move beyond them once and for all:

> For the soul it is obviously not enough to simply (easily, "just like that") *outgrow* metaphysics in a natural developmental process (metaphysics as the historical successor to myth), which would be no more than an "implicit" overcoming of it. It has to actively, systematically, in detail and in full awareness *work off* its own fascination and infatuation with the metaphysical, the mythic, the numinous, and the suggestive power of the imaginal—*through* pulling itself out of its neurosis, *really* stepping out of it and leaving it behind as the nothing that it is. The soul needs to concretely, as a hard-core reality, *put before itself* once more that from which its natural development has already long removed it, and to give it a new artificial presence so that it (the soul) is forced to also psychologically, explicitly depart from it.[64]

Underlying the radical ecopsychology project is a process by which the soul is "outgrowing," systematically and explicitly, the fantasy of unity proposed by ecopsychology. This the soul does by splitting off from itself in the form of the ecopsychological *I*: the ego that knows better and judges modernity "from the outside." Ecopsychology's logic of opposition is the procedure that makes the "shedding" process possible by placing before the soul, as a concrete hard-core reality, that which is to be overcome.

Conclusion

Ecopsychology beckons its own undoing from within itself. The self-contradiction inherent to its way of thinking calls forth its own sublation, for the unity it seeks to create in the world can only be achieved through the overcoming of the *mode* as which ecopsychology is, that is, the stance of the ego staked against the "spirit of the age." But the unity thus achieved has to be reconceived, for it is not the unity of the ensouled cosmos that the ecopsychologist so dearly seeks to recall. Rather, it is the unity of soul returned within itself, reconciled with its *actual* form, which in

cosmos delimited by the opposites of heaven and earth. "Modernity is characterized by the fact that man has emerged from his in-ness in a horizon, from his containment in a womb," in Giegerich, *Soul Always Thinks*, 218.
64   Giegerich, *What is Soul?*, 332.

this case is the form of modernity, ruptured consciousness, "earth-alienated mind." Such unity is not achieved by staking oneself against the historical rupture of modernity but by *owning up to it*, by taking responsibility for it as a constitutive aspect of who we are and by paying the price for it—where "paying the price" means

> without reserve and resistance allowing the irrevocable rupture of the unio naturalis or the loss of the unifying bond between the opposites to come fully home to consciousness as the soul truth of modernity, allowing it to work on, decompose, and distill the inherited logical form of consciousness with its traditional expectations. This would be tantamount to giving up the narcissistic illusion that our situation is merely the result of a faulty development, of our outrageous aberration from soul, of our crime (nostra culpa, nostra maxima culpa), as well as to giving up the unus mundus delusion.[65]

Only by paying the price in this sense can real unity be achieved—that is, *psychological* unity, the unity of soul reconciled within itself *as* ruptured soul, alienated, empty, meaningless. Real unity, the unity as which soul *is* always and already (even in its neurosis), is brought into being at the expense of ecopsychology and its radical project.

65 Giegerich, "Repentence Preacher," 207.

AFTERWORD

"...bringing them the plague" 2.0

Greg Mogenson

In a sentence precious to Psychology as the Discipline of Interiority on account of its figuring of the psychological difference, Jung declares that "behind the impressions of daily life—behind the scenes—another picture looms up, covered by a thin veil of actual facts."[1] For me the picture that looms up from behind the chapters of this book that have been drawn together to create this volume is that of the sea-voyage that was taken by Freud, Jung, and Ferenczi to America to lecture and receive honors in 1909. Standing on the deck as their ship made port in New York, Freud famously declared that they were "bringing them the plague." A handsome characterization, this, for the plague of psychological theories that the three of them would be introducing to America. Visiting Jung almost a lifetime later to verify that these words had in fact been spoken, the radical French psychoanalyst, Jacques Lacan, would subsequently base his much lauded "return to Freud" upon them.[2] Might an equally, or even more radical, "return to Jung" push off from this scene as well?

I say "more radical" here because while Freud and company crossed the Atlantic on a literally existing ship, the ship that this volume's authors crew upon *has no existence of its own prior to its being sailed!* Whereas actual sailing vessels are built in shipyards, only subsequently to be launched into the sea (perhaps with some psychoanalysts aboard and some theories in tow), psychology in the sense of Psychology as the Discipline of Interiority is different. The ship that it *is* has to build itself at sea, from what looms up or bobs up from behind the scenes of whatever the matter of interest may be that it finds itself submerged in on each

1 C. G. Jung, *The Visions Seminars: Book One* (Zurich: Spring Publications, 1976), 8.
2 For Lacan's comment on how Freud's so-called plague "proved to be anodyne in the land where he brought it" in that "the public [there] adopted/adapted it quite painlessly," see his *The Four Fundamental Concepts of Psycho-Analysis*. Alan Sheridan, trans. (Harmondsworth: Penguin Books, 1979), vii.

interpretative occasion. As Giegerich expressing this "sink or swim," or better, "sink *and* swim" dialectic puts it:

> there is no outside anchorage where psychology could make fast ... Psychology has only its own inside. [It] is only as its unconditional self-abandonment to its own internal bottomless sea. Ships float on the ocean that is all around them; psychology has to be a ship, too, and allow itself to be carried by what it *knows* not to be a solid ground to stand on, but an unstable element, "weak as water." The difference to literal sea vessels is that the ship called psychology has the ocean it floats on *inside* itself as the inner infinity and negativity of its own Notion. This is how "crazy" things are in psychology.[3]

Now this, I submit, is the real sea-faring! It is not enough that psychology book passage upon an actual ship like the *George Washington* which carried psychoanalysis to America. It has rather to be its own ship, "carried by ... an unstable element, 'weak as water'." Of course, it could certainly be argued that psychology had ship-character already in that earlier voyage inasmuch as it was in the ship of their ideas that Freud and company sailed and not just in the actually existing steam liner they shared with the other passengers. But even if this be granted, we have to realize that the *HMS Sexuality*, as that Freudian ship might be called, was not built at sea, but on the shoreline Freud liked to think that his psychology shared with biology, and that even to this day psychoanalysis has not fully cast off from such outside anchorage.

It was different, or was soon to become so, in the case of Jung. After casting off from Freud (or mutineer that he was, after having been made to walk that Captain's plank!), Jung came into his own as a psychologist via the "sink *and* swim" dialectic we learned about above. Blub! Blub! Blub! Down into the depths of his own "baseless enterprise,"[4] there to establish what he called his "psychology 'with soul'." Now by "psychology 'with soul'" Jung meant a "psychology based upon the hypothesis of an autonomous mind."[5] A very different ship, this, than the ship of sexuality! Indeed, as Jung jumping from the one to the other put it, "the sexual language of regression [that Freud prided himself on having brought like a plague to America—G.M.] changes, in retreating still further back."

> The so-called Oedipal Complex with its famous incest tendency changes at this [deeper] level into a "Jonah-and-the-Whale" complex, which has any number of variants ... Fear of incest turns into fear of being devoured by the mother. The regressing libido apparently desexualizes itself by retreating step

3   Wolfgang Giegerich, *The Soul's Logical Life: Towards a Rigorous Notion of Psychology* (Frankfurt am Main; New York: Peter Lang, 1998), 95.
4   An allusion to the title of Giegerich's article, "Jungian Psychology: A Baseless Enterprise. Reflections on our Identity as Jungians," in *The Neurosis of Psychology (Collected English Papers, Vol. I)* (New Orleans, LA: Spring Journal, Inc., 2005), 153–170.
5   Jung, *CW* 8, § 661, trans. modified.

by step to the presexual stage of earliest infancy. Even there it does not make a halt, but in a manner of speaking continues right back to the intra-uterine, pre-natal condition and, leaving the sphere of personal psychology altogether, irrupts into the collective psyche where Jonah saw the "mysteries" ("représentations collectives") in the whale's belly.[6]

What Jung in this passage from his *Symbols of Transformation* describes as "Jonah [seeing] the 'mysteries' in the whale's belly" is already his insight from *The Visions Seminars* about the other picture that "looms up" from behind the impressions and scenes of daily life. Crucial to grasp is that the soul truths that in this way psychology sights are not seen from the shore, nor even from that portable shore, the deck of a ship, but from within the waters of the psychic process itself. Expressing this in theoretical terms, Jung stresses what he calls our discipline's lack of an Archimedean point.[7] In contrast to other sciences which theorize from a position that is supposedly outside the phenomena that they are concerned with (for which reason they may be called "dry land" or "ship's deck" sciences), psychology is immersed in itself as in an infinite sea inasmuch as everything it says about its subject matter, the psyche, is but a further phenomenal expression of the psyche, strokes of the swimming it must learn in order to build itself at sea.

Have you ever been to sea, Billy? Have you ever left the shore behind and launched out into its infinite expanse? As I envision the plank-walking plunge that Jung took in departing from Freudian psychology, two amplificatory references come to mind. The first is from the *Splendor Solis*. Among the illustrations to that 16th-century alchemical manuscript is included an engraving that shows the figure of a king drowning in the sea. With a crown on his head, the drowning king flails about in the water with nothing to hold to. What better rendering of Jung's "whole man in the drink" psychology could there be than this?! My second amplification is drawn from a few lines of Joseph Conrad's novel, *Lord Jim*:

> A man that is born falls into a dream like a man who falls into the sea. If he tries to climb out into the air as inexperienced people endeavour to do, he drowns—*nicht wahr*? .... No! I tell you! The way is to the destructive element submit yourself, and with the exertions of your hands and feet in the water make the deep, deep sea keep you up.[8]

Now with these images in mind let us return to Giegerich's statement that "psychology has to be a ship, too." Drawing upon the same metaphor in another place, Giegerich reflects upon the commonality that in this respect psychology and life share.

---

6   Jung, *CW* 5, § 654.
7   Jung, *CW* 8, § 429.
8   Joseph Conrad, *Lord Jim*, Chapter 20.

the nature of psychology is such that, like life, there is no possibility of going back before or outside of it ... Just as a ship on the ocean that has been damaged by a storm confronts the sailors with the double task of continuing to steer ahead *while* repairing the damage with whatever means they have on board, so life and psychology confront us with a double task. There is no dry dock for us. Life and psychology are always already ongoing. We cannot first develop an insight into what life is about and how it should be lived and only then begin to live. While in the process of living life we have to try to make sense of it, and our actually lived life is itself our answer to the question of what sense to make of life. ... By the same token, we cannot first acquire a clear concept of soul and only then begin to do psychology. ... Why? Because the thinking about the soul would already be a psychological act. The reflection of life is an integral part of our living life itself. Becoming conscious of what a true psychology ought to be and what soul is *is* in itself an integral part of doing psychology.[9]

Just as "we cannot first develop an insight into what life is about ... and only then begin to live," so a true psychology cannot bring insights formulated on one shore ready-made to another, for to do so would be tantamount to draining the ocean of its ship-building depths, the voyage of its adventure character. The question arises: radicalizing Freud's comment about "bringing them the plague" in terms of the dialectic I have been describing as constitutive of a truly *psychological* psychology, what truths does Psychology as the Discipline of Interiority sight, what plague does it bring?

From my many teaching exploits during the past dozen and more years I have become accustomed to noticing that when I have had to introduce such Psychology as the Discipline of Interiority terms and conceptions as "the negativity of the soul," "absolute negative interiorization," and "logical movement," that many in the audience have suddenly gone pale. In traditional Jungian circles, where words such as "individuation" and "wholeness" reign supreme, this is especially so. Looking up from my notes I see that more than a few of the faces in the audience are staring back at me as if they were breathing through their hankies. No wonder I am put in mind of Freud's comment about "bringing them the plague"! But what *are* these terms about? What insights do they describe?

The editors of this volume have asked me to say a word or two about the close contact I enjoyed with Giegerich during the many years of my collaborating with him to bring out his *Collected English Papers* and several other books. Perhaps, I can take up the questions I just raised concerning the plague-like truth of Psychology as the Discipline of Interiority by obliging this request.

Similar to the audiences that I just described, many of Giegerich's insights had at first a disturbing effect upon my own understanding of Jungian psychology. To quickly convey this I would like to mention a dream I had during the course of an

9   Wolfgang Giegerich, *What is Soul?* (New Orleans, LA: Spring Journal, Inc., 2012), 2.

initial reading of his earliest English book, *The Soul's Logical Life*. The dream was of a creek behind my house overflowing its banks and washing my house off of its foundations—capsizing it as it were! Giegerich's book, suffice it to say, was both an exhilarating read and a catastrophic negation. But having owned to this I must hasten to add that the negation that it depicted in such violent terms was in truth not violent at all. On the contrary (as I only learned later to appreciate), its seeming to be so was only the first immediacy of the realization on my part that Jungian psychology was much more than the cozy theoretical home I had previously taken it to be.

My other anecdote again concerns a dream I had, along with Giegerich's reaction. It was from a time when I was fully immersed in his thought, reading his papers every day in my capacity as editor of his aforementioned *Collected English Papers*. In my dream I was out in the middle of the ocean. No shore could be seen in any direction, I was without a boat, and surrounding me on all sides as I sculled in the water with my hands and feet were the ominous black fins of a school of sharks! I mentioned this dream to Wolfgang at the end of an email that I had anyway to write to him about various editing matters. In his email reply back to me, my dream was the first thing he responded to:

> I was particularly impressed by the dream [...] you mentioned. Your being able to dream of finding yourself in the middle of the ocean surrounded by black sharks does you credit. I take my hat off to you. Total immersion in the bath and relentless exposure. No reserve.[10]

No wonder I was inspired to dub Giegerich "The Ahab of the Notion," in my "Whaling with Giegerich"[11] essay and in the same piece to give myself the name of the protagonist-narrator in *Moby-Dick*, Ishmael.

After this somewhat indirect approach of my sharing a few personal anecdote, let us return to the question of our psychology's truth. To be out at sea in the manner I have been variously describing is to be without an Archimedean point. It is only when our psychology is immersed so totally in the bath of what is that the other picture that is the mediator of its truth looms up. You have to be out there, like that drowning king, in order to see your topic or subject matter from within. You have to be totally immersed in the bath, making the deep sea keep you up with the exertions of your hands and feet, in order to see the great whale. The discipline of interiority is the discipline of Archimedeanlessness. We could also say: the discipline of landlessness, the discipline of a drowned book. And here now, as I scull amongst the shark fins, plague-like, whale-like, *there she blows!* In Melville's words from *Moby-Dick*:

---

10   Wolfgang Giegerich, email message to author, December 10, 2006.
11   Greg Mogenson, "Whaling with Giegerich: The Ahab of the Notion," *The Journal of Jungian Theory and Practice*, 6:1 (2004): 67–83. To be fair to Giegerich I should say here that in a personal email (December 9, 2003) he hastened to depart from my characterization. "I am not Ahab, I am ONLY me ..."

Glimpses do ye seem to see of that mortally intolerable truth; that all deep, earnest thinking is but the intrepid effort of the soul to keep the open independence of her sea; while the wildest winds of heaven and earth conspire to cast her on the treacherous, slavish shore? But as in landlessness alone resides the highest truth, shoreless, indefinite, as God—so, better is it to perish in the howling infinite, than be ingloriously dashed upon the lee, even if that were safety. For worm-like, then, oh! who would craven crawl to land! Terrors of the terrible! is all this agony so vain? Take heart, take heart, O Bulkington! Bear thee grimly, demigod! Up from the spray of thy ocean-perishing—straight up, leaps thy apotheosis![12]

---

12 Herman Melville, *Moby-Dick*, chapter XXIII, "The Lee Shore." In citing this passage I do not want to imply that Psychology as the Discipline of Interiority has anything to do with bringing about an apotheosis in anyone. That is too grand, too inflated. Cited in our context its last line is rather about the sighting a soul truth: "Up from the spray of thy ocean-perishing—straight up leaps [thy cognition of thy truth]."

INDEX

Abram, David 182

absence 3, 4, 12, 41, 87, 89, 131, 143, 195, 197

absolute negativity/absolutely negative 2–4, 7, 8, 11–12, 21, 35–6, 38, 41n63, 53, 62, 99, 124–27, 129n48, 130, 132n67, 133, 144, 165, 178–180, 179n30, 201; as departedness 41; interiorization 7, 125, 127, 201; and its *"geistig"* side 38; as pure consciousness 133

absolve/absolution 3, 118–19, 125–26, 129, 133, 186

abstract expressionism 116

Actaion myth 5

acting out 13n43, 29n32, 87, 91, 122, 122n15, 127, 129, 132, 195; the soul's logic 122, 122n15; a structure 91

active imagination 43, 89, 95, 134–35, 140–42, 140n25, 145–46

Adam/Adam and Eve 45, 116

Adler, Alfred 19–20

Adler, Gerhard 134–35, 135n9, 139–42, 140n25, 145, 147

afterlife 72–7

agoraphobia 137

alchemical gold 93, 151, 158

alchemy/alchemical xixn5, 4, 11–12, 11n31, 31, 35, 41, 43–5, 49, 50–4, 63, 75, 88, 111, 125n27, 130–31, 200; acid bath 12, 131; conjunction 45–6; decline of/end 49; "dross in the gold" 93; drowning king 200, 202; freeing the spirit Mercurius 6, 51–2, 125n27; Giegerich's

view of 44–5; heaven above, heaven below 31; Hillman's view of 119; historical task of 44; Jung's view of 43, 44; marriage 44; *Mysterium Coniunctionis* 17, 24, 27n24, 29, 35, 44–5, 47, 49, 50–3; *mundificatio* 125n27, 131; and nature 111; *nigredo* 119; "pictures" as moving toward a real notion of "image" 88; process of "silvering" 131; process of "yellowing" 119, 130–31, 131n60; *putrefactio* 5, 125n27; *separatio* 51; *solutio* 125n27

Aldrin, Buzz 178, 180n34

alienation 121, 122n16, 179, 189, 190, 192–93, 197; from earth/nature 189–90, 192–93, 197

Allais, Lucy 123, 123n19

"Allegory of the Cave" 6

Analytical Psychology xiii, xv, xviii, xix, 1, 3, 9n25, 21, 22n12, 28, 41, 45, 49–54, 59–61, 63, 65, 77, 87, 107, 150, 156, 201–2; applying theory to itself 1, 9; dissolution of xxi; Jungians 27n23, 115, 181, 201; missionary purpose and its shadow 115; post-Jungian 156; as psychology of contents 77; and the Shoah 150; as "show-and-tell" xv; uniqueness of 3, 9n25, 21, 25n18, 41

analytic training xx

ancestors 36–7, 178

ancient/archaic world 30, 35n46, 173

113; logical form/structure of 29, 51, 171, 197; modern 60, 121–22, 126, 137–38, 146, 192–93, 197; movement out of primordial existence 174; movement out of religious/mythological existence 137, 138, 176–77; natural 185n15; as negativity 170n3; as neurotic 126, 162n52; objective level of 120–21, 130, 170, 172–73, 175; opposites coming home to 197; ordinary xixn5; otherness within itself/self-contradiction 127, 130, 131, 173–74; as *procedere* 159n42; psychological 51, 103, 147n51; psychological difference 170, 172; pure 133; reflective 171, 175, 180; and rocket 175; seeing itself 46, 174, 174n13; as soul 2, 48–9, 136n12, 172; soul level/mode 5, 102; split in 154–55, 162n52; and technology 171, 172n8; transformation of 132; Western 135–36, 138, 191

content -s/content level 8, 11–12, 23, 25, 25n18, 27, 29–31, 39, 41, 48, 51, 59, 61, 76–7, 82, 86–7, 89, 91–3, 95, 99, 126, 129, 130, 141, 146, 166, 184–85; 'canned' 146; vs. form 82; of imagination/imaginal 91, 93, 141; Jung's psychology as psychology of 77; of neurosis/of psychosis 77, 166; as opposed to structure 92; pictorial 89; projected 61; semantic 12, 25n18, 29–31, 126, 129; of the soul's life 25; unconscious 59, 61, 77

contradictory/contradiction xiiin3, 2, 7, 9, 25, 29, 39–41, 62, 75, 81n39, 112, 116, 122, 23–125, 129, 130, 123n19, 147, 163, 165, 190, 196; absolute 124; of attempted reconciliation 122; of consciousness 130; of forgiveness 123–25, 123n19, 129, 130; in Jung's text 75; *see also* self-contradiction 103, 127, 131, 159, 196

contra-naturam 94, 99, 111–12, 173, see also *opus contra naturam*

copula 195n63

corpse 174

cosmos/cosmological 28, 30, 30n36, 31, 36–39, 60, 62, 141, 143–47, 164, 196, 196n63; vs. universe 37, 145–46

Councils of the Early Church 28, 31, 38

counter-transference xv

critical theory xviiin3, xx

critique 190

crucifixion 79, 127, 128

culture/cultural: ancient Greek 127n36; early Judaic 127n36; evidence of man's soul nature 36; expressions/phenomena;

135–36, 175; hunting 174; modern 136; and neurosis 12, 136; and objective soul 3–4, 45, 136, 139, 175; pre-modern 122n15; primitive/"older" 64, 87; as soul 135; technological 177; Western 29, 37, 121n 11, 136

cure: in case study of "Elizabeth" 145–47; and imagination's inability to cure itself 29; of "malnourished" Western culture as "trap" 29; of neurosis 11n36, 12n37, 135, 135n9, 146, 150–51, 158; transference 146; *see also* healing

daimon 25n16

Dante 28, 179

darkness 113–14, 140, 145, 173

death xviii, 95, 179n30; of alchemical King 45; alchemical yellowing 130, 131n60; of ego xviii, 115; of Eichmann 161, 161n49; of God 72, 127, 136–37, 190–2; Jesus' death 128; and moon landing 179; and Layard's Rule 110, 117; life after 72–5, 77; logical 5; of nature 191; as negative expression in suicide 109; perspective 76n30; as sublated in Psychology as Discipline of Interiority 117

deconstruction 147

deep ecology 181, 187–88

democracy 136, 138

denial: of dissociation/disunity 160, 194; and forgiveness 128; of the psychological difference 56, 63, 65; of split incurred by ecopsychology 194–95

departed/departedness 3, 39, 76

depth psychology xiv, xvi, 59–61, 108, 115, 118–19, 172

Derrida, Jacques 118–19, 123–24, 124n21

dialectic -s/dialectical xivn5, xviiin3, xix, xxi, 1–2, 6, 7, 8, 11, 42, 48, 52–3, 68–9, 74, 76–7, 100–3, 109, 115, 117, 123, 125, 128, 129n48, 130, 132, 132n67, 185–86, 186n17, 196, 201; contradiction-and-union of presence and absence 41n62; liquidity of 8, 47–8, 50–1; logic xivn5, 7, 50, 131–32, 132n67, 186, 186n17; negation 100, 115, 125, 130; sink and swim dialectic 199; undialectical 42, 50, 101, 125, 128–29, 162n52, 173, 193

Dialectics and Analytical Psychology xii, 28n25

dialectical thinking xxi, 2, 7, 52–3; vs. imagining/imagination 7; *see also* psychological thinking

dignity 136, 151–52, 158, 166

discipline 2, 4–6, 20, 159, 202